WHO ARE DOUG HALL
& DAVID WECKER?

DOUG HALL started his entrepreneurial career at the age of twelve as Merwyn the Magician. After receiving a chemical engineering degree from the University of Maine, he entered the Brand Management Department at Procter & Gamble, where he rose to the rank of Master Marketing Inventor. After ten years, he retired to found Richard Saunders International and fulfill his version of the American Dream.

DAVID WECKER is a Richard Saunders International Trained Brain®. He writes a newspaper column for the *Cincinnati Post* and co-hosts a call-in talk show on WLW radio.

PRAISE FOR DOUG HALL AND
JUMP START YOUR BRAIN

"A HOW-TO THAT DELIVERS. . . . The (creativity) process it outlines may be used by a business person creating a new product, a husband choosing a birthday gift for his wife, a school planning the world's best fundraiser or an author searching for a plot. . . . The book not only outlines the process, but also describes applications that have worked. . . . The book is sprinkled with his promotional genius. . . . HALL KNOWS WHAT HE'S TALKING ABOUT."

—Cincinnati Post

"REQUIRED READING. . . . HALL REVEALS HOW YOU CAN RETRAIN YOUR BRAIN TO THINK OF MORE CREATIVE IDEAS. THE BOOK IS FUNNY AND PACKED WITH ANECDOTES."

—Entrepreneur **magazine**

"JUMP START YOUR BRAIN is not theory. . . . JUMP START YOUR BRAIN is unlike other creativity books in that the tools are accessible. Not just by the creative types in your organization, but by everyone who has a stake in the prosperity of your company."

—Peter de Jager, expert on creativity and change

"We've found Richard Saunders Invention® methods to be different than most. THEY WORK."

—Michele Wojtyna, Pepsi-Cola Company

"HALL'S UNCONVENTIONAL APPROACH HAS WON RAVES FROM SOME OF THE BIGGEST CORPORATIONS IN THE COUNTRY."

—CNN

"Eureka! has more stimuli, more focus on the people and on the interaction of the people. . . . I'd hate to go back to a regular brainstorming session after experiencing Eureka! I don't know anybody that does the crazy stuff Doug does. . . . He's a magician. . . . EUREKA! IS A MAGICAL ENVIRONMENT, separate from reality."

—Dr. Arthur VanGundy, international creativity expert, University of Oklahoma

"A USER'S MANUAL FOR YOUR BRAIN! . . . Shows you how to retain that spark. It will awaken your spirit of adventure. . . . [Hall] has an impressive track record, not only for producing ideas that pay but for teaching too-serious executives to relax and produce. . . . Should the author be taken seriously as he babbles joyfully through these pages? Emphatically, yes."

—Soundview Executive Book Summaries

"I KNOW OF NO ONE WHO BLENDS KNOWLEDGE, CURIOSITY, AND CREATIVITY MORE PRODUCTIVELY THAN DOUG HALL."
—**Dr. Lynn R. Kahle, professor & chair, University of Oregon**

"DOUG'S UNIQUE SKILL IS IN ORGANIZING CHAOS INTO A COMPELLING IDEA THAT CLICKS ON THE LIGHT SWITCH."
—**Austin McNamara, group vice president, Chiquita Brands International**

"HALL SHOWS AND TELLS HOW TO TAKE THE KIND OF FRESH, CHILDLIKE, AND FUN LOOK AT THE WORLD THAT SPARKS ORIGINAL IDEAS."
—*Cleveland Plain-Dealer*

"IF CREATIVITY IS THE MENTAL SEX OF OUR LIVES, A EUREKA! SESSION IS AN ORGY." —**Barb Korn, group director, Ralston Purina Company**

"THE EUREKA! EXPERIENCE IS THE FRESHEST BREATH OF AIR I'VE HAD IN A VERY LONG TIME. The fact that something so much fun could both be productive and add value gives me hope for the broader corporate environment of the future."
—**Sharon Hall, general manager, Avon Products**

"I always knew you could have fun while you're being creative, but NOT UNTIL I WAS IN DOUG'S EUREKA! SESSION DID I REALIZE JUST HOW MUCH FUN YOU COULD HAVE."
—**David Moret, manager of new product development, Pepsi-Cola Company**

"DOUG BRINGS OUT (OR BACK) THE KID IN ALL OF US . . . TO FIND OBVIOUS SOLUTIONS THAT ARE INTUITIVELY OBVIOUS TO AN 8-YEAR-OLD BUT NOT TO A 40-YEAR-OLD."
—**Chuck Hong, director of R&D, Procter & Gamble**

"EXPLICITLY AND BUOYANTLY DESCRIBES HOW TO GENERATE FRESH THOUGHTS. . . . HALL'S IDEAS CAN BE ADAPTED TO ANY FIELD OR PROFESSION." —*Dayton Business News*

"Doug Hall is a mind to be reckoned with. Only a few decades back he would have been called eccentric. TODAY, THOSE WHO HAVE EXPERIENCED HIS MAGIC CALL HIM GENIUS. I met Doug expecting a brainstorm. What I got was a brain typhoon!"
—**David Reiss, president, Affinity Memberships, Inc.**

more . . .

"FINALLY, A NEW PRODUCT CONCEPT PROCESS THAT'S FAST, TESTABLE, AND DELIVERS RESULTS!"

—**Bill Harnew, senior product manager, Unilever U.S.A.**

"Suddenly (at the Eureka! mansion), despite your best intentions to remain cool and above it all, YOU FIND YOURSELF NODDING WITH AGREEMENT AT THE CRAZIEST IDEAS AND RESISTING THE CONVENTIONAL."

—**James Taylor, managing director, Yankelovich Partners**

"THE GREAT THING ABOUT DOUG IS THAT, ASIDE FROM BEING TREMENDOUSLY CREATIVE, HE HAS GOOD BUSINESS SENSE AND UNDERSTANDING. He is practical and very responsive to client input."

—**Michelle Greenwald, senior vice president of marketing, Mattel Toys**

"OVER THE PAST YEAR, ITS EUREKA! DIVISION . . . HAS DEVELOPED MORE NEW PRODUCTS (OR OFF-SHOOTS OF EXISTING ONES) THAN ANY OTHER ORGANIZATION IN AMERICA."

—*New York* **magazine**

"Upon arrival at the mansion for a Eureka! session, it's hard to believe anything will be accomplished—but WORK HARD/PLAY HARD WORKS. WE'VE GOTTEN SOME GREAT IDEAS. . . . I love the go-carts."

—**Sheldon Roesch, VP/general manager, Pepsi-Lipton Tea Partnership**

"WERE THERE TIMES I WANTED TO STRANGLE DOUG? ABSOLUTELY. He was what I call a 'high-maintenance subordinate.'"

—**Barb Thomas, Doug's first boss at Procter & Gamble**

"WORKING WITH DOUG HALL AND HIS LUNATIC FRIENDS HAS BEEN THE MOST UNCIVILIZED EXPERIENCE OF MY LIFE. . . . IF THERE IS A BETTER WAY TO CREATE NEW IDEAS, I HAVEN'T FOUND IT. . . . BY THE WAY, DOUG IS NOT NEARLY AS TALL AS HE APPEARS IN THE BOOK."

—**Mark Michaud, Coors Brewing Company**

"DOUG IS FUNTASTIC! He takes your brain, teases your senses and toasts newborn ideas as they flow forth! DOUG IS THE PIED PIPER OF IDEAS! HE EXUDES ENERGY, FUN AND WISDOM; Doug has created a magic kingdom in the true Disney sense—THE EUREKA! MANSION IS A PLACE WHERE DREAMS ARE BORN!"

—**Diane Iseman, president, Iseman & Associates**

"DOUG IS AN EVANGELIST TO THE DORMANT CREATIVE SPIRIT we have within each of us. A crusader redeeming our inventive spirit. Inspiring within each of us to embrace the passion each of us had as a child to originate thoughts, which is the birthing place of ideas."
—**Tina Mims, corporate manager, strategic marketing, Southwestern Bell Corporation**

"Doug should work for TWA as a baggage handler—he's that skilled at removing all the baggage . . . and you can't get there if you don't. Creativity is notorious for the not-invented-here syndrome, and Doug gets everybody to sense that it was their idea all along. HE HAS TAKEN CREATIVE-PROCESS MANAGEMENT TO THE 22ND CENTURY."
—**Watts Wacker, futurist, Yankelovich Partners**

"DOUG'S CREATIVITY INVIGORATES NOT ONLY THE BUSINESSES HE TOUCHES AND CREATES, BUT THE PEOPLE HE WORKS WITH."
—**Marilyn O'Brien, president, Insights Research**

"Doug is like a biologist continually setting up new cross-breeding experiments. He thinks if he puts an engineer, a poet, two suits, a gardener, an actor, his kids, and the right stimulus in the same room, they'll mate. THE CRAZY THING IS, IT WORKS."
—**Mike Katz, CEO, Creative Consultants**

"Doug is basically a big, barefooted daddy. SORT OF LIKE THE FOUND-ING FATHER OF A WHOLE NEW BREED OF CREATIVE KIDS. Corporate America, if you want to be fruitful and multiply profits, pay attention to papa."
—**Peter Lloyd, head honcho, The Right Brain Works**

"DOUG IS NOT AFRAID OF HIS MIND OR CREATIVITY—HE TRUSTS IN IT. THIS IS WHAT LETS HIM TAKE IDEAS OUT THERE, SOMETIMES BEYOND THE BOUNDS OF THE RIDICULOUS! THIS IS WHERE GREAT IDEAS START, THOUGH. I think most of us hesitate to go there for fear of failure or looking silly or both."
—**Kim Finnerty, marketing manager, Pepsi-Cola Company**

DOUG HALL

Retired Master Marketing Inventor,
PROCTER & GAMBLE, *and creator of the*
EUREKA!® STIMULUS RESPONSE™ METHOD
with **DAVID WECKER**

WARNER BOOKS

A Time Warner Company

Warner Books, Inc., 1271 Avenue of the Americas, New York, NY 10020

 A Time Warner Company

The following are trademarks of the Eureka! Institute:

666™, Battle of the Sexes™, B.O.S. Profiler™, Brain Brew™, Candid Comments™, Do One Thing Great™, Don't Sell Me™, Dr. Disecto™, Eureka!®, Flapdoodling™, Franklin Ledger™, InterAct®, Jump Start Your Brain®, Jump Start Your Business®, Kitchen Chemistry™, Law Breaker™, M.V.P.™, MacMerlins™, Magic Moments™, Mind Dumpster™, New Product Physics™, Pass the Buck®, Pin Pricks™, Skybridging™, Stimulus Response™, Tabloid Tales™, Trained Brain®, Winning Ways™.

Brain Programs Copyright © 1991, 1992, 1993 by Doug Hall.

AcuPOLL, BrainScan, and Reality Check are trademarks of AcuPOLL Research, Inc., and are used with permission.

Illustrations from *Big Bird's Color Game* Copyright © 1980 Children's Television Workshop and Jim Henson Productions, Inc. Illustrations by Tom Cooke. Reprinted by permission of Children's Television Workshop.

Originally published in hardcover by Warner Books.
Printed in the United States of America
First Trade Printing: January 1996
10 9 8 7 6 5 4 3 2

Library of Congress Cataloging-in-Publication Data
Hall, Doug
    Jump start your brain / Doug Hall with David Wecker.
    p. : ill. ; cm.
    ISBN 0-446-67103-7
    1. Creative ability in business. 2. Success in business.
    I. Wecker. David. II. Title.
HD53.H35 1995
650.1—dc20   94-18929
                                                  CIP

Book design by Giorgetta Bell McRee
Flap photo of Doug Hall and David Wecker by Gil Gray
Cover design by Lauren Avery, WBR Design

Dedication

This book is dedicated to my high school sweetheart, my best friend, my wife, the mother of our children, Debbie Hall—the only person on this good earth for whom I will make the supreme sacrifice. At her bidding, I will wear a tie.

This book is written for the sixty-something man who told me he'd devoted thirty-five years to corporate America and, after hearing my Jump Start Your Brain lecture, realized how far he'd sunk into conformity. How he'd allowed himself to be pushed into the dull, gray, emotionally numb corner of tradition. How he'd adjusted his life to fit the day-to-day world and, finally, had stopped dreaming. How he knew he'd lost the fire but on that day, he thought I'd helped rekindle a spark.

It was one of those misty moments you have sometimes. I saw a broken man, coming into the homestretch of his life, looking back. I saw a man who, once upon a time, could have been anything he'd set his mind to be.

It doesn't matter to me if I sell ten books or ten million. What's important is that the message of hope, independence, imagination, and self-reliance makes a difference for you.

> *Baa baa black sheep, have you any thoughts?*
> *Yes sir, yes sir, to chuck what I've been taught*
> *about channels and protocol and toeing the line.*
> *You've got to make waves to do something fine.*

RICHARD SAUNDERS

CONTENTS

Contents

ACT I

Brain Training: Welcome

There once was a magician named Doug;
From his mirror stares Ben Franklin's mug.
For Doug, ideas crackle, they snap, they spew
And become inventions, like board games and Brain Brew.
When Doug Meets Disney, creativity n'er wanes,
For our team explodes when he "Jump Starts Our Brains"!

Doug Hall is crazy and brilliant. Doug Hall is a masterpiece.
Doug Hall emits ideas like frying bacon emits grease.

ELLEN GUIDERA
Vice President, New Business Development
Disney Consumer Products

Act I

Brain Training: Welcome

If you would not be forgotten, as soon as you are dead and rotten, either write things worth reading, or do things worth the writing.

BEN FRANKLIN

I'll warn you up front: *Jump Start Your Brain* is not a scholarly work. It's sewn together with lots of grins, a few smirks, and all the stuff I know about inventing new to-the-world ideas. My aim is to educate a little, entertain a little. Our corporate namesake, Ben Franklin, had a similar philosophy. In fact, some historical accounts suggest that the reason he wasn't asked to write the Declaration of Independence was for fear he'd slip a joke into it.

My credentials aren't academic. I'm neither a consultant nor a theoretician. I'm a practicing inventor, entrepreneur, magician, juggler, publisher, writer, market researcher, chemical engineer, advertising creative, Eagle Scout, marketing executive, husband, and daddy. I'm a short balding kid in sneakers and blue jeans who helps com-

panies like Pepsi-Cola, Procter & Gamble, Nike, AT&T, Walt Disney Consumer Products, and U S West invent business-building ideas.

To paraphrase the guy in the commercial, you may not know me, but you know my work. Surveys show that the average American home contains eighteen brand-name products that my team has helped jump-start.

This is a book about maximizing your brain power and your productive creativity. I'm not talking about theoretical creativity. I'm talking about applying creativity to invent ideas that lead to purposeful end results, that is, ideas that fulfill actual needs, earn profits, and change the world.

My life and the focus of my company—Richard Saunders International—have been on the practical and the actionable. I take pride not in the theoretical creativity or originality of our ideas, but in their practical applications and profitable nature. Inventing is focused on results. Inventing is what changes history.

The classic approach most humans take when looking for solutions to problems is a procedure I call Braindraining. It works like this:

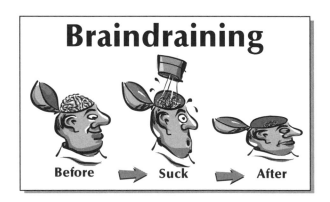

Braindraining

Before → Suck → After

Humans sit in a room. One of them says, "Ready, set, create!" With that, they desperately try to suck solutions from their heads. They squint, grind their teeth, and sweat profusely, all in hopes of squeezing a few angry pellets of ideas from their straining craniums. In short, they use their minds as mere reference libraries. This SUCK method of creativity will shrivel your brain like a prune in the desert sun. It's not good for you.

The methods described in this book are good for you. And they work. They're the collective outcome of twenty years of searching for a better, more efficient way to think. My goal was to arrive at a simple, fundamental theory to explain how the human mind goes about the business of creating, a theory that would explain as simply as Einstein's $e = mc^2$ how to jump-start human creativity.

I call the methodology Eureka! Stimulus Response. Validation studies by Dr. Arthur VanGundy of the University of Oklahoma, one of the nation's leading authorities on the creative process, have found the Eureka! Stimulus Response method cranks out over 1,000 percent more new ideas than the aforementioned Braindraining technique the average American uses today. Even more impressive in VanGundy's study is that Eureka! Stimulus Response generated 558 percent more "wicked good" ideas; that is, super smart ideas, with above average marketplace potential.

Stop. Read it again. The Eureka! Stimulus Response invention method can make your brain up to 500 percent more productive! It's like having five brains in one head!

Over the years, I've read many insightful books on creativity and thinking from Edward de Bono, Tony Buzan, Alex Osborn, Betty Edwards, Ned Hermann, Dr. Arthur VanGundy, Joyce Wycoff, Richard Bach, Chic Thompson, SARK, Guy Kawasaki, David Ogilvy, James Adams, and my personal favorite, Ben Franklin. Each offered a wicked good system or a method to open the doors of my mind a bit wider, a nudge at a time. After reading, I was smarter, but I was still left looking for a fundamental principle that would, with a single push, make it possible to swing the doors all the way open.

Over the years I have conducted experiments, run research, interviewed business leaders, interviewed experts in the field of creative behavior. I've even had a half dozen different creativity experts attend Eureka! Stimulus Response sessions to stimulate and exchange thoughts, theories, and ideas.

This work led me to a basic formula I call the Eureka! Stimulus Response Theory of Creativity. In short form, it reads like this:

$$\mathcal{E} = (S + \mathbf{B.O.S.})^F$$

Which is short for:

$$Eureka!_{\text{® Inventing}} = (Stimulus + \mathbf{B}rain\ \mathbf{O}perating\ \mathbf{S}ystem)^{Fun}$$

Put simply, the big idea—the Eureka!—comes from blending stimuli with your personal Brain Operating System, all multiplied by a factor of adventurous fun.

With the Eureka! Stimulus Response method, your brain is used more like a processing computer, less like a reference library. Instead of withdrawing ideas from a finite collection of thoughts, your brain reacts off stimuli to create new associations, new Eureka!'s.

6

Stimuli act like fertilizer for your brain; they set up chain reactions of ideas, many with the potential for brilliance.

Eureka! Stimulus Response allows you to plumb the depths of your Brain Operating System, or B.O.S. for short—a term I use to describe the lens through which you filter, perceive, and react to stimuli. Your B.O.S. is a function of your collective experiences that you bring to every situation. It's what's behind your eyes that makes you see things the way you do. It's your mental fingerprint.

This method starts with your B.O.S. and supercharges it with multidimensional stimuli to excite and agitate original thoughts.

Stimuli can be anything you see, hear, smell, taste, or touch. Stimuli are anything that spurs your brain to make new connections, new associations, and new-to-the-world ideas.

A stimulus can be as simple a matter as looking up a synonym in a thesaurus or as complex as searching an on-line computer database for articles and academic studies on the mating habits of the duck-billed platypus. It can be as everyday practical as flipping through a cookbook for ideas for dinner for your in-laws or as business-focused as purchasing a competitor's products and conducting personal, real-world test-drive experiments with them.

Warning: The methods and systems you'll learn here are industrial strength. They're designed for big thoughts, big ideas. Do not venture into these waters unless you're intent on making a real difference. You're about to embark on a grand adventure in which you will come face to face with fear, uncertainty, and doubt. But take heart. With a little courage and imagination, you'll reach new highs and new levels of awareness as you unleash the forces of your brain.

Beware: Once you've opened your brain and realized your potential, you'll never be satisfied with mindless mediocrity again. After experiencing Eureka! Stimulus Response you'll be filled with discontent and anger at the thought of averageness, normality, and head-in-the-sand scaredy-catness.

The book's title sums up the corporate mission of my company—and of this book. The intent here is to help you get the maximum horsepower from your own particular combination of imagination and intellect, in whatever proportion they exist inside your skull; to help you establish a dream and turn it into reality.

This little piggy went to market,
This little piggy stayed home.
The first little pig had a wicked good idea,
The second little pig had none.
And the first little pig laughed,
Hee, hee, hee, hee,
All the way to the bank.

RICHARD SAUNDERS

I call my creative methodology Eureka! Stimulus Response. That's Eureka with an exclamation point! The name provokes energy. It also recognizes the phenomenal power of stimuli to activate new thoughts. It invokes the moment of inspiration, the instant in which something new is born.

A stimulus was, in fact, responsible for the creation of the word *Eureka*. In the original Greek, *Eureka* means "I have found it!" According to Greek legend, a mathematician and physicist named Archimedes coined the term after being stimulated in a hot tub.

He was settling in for a long soak one day around 250 B.C. At the time, he was preoccupied with finding a way to determine the proportion of real gold to ordinary metal in King Hieron's crown. See, the king thought he might have been shorted on the crown deal. He wanted to make sure the crown he was wearing was pure gold and not some cheap imitation. At the time, the weight of gold per unit volume was well known. But given the intricate nature of the crown's design, what with all its curlicues and whatnot, it was impossible to measure its volume.

Anyway, as Archimedes was lowering himself into the tub, he

noticed his bathwater rising in proportion to his entry into the tub. The lower he sunk, the higher the water rose, until it overflowed.

The stimulus of the overflowing hot tub gave Archimedes a revelation. He suddenly realized he could measure the volume of the crown by simply dunking it in a tub filled to the brim, then measuring the water that overflowed.

He leaped from his tub and ran naked into the street hollering, "Eureka!" Thus, in the white-hot grip of inspiration, Archimedes also invented streaking. And it didn't end there—the hot tub stimulus further led Archimedes to the discovery of the law of specific gravity and the general science of hydrostatics.

Yes! You, too, can benefit from Eureka! Stimulus Response Thinking. You don't have to think of home, and you don't have to click your heels three times. Anyone can learn from Eureka! Stimulus Response. All kinds of folks with all kinds of backgrounds have applied the Eureka! Stimulus Response principles in their careers, their homes, their lives.

If you have a brain and you'd like it to function better, faster, and smarter, you've come to the right place. It doesn't matter if you're a chief executive officer, a plumber, a Cub Scout den mother, an astronaut, a hamburger flipper, or an ichthyologist; the methods described herein will change your life if you take them to heart and put them to work.

You may never care to invent a new product or service for a billion-dollar company, but the methods you'll learn here will show you how if that's how you'd like to set your personal compass. Or maybe you're more interested in finding a new fundraiser for your PTA, solving the federal deficit, or reinventing the claw hammer. Whatever race you're running, the Eureka! Stimulus Response system will get you there faster and more effectively. Think of Eureka! Stimulus Response as a supercharger for your brain.

These methods don't happen in baby steps. They happen in quantum leaps. You'll see results in a hurry.

Through these pages, you'll also meet my Trained Brains—a collection of eclectic, eccentric entrepreneurs and adventurers who, in working with corporations around the world, have a proven ability to invent new-to-the-world ideas. When a company hires me to invent ideas, I always turn to the Trained Brains. They're my collection of different Brain Operating Systems.

They're my posse; my band of merrymen and merrywomen; my wing and my prayer; my partners in crime against corporate convention. They're hopeless romantics, incurable daydreamers, optimists, and willing adventurers blessed with sweet, gentle souls. They go eagerly where no imagination has gone before.

They don't fit in, but they never feel left out. They avoid the beaten path and the well-worn rut as a point of pride. They see the world through rose-colored kaleidoscopes. They're often naive, sometimes gullible, and inclined to make errors of judgment and social grace. They're like children that way.

But they laugh a lot. They're young for their age. They long ago stopped heeding the advice of their elders to straighten up and fly right. Their eyes are wide open with wonder. Somehow, they've been able to resist the corrosive forces of cynicism. They have a pure, simple way of seeing and an ability to extract the fresh from the mundane.

Most of all, they have a gift for shaking it up, twisting it around, and making something new happen.

By the time you've finished this book, you'll know what it takes to be a Trained Brain. Indeed, you'll have all the tools you'll need to be one yourself.

The book is cast in the first person, but it's an all-encompassing first person. It's not just me. It's the collective voice of the entire Richard Saunders International team. I believe passionately in the premise that leaders lead, but teams make things happen. People often ask what I've invented, having inferred that I'm a one-man shop. I tell them I've invented nothing, zero, zilch. Everything I do involves a team effort, a collaboration of the world's finest clients with my Trained Brains, writers, artists, and market researchers.

> *We must all hang together or most assuredly we will all hang separately.*
>
> BEN FRANKLIN

The mainstay of our work at Richard Saunders International is the Eureka! Stimulus Response inventing service, which is aimed at helping clients jump-start their businesses; that is, develop actionable, creative solutions to their business problems. Jump-starting is a matter of helping clients find a vision for making more profits, which in turn is a matter of building within the corporation the positive entrepreneurial energy it takes to succeed—as in "be the best"—in today's business world.

As mentioned earlier, surveys indicate that you have, on average, eighteen products in your home that I've had a hand in jump-starting. In many cases, due to our clients' corporate security policies, we are regretfully unable to identify these products. While the thinking that went into, say, the positioning for a new toilet paper may not seem to be on the same plane as an issue of national defense, Real World Adult corporate types disagree and, in fact, often require me to sign a confidentiality agreement.

A second service that a spin-off company of Richard Saunders

offers is AcuPOLL Research, a digital research system whereby honest-to-gosh Americans record their opinions on new or established products. AcuPOLL poses such questions as:

- How interested are you in buying this service or product?
- How new and different do you think it is?
- How often would you purchase a product or service?

Tracking studies indicate AcuPOLL has an 89-percent accuracy rate when it comes to predicting winners and losers. In a recent twelve-month period, AcuPOLL also tested more than two thousand ideas—making it the leading concept testing service in the nation in terms of the number of concepts tested.

The successful invention and implementation of a great idea requires melding and blending the appropriate resources of my team with those of the client team.

At Richard Saunders International, we don't assume the role of client manager. Instead, we act as guides, motivators, coaches, and teammates to help clients reach their goals.

Our roles vary with the needs of the client.

Sometimes, we invent the idea and assist in business design and development, as we did with Duncan Hines Pantastic Party Cakes, Air Heads Tongue Twisters, Eveready Generator Battery Chargers, and Eveready Eversafe.

Other times, we simply help corporations create and focus their marketing strategies and marketing communications, as with Lipton Originals Iced Tea, Crystal Pepsi, Eveready Greenpower, Oil of Olay, Frito-Lay Snacks, Folgers Coffee, Southwestern Bell Yellow Pages, and Hawaiian Punch.

About a third of our work is devoted to inventing new products or services. The remaining two-thirds is focused on finding ways to increase sales for established businesses, which is one of the most efficient methods for increasing corporate profits.

In all cases, we focus on results. We don't consult, spew theory, "do suits," or woo clients at fancy French restaurants. We create tangible business-building concepts with quantified sales potential.

Among the organizations and/or brands we've had the honor of providing creative, technical, educational, and/or marketing assistance to are:

Procter & Gamble	Quaker Oats
Colgate-Palmolive	Avon Products
NBA/Gatorade	Darden Business School
Anheuser-Busch	Planters/Lifesavers
Walt Disney Consumer Products	HoneyBaked Ham

Apple Processors Association	Hussmann Corporation
Young Presidents Organization (Amsterdam)	Hillshire Kahns
	National Leukemia Society
Folgers Coffee Company	Western Union
Reynolds Metals	Seagrams
Random House	Pepsi-Cola
Ralston Purina	Southwestern Bell
DowBrands	Continental Baking
Advertising Age	Thomas J. Lipton
Coors Brewing Company	M&M Mars
Cincinnati Symphony	Kraft/General Foods
Nike	Ocean Spray
AT&T	American Marketing Association
Nabisco Brands	*Wall Street Journal*
Van den Bergh Foods	Borden, Inc.
Campbell Soup	Marketing Intelligence Service
John Morrell Meats	Binney & Smith (Crayola)
Eveready Battery Company	Slush Puppie
Van Melle Candy	Waste Management
Sweetheart Cup	3M
Cincinnati Bell	BOSE
International Data Group	Western Publishing
Frito-Lay, Inc.	University of Maine
Pillsbury	Chattem Consumer Products
Playtex Family Products	Montgomery Inn (Ribs King)
Parker Brothers	Green Giant
Celestial Seasonings	Congressman Rob Portman
U S WEST	Gatorade

As I travel the country, I sense something out there that's turning the established ways upside down. I see people inside and outside the corporate realm who are taking matters into their own hands.

> *If you love life, then do not squander time, for that is the stuff life is made of.*
>
> BEN FRANKLIN

In spare rooms at corporate technical centers, in dank cellars and in garages cluttered with bits and pieces of dead cars, average Americans are fighting the system with the most formidable weapon they have—their power to think, imagine, and invent.

Inventions are America's lifeblood. The best ones come from the little guy who has put his personal savings or corporate reputation on the line, tinkering away to make his whacked-out vision a reality.

This book is designed to help people like that, people who have a dream, and to light a spark for those who want to escape conformity. It's a blueprint for conquering fears, cultivating gumption, taking risks, and taking control. It's a ticket to change your life. And the world.

> *Up, sluggard, and waste not life; in the grave will be sleeping enough.*
>
> BEN FRANKLIN

This book is also for those responsible for providing leadership. I believe that people of all collars—white, blue, pink, or polka-dot—want to do the right thing. But they don't have the tools.

My dad, M. Bradford Hall, spent a year working with world-renowned quality expert W. Edwards Deming. What he told me of his experience shaped my attitudes toward business.

> *Fifteen percent of all business problems are attributable to workers and supervisors—not following directions, absence from the job, and pushing the wrong button. The remaining 85 percent are faults of the system that only management can solve. Examples are poor product design, poor equipment design, poor instruction. The days when top managers can sit in their plush offices and honestly say, "If the workers did a better job, we would produce more and make more money," are gone forever.*

Books of this sort are generally read by those on the lower rungs of the corporate hierarchy. But it's the folks at the top who most need to hear the entrepreneurial message contained in these pages, that of empowering people and doing the right thing. To help ensure they do hear it, I'm sending copies of *Jump Start Your Brain* to some of the King Kahunas of the *Fortune 500*.

> *There once was a CEO who lived in a shoe,*
> *He was so laced to tradition, he didn't know what to do.*
> *Wouldn't know an idea if it hit him in the head,*
> *In no time at all, he was deep in the red.*
>
> RICHARD SAUNDERS

I wrote this book, too, to inspire you to reclaim your freedom and recapture your sense of adventure and lost innocence.

> *We all started out creatively free. Remember the sand-box? All you needed were bare toes in warm sand and maybe a good bucket.... At school, things may have changed.... The chairs were in rows, and tree trunks were to be colored brown, not purple. If you lived in a world of purple tree trunks, you probably learned to hide it.*
>
> SARK, friend & author,
> *A Creative Companion*

Finally, I wrote this book for the giddy feeling that comes over me when I see someone enjoying a product I've had a hand in giving birth to. That's why I plan to give away portraits of Ben Franklin to the first twelve people I see reading *Jump Start Your Brain* outside Cincinnati. To save printing costs, I intend to use the portraits that the U.S. Treasury prints on its $100 bills.

Jump Start Your Brain invented itself. A group Eureka! Stimulus Response invention session was convened to invent more than fifteen hundred bookworthy ideas. The title and subject matter were selected by John Q. Public, via AcuPOLL research.

> *I am very sensible that it is impossible for me, or indeed any one writer to please all readers at once. Various persons have different sentiments, and that which is pleasant and delightful to one, gives another disgust.*
> BEN FRANKLIN

AcuPOLL Research tells me you're interested in learning how to think smarter, faster, and better. You want how-to advice. You don't care to read an academic treatise—you want practical, easy-to-implement methods for increasing your brainpower, presented in short, inspired bursts.

To that end, *Jump Start Your Brain* is designed to be a statement of countercorporate culture. It's meant to be a quick, greasy-slick read. At last count on my Macintosh PowerBook 180, the text was down to 4.56 characters per word.

Friends have asked why I'd give away my secrets. The reason is, it's the right thing to do. It's an attitude I picked up while kicking around in juggling circles. The philosophy among jugglers is that if I teach you a trick and you teach me a trick, we're both enriched.

Then, too, there are these sentiments from two authorities for whom I have the greatest respect:

> *He offered me a patent for the sole vending of them [Franklin stoves] for a term of years: but I declined it from a principle which has ever weighed with me on such occasions, that as we enjoy great advantages from the inventions of others, we should be glad of the opportunity to serve others by any invention of ours.*
> BEN FRANKLIN

> *When you share ideas, you have more.*
> KRISTYN HALL, age 5,
> my daughter

Act I: Brain Training: Welcome

Jump Start Your Brain is presented in three acts:

• **Act I, Brain Training.** The focus here is on setting your mental gyroscope to inventing new-to-the world ideas. Act I details the Eureka! Stimulus Response principles for rediscovering a child-like sense of wonder and adventure for fun and profit—emphasis on fun and profit. Act I defines the Eureka! Stimulus Response process that can increase the powers of your imagination.

• **Act II, Eureka! Stimulus Response Explosion.** This section lays out the same practical, can't-miss Brain Programs I use to invent major, industrial-strength ideas for some of America's biggest corporations. Each Brain Program is detailed and explained so you can put them to work for you immediately, without any snags.

Excuse me for a moment, would you?

Okay. I'm back. Where was I? Oh, yeah ...

The notion of a "wicked good" idea, by the way, is a common thread connecting the three acts. It's a term borrowed from my boyhood in Maine. In the north country, when something particularly impressive or novel or magical comes along, it's not just cool or awesome. It's, well, wicked good.

• **Act III, Go4it!** Even the most glorious, magical idea won't do you much good if you can't make it real. Act III is designed to give you a shot of inspiration adrenaline before you and your idea set sail in the real world. Act III also includes my Ten Commandments for moving your idea forward from diaphanous abstraction to three-dimensional reality.

Speak Little. Do Much.

Words may show a man's wit, but actions his meaning.
BEN FRANKLIN

DISCLAIMER: Every account you'll read here is essentially true in terms of the events they describe and how they unfolded. But I've taken the liberty to make two modifications to historical accounts:

1. Certain identities or products have been obscured in the interest of client confidentiality or to protect the guilty. This is a book about hope, faith, and believing in yourself. You won't find tales tattled here. Sorry, *National Enquirer*. Maybe next time.

2. As Ben Franklin was famous for doing, I've editorialized some stories, adding a joke here or a twist there to make a point. My goal is to teach and inspire—not to brag or bore you with my life story.

One final note: These pages are sprinkled liberally with quotes from friends, colleagues, and associates. Here and there, I've included nuggets that came to me on a moonlit night from my personal poltergeist, Richard Saunders, which by an eerie coincidence happens to be Ben Franklin's pen name. Although I can't prove conclusively that it's the same Richard Saunders, I can believe it so. I mean, it's a free country.

Act I: Brain Training: Welcome

In his epitaph, the real Richard Saunders put it this way:

> *The Body of*
> *B. Franklin,*
> *Printer;*
> *Like the Cover of an old Book,*
> *Its Contents torn out,*
> *And stript of its Lettering and Gilding,*
> *Lies here, Food for Worms.*
> *But the Work shall not be wholly lost:*
> *For it will, as he believ'd, appear once more,*
> *In a new & more perfect Edition,*
> *Corrected and amended*
> *By the Author.*

My dream is that this book will serve as that "new & more perfect Edition" until a newer and more perfect one comes along. In either case, it's what I am. I hope it widens your eyes, renews your hopes, strengthens your resolve, and helps you realize a dream.

Cheers,

DOUG HALL
October 9, 1994

CHAPTER 101

Who Am I and What Am I Doing Here?

The advance intelligence was not encouraging. It was, in fact, a little intimidating.

I would be facing 132 of the top marketing and research executives of Anheuser-Busch. The occasion was the annual strategy session for one of America's most esteemed and beloved makers of fermented grain beverages. My mission: Arrive early to crank up their craniums and otherwise fire up this bunch of suits.

The word I had on the Budweiser folks was that their notion of "relaxed" was to take the hangers out of their shirts and blouses before getting dressed in the morning. I'd been told they were a rigid bunch; not prone to laughter, not given to childlike flights of frivolity, and certainly not inclined to suffer fools gladly. In short, they were not the sort of individuals who, by any contortion of the imagination, were accustomed to dealing with a guy in a straitjacket telling them that they ought to try howling at the moon once in a while.

Ulp!

Such were my thoughts as I was strapped into my canvas, leather-strapped straitjacket outside the lecture hall where my Anheuser-Busch audience awaited, seated on chairs under which, that very morning, I had hidden 132 individually packaged, grade-A rubber, imported-especially-from-Taiwan whoopee cushions.

As I stood there awaiting my cue in the wings of the conference hall at the Westin Hotel in Vail, Colorado, it occurred to me that

21

I'd taken the long road to get there. But it felt like I'd arrived in a hurry.

I was born of a middle-class family in Portland, Maine—253 years to the day after the birth of Benjamin Franklin, a circumstance that has tinted my outlook and, to a great extent, influenced who I am.

> *Doug was the same as a child as he is now—reaching out to everything. He was like my grandfather, Frank Emerson, who worked for years trying to invent a perpetual motion machine.... My grandmother Emerson was left practically strapped when he died. But like my grandfather, Douglas has the courage of his convictions. He is a good boy, too. When he was in college, he would send me a letter every week....*
>
> HAZEL LOUISE EMERSON HALL,
> my grandmother

At the age of twelve, I developed an addiction to magic. I called myself Merwyn the Magician, after my dad, who was not a magician and who deeply regrets the fact that his name sounds a lot like Merlin. My younger brother, Bruce, joined the show as Boo Boo the Clown. It was during those days that I invented and shipped my first products—Merwyn's Magic Bunnies, Boo Boo Balloon Animal Kits, and Merwyn's Juggling Kit. We performed at carnivals, dinner theaters, county fairs, and high school football halftime shows throughout New England.

> *Doug is a doer. He was always able to entertain himself. He used to make all his own magic tricks. I'll never forget the time he cut a big hole in the trunk where I kept my college mementos so he could cut a girl in half. I was not pleased.*
>
> JEAN HALL,
> my mom

I like thinking of possibilities. At any time, an entirely new possibility is liable to come along and spin you off in an entirely new direction. The trick, I've learned, is to be awake to the moment.

> *Doug's mind runs at full speed at all times. One night, after he and Debbie had been dating a few years, he told me he had an idea for a way to earn money at college. He was going to make pizzas, and he wanted to know if he could use my kitchen to experiment. I said sure ... the night arrives, and he shows up with ten pounds of flour and all the fixings. We had pizza coming out our ears. It was OK pizza, I guess. But Debbie went to bed sick that night.*
>
> LILLIAN CHAPMAN,
> my mother-in-law

> *It's what? Twelve years later? And I still have indigestion from that pizza.*
>
> WALTER CHAPMAN,
> my father-in-law

I decided not to get into the pizza business in college. Instead, I formed Campus Promotions International, a little company that marketed beer mugs, T-shirts, and just about anything you could print a logo on to four different campuses. I published a vinyl phone book cover, the kind with the ads all over them. Money was tight, so I took lots of items in trade. Got a diamond ring from a jeweler that way. Gave the ring to Debbie when I proposed.

> *Bringing up Doug was a scary job. This was a kid who could go any direction he wanted.*
>
> M. BRADFORD "BUZZ" HALL,
> my dad

The University of Maine spat me into the world in 1981 with a degree in chemical engineering and a hankering to get into marketing. I'd worked as a summer engineer at Procter & Gamble's

Mehoopany, Pa., Paper Plant in the pulp mill, where I learned two lessons:

- P&G was a wicked good company.
- High-volume pulp digesters are not appropriate settings for free-spirited inventing.

Having decided chemical engineering was not my life's mission, I applied to P&G's advertising department. At the interview, I performed a few illusions, figuring that any company that couldn't appreciate a magic trick or two was not a place where I wanted to work. When the man interviewing me, Mark Upson, called in his secretary and asked me to do the tricks again, I decided P&G was all right by me. I got the offer and hired on with Coast soap, a fine deodorant bar. Didn't know the first thing about big-time professional marketing.

> *Were there times I wanted to strangle Doug? Absolutely. He was what I call a "high-maintenance subordinate." You had to watch him like crazy. He'd be nodding at what I was saying, but his mind would be somewhere else. Linear he's not. He's more like a helicopter pilot— he sees the same thing you see, but from a different perspective....*
>
> BARB THOMAS,
> my first boss at P&G

P&G was a great place to work. The company prides itself on doing the right thing. Most of the people are highly intelligent and committed to excellence. Diversity is encouraged and rewarded. I moved up through the ranks of brand management through tiers of increasing responsibility. I also threatened with some regularity to quit. In fact, I did leave for a few months in 1985, but returned with the assurance I would never again have to work under adult supervision. It was around that time that I became the company's first and only Master Marketing Inventor, leading an all-star team of corporate mavericks in the creation of new-to-the-world inventions.

Act I: Brain Training: Welcome

Doug's divergence paid off a number of times in the context of inventions that would not have been discovered simply by taking incremental steps forward from where we were.

BARB THOMAS

It was once calculated that my team at Procter & Gamble took a product to market with 10 percent of the staff in 16 percent of the time and at 18 percent of the cost of a similar project in another part of the company. It wasn't that we were any smarter. It was because we weren't faced with the same constraints, rules, or regulations that they had in the normal channels.

It was a wild time. We wore jeans and sneakers, worked sixteen to twenty hours a day, and loved it. The company loved it, too.

Doug brings an extraordinary degree of creativity, entrepreneurial instinct, and energy to his work. He has brought eight product concepts from invention to shipping, all within calendar 1990 ... with a ninth project soon to follow. This has to be something of a record.
From my final personnel review at P&G

The corporation acknowledged and respected my efforts. But for all that, it's still a corporation. And as with all corporations, certain rules of protocol are to be followed. The review continued:

Doug has just one key opportunity for improvement: he needs to treat the "system" with more respect.... (he) takes almost malicious pleasure in "beating the system" by developing new product concepts faster and cheaper than if work were done through traditional channels.... It does not help to rub people's noses in their inefficiencies, their cost of operation or their tortoiselike speed.... Finally, and of much lesser importance, Doug has a too-low tolerance for paperwork, memo writing, budgeting, and similar administrative errata which, until successfully addressed, will limit his effectiveness in conventional management assignments.
More of my last personnel review at P&G

Guilty as charged. I have a fundamental disrespect for inefficient operations, high costs, and slow speed. The point regarding administrative issues is also apt.

> *Doug has messed up our checking account twice. He may be able to come up with big ideas, but if he takes our checkbook one more time, I'll garnishee his wages.*
>
> DEBBIE HALL,
> my wife

All good things must come to an end. I awoke one morning and realized it was time to get on with the next phase of my life. A lot of people wait until they're sixty-five to retire from the corporation and start living the good life. I retired at the age of thirty-two. My letter of retirement from Procter & Gamble read as follows:

To Whom It May Concern:

Effective February 13, 1991, 10 years to the day from my first interview with the Bar Soap Advertising Department, I retire from Procter & Gamble and from working as an employee at any and all corporations.

I intend to create my own company, one that is dedicated to offering inventive excellence at unprecedented speed. I plan to fulfill the classic American dream of independence and self-reliance. It's the dream my forefather, John Hall, had when he left England and helped found Boston in 1620; the dream Lyman Hall had when he signed the Declaration of Independence, risking his life, his family, and his fortune. It's a dream to found, build, and create a new way of life, a new type of company that is the best in the world.

My tenure at Procter & Gamble has been outstanding. I truly believe that, from an employee's perspective, there is no finer company anywhere. My dream is that, one day, those who work for me will say the same. I wish the company and all those I've worked with great happiness and success.

Sincerely,

Doug Hall
Entrepreneur

P.S. There's no need to search for "guilty" parties that may have "caused" my retirement. No person or persons caused me to leave. I am leaving to pursue the same dream as William Procter and James Gamble in 1837.

I borrowed Ben Franklin's pen name for my new company, Franklin having published *Poor Richard's Almanac* under the name Richard Saunders. And that, in a nut, was the birth of Richard Saunders International.

You might say Ben is my spiritual mentor. The connection came from my days as a student at the University of Maine, where I blended my involvement in student government politicking with a major in chemical engineering, operating my own magic and juggling business and launching my promotions company, Campus Promotions International. Franklin was a renaissance man; I was a renaissance student.

The comparisons don't end there:

- We share the same birthday, a scant 253 years apart.
- We both have backslidden hairlines.
- We both have wives, the true loves of our lives, named Debbie.
- We both like to fly kites and play practical jokes.
- We both have far-flung interests ranging from science to business to politics.
- My forefather, Lyman Hall, signed the Declaration of Independence with Franklin.
- Our profiles and physiques are strangely alike, although I think Franklin may have had one or two more chins.

The *Wall Street Journal* noticed the similarities, too:

> *[Hall and Franklin] sort of look alike, especially when the balding and bespectacled Mr. Hall wears colonial-style shirts with puffy sleeves.*
>
> Wall Street Journal,
> March 2, 1993

It required a leap of faith to leave the comfy corporate womb for the life of an around-the-clock, let-'er-rip, freelance corporate inventor/entrepreneur. The hardest part, really, was the leaping. I've since discovered the answers to two pressing questions, to wit:

No. 1: Is it a good idea to take the road less traveled—or in my case, as the founder of a company inventing products for big corporations, to hack a completely new road through the jungle? Would it be worth all the bumps?

Answer: Yes, indeed. The bumps are what make it fun. The journey is the reward.

No. 2: Can a hardworking boy or girl make it on an idea, a prayer, and an American dream? Yea, though you walk through the shadow of corporate conformity and me-tooism, is raw inventing alone enough to carry you over the top? Or, to put it another way, is what you want to do what you should do?

Answer: Yes! Yes! And again I say YES!!!

The media and my business associates have tagged me with a number of labels: P&G Marketing Whiz (*Wall Street Journal*); Counterculturist Entrepreneur (*New York Magazine*); Goof Ball, Corporate Guru, and Barefoot Chief (*Dateline NBC*); Modern Day Ben Franklin (Joyce Wycoff), Think Tank Genius and Mr. Wizard (*The Cincinnati Post*); Pied Piper of Ideas (Diane Iseman of Iseman & Associates); Wizard of Oz (Page Thompson), and Evangelist to Dormant Creative Spirits (client Tina Mims).

Aw, shucks. The bald fact is, I'm an ordinary balding guy from Maine. The difference is, I'm not afraid to think great thoughts, and I have sufficient supplies of energy and enthusiasm to turn them into reality.

Look around. America has become a gray nation of gray people working in steel-and-concrete fortresses with armed guards at every door. We grind away in ergonomically correct office cells with windows that won't open, laying our lives on the corporate altar. Meanwhile, institutions are crumbling; our IBMs and GMs are falling apart. No longer can we trust the corporate system to trickle down what we need.

In the 90s, it's our turn. Smaller, not bigger, is better. The 90s are shaping up to be the decade of the little guy.

America has lost its edge—or thinks it has. Actually, the edge is still there, but it needs sharpening. The rust needs to be sanded from the blade. Americans need to rediscover their ability to create. As in ideas.

This country was built on entrepreneurial ideas. It was itself a wild and crazy idea from the beginning. It attracted people who had ideas. The song of the New World appealed to the discontented, the pioneering, the imaginative—not the slow, the lazy, the leaden of foot.

The first Americans comprised the lunatic fringe of their day.

> *The American Revolution was run by radical revolutionaries. It took historians to identify them as brilliant.*
> RICHARD SAUNDERS

The early Americans were forced by circumstances and environment to be creative. Survival was as much a matter of inventing solutions as a factor of fitness. Every step of the evolution of the United States—from the first mud and-log settlements, through the Industrial Revolution, and on into the computer age—began as a figment of somebody's imagination.

But the New World has grown old. These days, there doesn't seem to be much need to be creative. These days, all you have to do is add water or change the channel or pop it in the microwave. That and show up for work on time. No sweat, man. You don't even have to think about it.

Aren't you bored?

Can't you hear that little voice in the back of your head, the one that comes to you on the drive home after work or when you're lying in bed late at night and tells you there must be more than this?

There, there. You're not alone. Millions of good, decent people are bored. But they don't realize it. They don't have a hint. They've grown accustomed to the pace.

Why be normal? What's the point?
RICHARD SAUNDERS

But you have an advantage. Two advantages, actually. The first is, you've acknowledged that you're ready for change. Which means you've made change possible.

The second advantage? You're looking at it. Or rather, you're reading it.

Jump Start Your Brain is a book for people who want a New World. Maybe it's within the context of their current job, current life setting. Maybe it's an entirely new and different world of their own making. It's OK to stay in your current environment, and it's equally OK to leave. The important thing is that it be your own choice. Either way, this book will show you how to find new ideas, how to make them real, and, in the process, how to conjure a fresh entrepreneurial reality for yourself.

Jump Start Your Brain will tell you how to get the most out of that forty-nine-ounce sponge God put inside your head. Think of it as a user's manual for your brain. The approach is sort of like unscrewing the top of your skull and diving in. No sticking your toe in the water, no hedging of any kind. The idea is to abandon yourself to the whimsy impulse.

At Richard Saunders International, we abandon ourselves to the whimsy impulse on a regular basis. Our clients spend considerable amounts of money to have us show them how to do the same thing in our Eureka! Stimulus Response Invention sessions.

We help clients and corporations free their entrepreneurial spirits. We help them recapture the energy and enthusiasm that the founders of some of today's most powerful corporations—men like William Procter, James Gamble, Henry Ford, Bill Gates, and Thomas Watson—had when they were entrepreneurs themselves.

The scene of these crimes against corporate conformity, the headquarters of Richard Saunders International and its sister market research firm, AcuPOLL, is the Eureka! Mansion, a 150-

something-year-old Greek Revival home listed on the U.S. Historical Register and located barely within the gravitational pull of Cincinnati.

The place is stocked with wall-to-wall toys and games, an adult-sized swing set, a sand volleyball court, and an off-road go-cart course. It's a spot in the country where corporate vice presidents, market researchers, and assorted other Real World Adult executives can learn to think in Play-Doh terms, take shots at each other with Nerf weaponry, and, generally speaking, rediscover their funny bones. Our clients have come to think of the Mansion as a "corporate detox center."

As the chief tour guide for these Eureka! Stimulus Response safaris, I go to extremes to create the ultimate creative environment. I've developed a variety of techniques that make it possible for even the stodgiest, most pinstriped Real World Adults (RWAs, for short) to return to an innocent, childlike, entrepreneurial mindset—the source of the best ideas, the freshest perspectives, the concepts that sizzle and pop with originality.

If they can do it, you can do it. I'll give you all the tools you'll need. I'm not talking about theorics here—I'm talking about practical techniques for thinking smarter, better, faster. Each one is spelled out in simple, easy-to-grasp terms.

Largely because of these techniques, consider that:

- Richard Saunders International and AcuPOLL Research have become the leading new product invention firms in the United States. In one year, we test more new product ideas than Procter & Gamble tests in ten.
- My creative, research, and/or training groups have had the privilege of working with America's brightest managers and businesses.
- We've had the opportunity to conduct Eureka! Stimulus Response sessions from San Diego to Epcot Center in Orlando to Drachten in the Netherlands.
- The work of myself and my companies has been reported in print, on television, and radio, including *Wall Street Journal*, *Dateline NBC*, *The New York Times*, *CBS This Morning*, and *New York Magazine*.

- After going out on my own, I'm earning twice as much in one year as what Procter & Gamble paid me during the entire ten years I worked there.
- I'm a self-made millionaire living my own American dream, and I don't have to wear a tie. Sometimes I have to pinch myself.

When Doug first came in for a visit, our receptionist called up and said, "There's a man here in the lobby wearing blue jeans," which was a tip-off. Next, I learned about Dick Saunders. Then a bunch of us crawled around on the floor and acted like dogs for a day. Finally, we developed and introduced what looks like a successful new product. Go figure!

JIM HOLBROOK,
business director

All of which brings me back to my whoopee cushions and the 132 Anheuser-Busch marketing and research executives.

Having escaped from my regulation Acme straitjacket at the outset of my lecture, I went straight for the jugular. Or the things they wrapped around their jugulars on a daily basis—their neckties. These silken accessories from hell are in reality neck tourniquets that serve mainly to impede the circulation of blood to the brains of those who wear them. At the same time, they cause a buildup of hot air to the cranium, resulting in an unhappy condition known as "Fatheadedness."

I shared this information with my audience, along with a brief description of an experimental device, approved for use in Mexico but not yet in the United States, that was reportedly capable of curing Fatheadedness among necktie-wearing Real World Adults.

To my surprise, the A-B bunch applauded. I told them that if they'd reach under their seats, they'd find a sample of the aforementioned device, ready to be inflated and sat upon.

It was my first gang whoopee. I felt like Leonard Bernstein conducting the New York Philharmonic as these beer marketers and researchers blew up their grade-A rubber bladders from Taiwan and, at the count of three, descended posterior-first in unison.

A mighty *buh-rrrrraaapppppp!* filled the room, followed by peals of childlike laughter.

I'm not sure what the long-term effects will be. But I can tell you that, at least in the short term, a whole lot of hot air was released in that moment.

Steve Burrows, vice president of brand management for Anheuser-Busch, the man to whom my audience of 132 reported, agreed:

> *I think the best endorsement of [Doug's] impact on the group was that, throughout the balance of our planning week, I frequently heard people saying things like, "C'mon, get out of the box!" I saw the process of protecting newborn ideas in action. [Doug] helped us achieve our planning objectives and loosen up some very intelligent brains.*

CHAPTER 102

Recapturing Innocence

While we may not be able to control all that happens to us, we can control what happens inside us.

BEN FRANKLIN

The world ages us too quickly. We grow up too fast, we stop dreaming too early, and we develop the ability to worry at far too young an age. For too many of us, the ability to worry becomes a finely honed skill that narrows our vision and keeps our hearts from soaring.

Powerful forces weigh us down. Gravity makes us sag, mortgage payments are a drag, and we live in fear of our cholesterol levels. Our spirits are flattened under a steamroller of power lunches, secondhand smoke, rush-hour traffic, fiber-deficient diets, IRS regulations, office politics, and countless other existential dilemmas. On one hand, we're advised to make out living wills. On the other, we measure our lives in deadlines, arbitrary notches in time that, inch by inch, bit by bit, make us deader and deader.

The world pumps us full of experiences that grind away at innocence and creativity. Experience teaches us to doubt and distrust, to scoff and roll our eyes. In no time at all, the world can turn a child into a Real World Adult. At that point, there's not much of you left; there's only a job title on an office door, a number on a badge, a face in the crowd.

It's all so ... so ... yucky.

Think back. Remember when you were little and the world was a glittering place of limitless possibilities. Everywhere you looked, you found something new and different. As far as you knew, you could do anything because nobody had told you otherwise. You could fly and you could walk through walls. You and your invisible friend could touch the sky.

> *A child's word is made of spirit and miracles. We some-times think that children should follow us, listen to us, become like us. Follow a child closely for an hour. Not to teach or to discipline, but to learn, and to laugh.*
> SARK
> *A Creative Companion*

Or to put it another way:

> *The secret of genius is to carry the spirit of the child into old age, which means never losing your enthusiasm.*
> ALDOUS HUXLEY

The whole point of growing up in America is to become a grown-up. It's too bad, really.

We embark on our lives as small, helpless individualists, each with our own way of understanding the world, each with our own separate reality. Everything we see, hear, touch, taste, and feel is new and distinct. We're so busy exploring that we're incapable of boredom.

When we're small, we are able to invent our own answers. For example:

One day, I was reading *Big Bird's Color Game* to my three-year-old, Tori. On one page, Big Bird was shown thinking of something orange that's good to drink. I bet you can't guess what it is, so said Big Bird in his word balloon.

On the next page, Tori had a choice of a half-dozen orange-colored items—a butterfly, a T-shirt, a jack-o-lantern, a toy boat, a tiger lily, and a glass of orange juice.

Which one did you pick? Tori picked the tiger lily because of its long stem, which she took to be a straw. When you're three years old, "good" equals "fun." And it's a whole lot more fun to drink through a straw than from a plain old glass. The tiger lily might not have been the answer Big Bird had in mind, but it was a valid response to the question.

Kids aren't simply adept at coming up with their own answers. They're good at insisting on their accuracy. Sometimes they can believe them into reality. Consider an incident that occurred when my other daughter, Kristyn, was taking one of those pre-screening evaluations for kindergarten. The nice lady administering the test showed Kristyn a picture like this:

What does it look like to you? Kristyn decided it was a windmill. The nice lady explained that, no, it was an airplane propeller—at which point, Kristyn launched a ten-minute counterclaim. She argued that, with all due respect, the picture she had been shown was most definitely and undeniably of a windmill.

Afterward, the nice lady explained to my wife that, technically, she should have subtracted points from Kristyn's score for her answer.

"But she convinced me," the nice lady said. "I guess it is a windmill after all."

What happens to us? How do we lose the ability to invent answers? In the transition from innocence to experience, why do so many circuits in our brains slam shut?

It's because, early on, we're told to stay inside the lines when we color. Learning to stay inside the lines when you color is the first step toward becoming a grown-up.

Or in other words:

As education increases, imagination decreases.

Before long, we're remanded to the custody of an educational system dedicated to exposing every one of us to the same body of information, so that we all know exactly the same set of facts, theories, and hypotheses. Marvin Camras of the Illinois Institute of Technology Research Institute, the inventor of magnetic recording and holder of more than 500 patents, said it well in an interview in the wicked good book *Inventors at Work*, by Kenneth A. Brown, published by Tempus Books of Microsoft Press:

> *I think little children tend to be creative, but the more education you get, the more the inventive spark is educated out of you. In our educational process, you have to conform. Educators don't like you to go off the beaten path. In math, for example, you have to follow the style that someone suggests. After you've gone through more and more education, you conform more and more. You might even say that you're discouraged from inventing. Of course, different people have different natures. Some people can invent in spite of their education.*

We read from the same books, take the same exams, and drink from the same Cup of Knowledge. This cup has been passed around quite a bit. In the process, we inevitably consume a certain amount of backwash.

Semester by semester, school whittles away at individuality. It pushes us through the same funnel with but one goal: to turn us into Graduates. These are people who wear matching caps and gowns, who stand in line to receive matching certificates, and whose heads have been programmed with matching thoughts.

Never let formal education get in the way of your learning.
MARK TWAIN

As we march toward Real World Adulthood, we become increasingly categorized, polarized, and depersonalized. We learn to wear uncomfortable uniforms so we can be identified quickly and efficiently. We take the safe road—the one in the middle. We accept conventional wisdom and toe the company line.

This is not to say there's no value to growing up. We need Real World Adults to beat back the wilderness. But we pay a price. To give our lives focus, we put on blinders. We starve our imaginations. We fall out of sync with our inborn ability to see what no one else can.

We reduce our options even further when we assign names and titles to things. While names and titles help us communicate, they also lock us into well-worn patterns of thought. We limit ourselves to only one right answer. Because the moment you label a whirligigwhatchamacallit a propeller, you fence in your possibilities.

Consider the snowflake, a fleeting moment in ice. We tend to think a flake is a flake is a flake. In reality, of course, no two are the same. Of the bazillions of snowflakes produced during the average blizzard, each is a delicate, intricate, completely distinct frozen sculpture unto itself. But once you label it a snowflake, it becomes just another bit of white fluff. No big deal.

Which picture is prettier? Which would you rather see?

Recapture the innocence of childhood and you'll open the windows in your brain. Once the windows are open, you can't keep imaginative ideas from entering.

The best ideas come from childlike minds, the psyches that are naive and unafraid. The essence of the Eureka! Stimulus Response mission is to rekindle that way of thinking, so that you see, hear, smell, taste, and touch as if for the first time.

Recapturing innocence and opening our minds is more than just a means for getting greater pleasure out of life. It's a method for capturing the spirit of entrepreneurial thinking and enthusiasm that made this country great.

It's the key to jump-starting your brain.

Consider your last five jobs or significant life roles. Chronicle them here:

Job 1: _____

Job 2: _____

Job 3: _____

Job 4: _____

Job 5: _____

Think back to your first thirty days on each. Try to recall the rush of ideas you had, the problems you saw, the solutions you imagined. If you're a parent, remember the thoughts you had before your child arrived. Remember how you were determined to be the perfect parent? Remember how you weren't going to make the same mistakes your parents made?

Odds are, you were a fountain of energy and enthusiasm. Chances are, you were a major fireworks display of ideas. Why? Because you were new, naive, and innocent.

One of two things happened. You ran with your ideas because you didn't know any better, or your ideas flickered and died because you kept your mouth shut. And that was the end of that. Because pretty soon, you became educated. You learned to keep your thoughts to yourself. You became politicized.

Where are those thoughts now? Whatever became of them? What do you wish you'd done with them?

You've arrived at the point of departure. Welcome aboard The Retrogression Express, a train of thought that travels at the speed of laughter. We'll use a method of negotiating the universe and points beyond that I call The Eureka! Way of Life.

> *You just open yourself up to become like a child. All of a sudden, the world is a wide-eyed experience again. You start feeling again, and you see the world through the eyes of a five-year-old. Once you get rid of preconceived notions, ideas can start to cross-pollinate.*
> ERIC SCHULZ,
> Buena Vista Home Video
> (The Walt Disney Company)

Let's spend the next three pages putting together a scrapbook. Call it "Me Throughout My History." Find three photographs of yourself—one as you are today, one when you were getting ready to graduate from high school, and one when you were just starting elementary school. Paste the photos in the spaces provided on each page. Fill in the blanks with the appropriate answers. Take your time. Be honest. After all, whose life is it?

The Littlest You: Entering School

Insert photo here

"Entering school"

Please answer the following questions:

1. What was your nickname? _____

2. Who were your heroes? _____

3. What did you like to do more than anything? _____

4. What were you known for being good at? _____

5. What did you want to be when you grew up? __ _____

6. Who was your best friend? _____

7. What were your greatest fears? _____

8. What was the kindest, most generous act you committed during this time? _____

9. What was your favorite toy? _____

10. Were you happy? If not, why not? _____

The Middle You:
Graduating from High School

Insert photo here

"Graduating from High school"

Please answer the following questions:

1. What was your nickname? _____

2. Who were your heroes? _____

3. What did you like to do more than anything? Besides that, I mean. _____

4. What were you known for being good at? _____

5. What did you want to be when you grew up? _____

6. Who was your best friend? _____

7. What were your greatest fears? _____

8. What was the kindest, most generous act you committed during this time? _____

9. What was your favorite toy? _____

10. Were you happy? If not, why not? _____

The Current You

Insert photo here

"Current you"

Please answer the following questions:

1. What is your nickname? _____

2. Who is your hero? _____

3. What do you like to do more than anything? _____

4. What are you known for being good at? _____

5. What do you want to be when you grow up? _____

6. Who is your best friend? _____

7. What are your greatest fears? _____

8. What is the kindest, most generous act you
   recently committed? _____

9. What is your favorite toy? _____

10. Are you happy? If not, why not? _____

Look at yourself. Gee, you were a pretty nice-looking little kid. What else do you remember about the littlest you?

Back then, you probably weren't thinking much about money or bosses or sex appeal. You probably weren't concerned with practicalities. You whined on occasion. You pouted. Hopefully, you didn't worry much, if you worried at all.

Maybe you wanted to fly or be invisible or see through walls. Maybe you wanted to swing from a skyhook. Maybe your hero wore a cape. Maybe you couldn't wait for your next birthday. Maybe you had a hard time getting to sleep the night before Christmas.

The other morning, Kristyn decided to become an artist when she grows up. The day before that, she was going to be a nurse. The day before that, she was going to be a painter. Tomorrow, she may want to be a cowboy astronaut Barbie trapeze artist.

Hurray for Kristyn! To her, everything is possible. It may not be the most practical point of view, but it beats being a Real World Adult. Maybe you dimly remember living in that other world a long time ago. Maybe you don't, but you think you might be able to do some good if you could go there.

Step outside yourself. Be objective. If you could materialize all three versions of yourself, which would be the most confident? Which you would have the most faith in the future? The most hope? Which is the most trusting? Which you would have the freest spirit? Which would laugh the hardest? Which would hate bedtime the most? Which would be the most amazed and/or amazing?

If you knew then what you know now, which of the three versions of yourself would you most like to spend a day with?

Do the next best thing. Spend a day with a child. If you don't have a child of your own, borrow one—ideally, a child between the ages of four and seven. Borrow one of your neighbor's kids, your grandchildren, or a small cousin. You want a child with no grown-up tendencies whatsoever.

Go for a walk, take a ride, share a Special Day with a child. Special Days are big occasions at my house. On Special Days, the kid is boss. The kid decides what to do and where to go.

You're running a risk here. You're risking floating a paper boat

on a pond at the park, building a kite from scratch, going to a secondhand thrift store and buying a bunch of dress-up clothes. You're running the risk of lying down on your back in a grassy meadow, putting your hands behind your head, imagining faces and horses galloping in the clouds.

Whatever your child does, make sure you do it, too. Don't just stand there like a lump on a kosher dill. And ask your child lots of questions. Find out everything you can about your child. Ask your child the questions you answered in your personal scrapbook. Don't be afraid to ask silly questions. Have some laughs.

Read a book to a child. Find a book with no connection with reality, preferably a tome by the late Dr. Seuss, arguably one of the great creative minds of the twentieth century. His characters and stories will live forever because they aren't like anything anywhere anyhow.

Wait a minute. I've got an idea. Drop everything. Grab your coat, run to the library or nearest bookstore, and pick up a pile of Dr. Seuss's greatest works. Here are a few suggestions, along with brief critiques. I recommend you purchase the following volumes for your personal library:

1. *Oh, the Places You'll Go!*
   The world is a big place, filled with colors, shapes, and possibilities. It's dangerous and scary, but you'll succeed if you only get going.
2. *The Sneetches and Other Stories*
   This collection of stories exposes the silliness of prejudice and stubbornness, emphasizes the importance of a name, and equips you to battle your fears.

3. *Oh, the Thinks You Can Think!*
The doctor prescribes methods for stretching the imagination, à la "Oh, the THINKS you can think up if only you try!"

4. *If I Ran the Zoo*
Lions and tigers and that kind of stuff aren't quite good enough for young Gerald McGrew. So he stocks his zoo with Bustards and Flustards from Zomba-ma-Tant, as well as a Joat, a scraggle-foot Mulligatawny, and numerous other species you don't see every day.

5. *The Cat in the Hat*
A classic book about defeating boredom. It's the story of Thing One and Thing Two and all the things that they do.

6. *There's a Wocket in My Pocket!*
A guide to the fauna hiding in your house. Under the bed, in the closet, up the chimney, behind the sofa ...

7. *Dr Seuss's Sleep Book*
A magical book that's 99.44-percent guaranteed to bring on yawns. Do not read while operating heavy equipment.

8. *The Lorax*
An environmentally conscious fable of high drama about the Oncle-ler and the damage he did to the Truffula Trees for the sake of his lousy Thneeds.

9. *Did I Ever Tell You How Lucky You Are?*
The old man in the Desert of Drize shows us how good we really have it.

10. *On Beyond Zebra*
The doctor discovers a slew of letters beyond the traditional alphabet's twenty-six.

Aside from literary pursuits, another means of recapturing innocence is to kick loose from your day-to-day modus operandi. Take a mental vacation, even if it's for only five minutes.

You can hook yourself up to a biofeedback machine or go floating in a sensory-deprivation tank. But there are plenty of simpler, less expensive ways to kick loose, many of which are available at your local toy store.

Here are some of my favorite prescriptions for restoring the spirit and innocence of your once childlike mind-set:

- Inhale the contents of a helium balloon, then abuse your company's intercom system.
- Buy a joy buzzer, pepper gum, black soap, and fake dog poo and learn to use them properly.
- Climb a tree.
- Fly a kite. Pretend you're the kite.
- Hang by your knees from monkey bars.
- Roll down a hill.
- Swing as high as you can.
- Write a letter in crayon.
- Visit a fun house.
- Play catch in the office or in the hallway.
- Go wading.
- Make a dart board of negative thoughts and shoot them.
- Throw water balloons, shoot squirt guns, get wet.
- Spin until dizzy.
- Hold a pie-eating contest with yourself.
- Assemble a company kazoo band.

Most of the aforementioned prescriptions carry a degree of risk, at least initially. There's a chance you might feel, well, silly.

Don't worry. It's just the Real World Adult in you rebelling. Fight back. Take back control of your imagination. The key to achieving a childlike state of mind is to engage in childish behavior. You can do it. After a while, you won't feel silly at all. You'll be on your way to the best of both worlds.

> *There is too much sadness to hold your mouth down.*
> *When I see people like that, they hold their lip just so,*
> *and I go up to them and just say, "Boo!" People today*
> *are in a rut. They're afraid to think.*
> HAZEL LOUISE EMERSON HALL,
> my grandmother

My friend SARK put it this way:

HOW to Be an ARtist

STAY loose. learn to WATCH snails.
plant impossible GARDens. invite
someone Dangerous to teA. MAKe
little signs that say Yes! and post
them All over your Hous e. MAKe friends
with Freedom & uncertainty. look
Forward to DreAM s. Cry During Movies.
swing As HiGH As you can on A
swingset, By Moonlight. Cultivate
Moods. refuse to "be responsible."
Do it For love. TAKe lots of naps.
Give money AwAy. Do it now.
the Money will Follow. Believe in Magic.
laugh A lot. celebrate every Gorgeous
Moment. TAKe Moonbaths. HAVe
wild imaginings, transformative
DreAMs, and perfect CALM. Draw on the
wAlls. reAD everyDAY. imagine yourself
MAGic. Giggle with children. listen to old
people. open up. Dive in. Be Free.
Bless yourself. Drive AwAy Fear. plAY
with everything. entertain your inner
CHild. You Are innocent. Build A Fort
with Blankets. Get wet. HuG Trees.
write love letters.
♥ ©SARK 89

To reconnect with your earlier self, ponder this essential
Eureka! truth—to wit:

To thine own self, be the true you.

It's your call. It's your life, too. Totally and irrevocably.

CHAPTER 103

Recapturing Adventurousness

The spirit of adventure is the fuel that drives the creative engine. It awakens the imagination, fires up the adrenaline, and ignites the willingness to try.

It makes it possible for you to move forward, to take that leap of faith into the fiery fray. Without it, your life would register on an oscilloscope as a flat, horizontal line. With it, you can push back entire frontiers. Nothing adventured, nothing gained.

> *America basically conforms to an apple pie, Mom, family around the kitchen table–oriented population. Anything you can produce, invent, or do to better the way of life of many can be turned into a two-way profit. Think on those things. Hitch your wagon to a star; get going!*
>
> HAZEL LOUISE EMERSON HALL,
> my grandmother

Adventures can happen on many different and not necessarily grand scales. You don't have to be a Magellan, a Freud, an Einstein, or a Lewis and Clark to blaze a trail. You might be an assistant brand manager negotiating a better idea through a byzantine maze of corporate bureaucracy, a soccer coach working to motivate a bunch of ten-year-olds who have yet to win their first game, a suitor trying to string together just the right words so that the woman of his dreams will accept his proposal of marriage.

Entrepreneurs, in particular, are the modern equivalent of the great adventurers of history. Both explore new horizons of the mind, the world, and the realm of possibility.

The lead dog gets the best view. The rest of the dogs' view is butt ugly. Of course, the lead dog is also the first to fall into the ravine.

RICHARD SAUNDERS

As part of our continuing investigation into the invention process at Richard Saunders International, we do a lot of academic studies. In one such effort, we pooled random groups of people and asked them to come up with new ideas for eyeglasses, using a selection of Eureka! Stimulus Response Brain Programs.

They were given forty-five minutes to complete the task. Afterward, they were also were asked to answer 100 questions designed to provide profiles of their values, personalities, and attitudes.

Mike Kosinski, AcuPOLL's director of statistical analysis and, in my opinion, the sharpest stat cracker in research today, compared the quality and quantity of each person's creative output with his or her personal profile. The overwhelming conclusion:

The power of creativity is tied most directly to an adventurous mind-set. The strongest correlation between quantity and quality of ideas turned out to be a person's sense of adventurousness. The people we tested who regarded themselves as having an adventurous spirit created an average of 72 percent more wicked good ideas in forty-five minutes than those who saw themselves as more cautious. In other words, to jump-start your brain, you have to embrace a spirit of adventure. Indeed, a simple embrace may not suffice—I suggest a big-time bear hug.

An analysis of the profiles of those who saw themselves as being more adventurous led me to the following conclusions. Those who are more adventurous:

- *Exhibit a high level of discontent with the status quo.* Adventurers ask themselves, "Is this all there is?" They see their laurels as stepping-stones, not resting places.

  Their open-endedness is tinged with a dash of pessimism, tempered with an edge of cynicism. Their discontent spurs innovation. Henry Ford gave us the mass-produced automobile. But it took Charles Kettering to invent the self-starter, thus making it possible for us to turn over our engines with an ignition key instead of a hand crank.

- *Are by nature spontaneous.* They're ready, willing, and eager for new experiences, if for no other reason than for the exhilaration of it. They have a lot in common with the fool, whoever it was, who came up with the idea of climbing to the top of some craggy precipice, strapping bungee cords to his or her ankles, yelling "Geronimo!" and leaping headfirst.

  Anyone I know who has had the bungee experience invariably tells me it was "a huge rush." But I doubt that it compares to the feeling that seized the heart of that first jumper when he or she went sailing into space for the first time. Anyone who jumped after that point was simply following.

- *Calculate the risks, then move forward with eyes opened wide.* Adventurers weigh the odds, study the obstacles, and plan for contingencies. Adventurers are not daredevils.

  Christopher Columbus had good reason to believe the planet was not flat when he set sail for the New World; he noticed that the masts of departing ships appeared to shorten as they approached the horizon, a phenomenon he took to mean that there was a curvature in the earth's plane.

- *Have generally liberal attitudes*—not necessarily so much in political terms as in their overall outlook toward the new and diverse. Our research indicates adventurers are more forgiving, more adaptable, more open to fresh ideas. They're comfortable in more different settings, able to function equally well under wildly extreme circumstances. Given the opportunity, a proper adventurer can get along with an aborigine on a desert island as easily as with a bejeweled head of state in a "ballet roost." Or an aborigine in a "ballet roost."

  Likewise, adventurers don't require perfection. They're

absorbed with the process, with what's happening at the moment. The sculptor Korczak Ziolkowski spent three and a half decades blasting away, ton by ton, on a granite mountain in the Black Hills of South Dakota, slowly shaping it into a colossal statue of the great Sioux chief Crazy Horse, astride a mustang, his left arm outstretched toward the horizon.

In terms of sheer magnitude, Ziolkowski's project remains the most ambitious undertaking in the history of art. It's 641 feet long and 563 feet high. All four of the sixty-foot-high presidential heads of nearby Mount Rushmore would easily fit under Crazy Horse's headdress.

At the time of Ziolkowski's death in 1982, when he was seventy-four, it was estimated that the project would require another five to ten years of blasting before any actual carving could begin. His widow, Ruth, and ten children have carried on his work.

Ziolkowski had a vision. But he was not focused on the thought that, someday, he would actually behold the finished sculpture. He realized early in the project that he probably wouldn't live to see it completed. What drove Ziolkowski was the process, the knowledge that with each detonation, each ton of rubble, he was inching toward his destination.

- *Have high levels of self-esteem.* Adventurers are predisposed to saying "I can." Or to put it another way, "What, me worry?" They can't help it. Repeated failures never daunt true adventurers. They view setbacks as lessons learned— and each lesson learned as another step forward.

  While they respect the accomplishments of others, they aren't intimidated by them. They tend to think that, if they applied themselves with sufficient dedication, they could do the same thing. In fact, the accomplishments of others often inspire them to reach farther. Paul McCartney was hugely impressed on first hearing Brian Wilson's landmark *Pet Sounds* album. So he sat down and wrote "Sgt. Pepper."

Even in the most regimented system, you can be a swashbuckling adventurer. I dedicated a decade of my life to Procter &

Gamble, one of the most blue-blooded, buttoned-down corporations in the world. But I wore my colors proudly; my office was festooned with a six-foot Bugs Bunny, a humongous Kermit the Frog, two eight-foot cardboard palm trees, and several surfboards. I forsook ties and suits and declared a personal embargo on all nonproductive meetings and paperwork. I filled the air with Grateful Dead tunes, thought big thoughts and made them real.

I hear you. You're saying, hey, that's fine for you. You're different.

So are you. That's the point. Be yourself. Whatever you are.

As we grow up, we become progressively more cautious. We learn not to touch hot stoves, but we soon begin confusing hot stoves with potential adventures. We fall into deep, cavernous ruts.

We encourage children to reach out to new experiences. We arrange dance lessons, swimming classes, soccer leagues for them. But we don't do as we preach. We're too quick to slap our own hands. As adults, we live predictable, restrictive lives.

Enough, already! Wake up! Dare to dare. If you want to grow, force yourself to climb out of your personal ruts.

If you want to jump-start your imagination machine, you have to feed it with new stimuli, new people, new experiences. Choke off the stimuli and you choke off your brain.

Take those first few tentative steps. Here are a dozen suggestions for climbing out of ruts. But be careful—as simple as they are, they can lead to unsettling levels of new stimulation:

1. **Be Adventurous.** Take a different route to work or school.
2. **Be Adventurous.** Spend $30.00 on magazines you've never read, about subjects in which you have no interest.
3. **Be Adventurous.** Buy the No. 1 paperback on the *New York Times* best-seller list and read it in one sitting.
4. **Be Adventurous.** Purchase the top three music albums. Lip synch the songs using your hairbrush as a microphone.
5. **Be Adventurous.** Buy the *National Enquirer* and the ultra-creative *Weekly World News*.
6. **Be Adventurous.** Have dinner at the fourteenth restaurant listed in the yellow pages.

7. **Be Adventurous.** Go to a bookstore and buy the first cookbook you see. Prepare the eighth appetizer, the eighth entree, the eighth side dish, and the eighth dessert listed in the table of contents. Have them with a chilled white wine. Even if the entree is red meat.
8. **Be Adventurous.** Look in the newspaper and find the movie with the greatest number of letters in the title. Go see it.
9. **Be Adventurous.** Ask the seventh person you talk to at work to lunch today.
10. **Be Adventurous.** Write the numbers of the channels on your TV or cable system on little scraps of paper. Put the scraps in a hat. Pull out a scrap and turn to that channel. Set a timer for five minutes and watch. Pay attention. When the timer runs out, pull out another slip. Repeat until your eyes are bloodshot.
11. **Be Adventurous.** Call the family member you have the biggest grudge against—a really long-standing hostile bout of bad blood—and say you're sorry and want to start over again.
12. **Be Adventurous.** Convince a Rolls-Royce salesman that you're wealthy and take a Corniche for a test drive.

I bet you'll surprise yourself. You'll discover you like things that you used to know you wouldn't. You'll tap into a whole new set of ideas, options, and perceptions. You'll start to climb out of your life rut. You'll be taking the critical first step to recapturing your lost spirit of adventure.

The key to becoming an adventurer is in learning to feel at ease with two of the most central elements of your life—chaos and uncertainty.

Too many of us have been lulled into thinking we need a pat destination before we embark. Or we think we have to know the answer before we ask the question. So we never take the first step. Or the question never gets asked.

But no matter how many travel brochures you read, you won't know how it feels to stand with your feet planted on the beaches of your destination until you get there. And you most assuredly will never get there until you've taken the first step.

Granted, you'll be risking failure. At the same time, you'll be enhancing your odds from "impossible" to "possible." You'll also be running the risk of accomplishment.

Hold it right there!

You're not listening. You're nodding your head, but you're not internalizing what I'm saying. You know in your mind that I'm right, but you don't know it in your heart, which is where all such knowledge has to be known before you'll act on it.

Put this book down right now and engage yourself in some off-the-wall act of spontaneity—something that makes your toes tingle, your palms sweat, and the hairs on the back of your neck prickle. Something that makes your heart gallop and reminds you you're alive. Step outside yourself.

Or try this. Pick up the phone and call the couple you always get together with on Friday night. Invite them to a Friday night Eureka! adventure. Tell them it will be a surprise. Do the Eureka! adventure as part of a group, since there's safety in numbers. Doing a Eureka! adventure night with friends also makes it more fun.

Do the following:

- Have appetizers at the fifth restaurant listed in the yellow pages.
- Have your entree at the thirteenth restaurant listed in the yellow pages.
- Have dessert at the twenty-third restaurant listed in the yellow pages.

- If this is all a tad too random and free-spirited for you, then have each person in your party write the name of a restaurant that they want to try but have never visited on a slip of paper and put the slips in a hat. Pull them out and have drinks, appetizers, entree, and dessert at the restaurants in the order they are pulled from the hat.
- If time allows, go to the late show with the greatest number of letters in the title. In the event of a tie, flip a coin.

WE INTERRUPT THIS BOOK UNTIL AFTER FRIDAY NIGHT. PLEASE PUT THE BOOK DOWN AND ENGAGE YOURSELF IN A SPONTANEOUS ADVENTURE. PLEASE.

There now. Doesn't that feel better? Aren't you the live wire? Once you got past the first blush, it wasn't so hard, was it?

Imagine how it would feel to live out an adventure every day, all day long. Imagine being able to transform the obstacles that life dishes out into opportunities. Imagine taking control of your circumstances rather than allowing your circumstances to take control of you.

Good for you, traveler. You're on your way!

CHAPTER 104

We Hold These Truths to Be Self-Evident

The Eureka! way of life requires that you be excited, aware, passionate, and enthusiastic. It requires that you not be brain dead.

Being Brain Dead is being staid, emotionless, dull, and terminally serious. If you want to experience brain death, invite a life insurance salesman to explain the difference between term and whole life insurance. Or make an appointment at a funeral parlor to discuss advance payment programs.

It's your brain. Use it or lose it.
RICHARD SAUNDERS

Under the Eureka! way of life, it's advisable to avoid prolonged exposure to the brain dead. Here are ten dead giveaways for spotting brain-dead individuals:

1. They have chapped lips from kissing the boss's butt.
2. They don't observe the holidays of April 1 and October 31.
3. Their fingers point in only one direction—away from themselves.
4. Their doors are closed, their shades are drawn, and they cast no reflections.
5. The family pictures on their desks are studio portraits, not snapshots.
6. They think Dr. Seuss is a pediatrician.

57

7. They're rude to waitresses.
8. They wish children would "just grow up."
9. They once had an original thought, but decided it was gas.
10. They get mad when you tickle them.

The brain dead are everywhere. I once encountered one at an outdoor summer concert of the Cincinnati Pops Orchestra. It so happened I had a half dozen bottles of soap bubbles on my person. A handful of ten-year-olds nearby looked bored, so I gave each a bottle.

It was an enchanted evening. As the fireflies flickered and the orchestra played an arrangement of Tchaikovsky's Symphony No. 5 in E Minor, opus 64, those of us who were so equipped blew bubbles.

Then we noticed Brain-Dead Man, sitting cross-legged on his blanket. As our bubbles floated by, he scowled and swatted at them.

My jaw fell open. The kids shrugged and took their bubbles elsewhere. Brain-Dead Man was to be pitied.

Those of us who embrace the Eureka! way of life are, generally speaking, not big on rules. For the most part, we regard the average rule as an item to break, bend, circumvent, spindle, fold, mutilate, limbo under, and otherwise grind into a fine powder.

But there are exceptions. And while the notions of recapturing innocence and embracing a spirit of adventure are overall life goals, a number of more tactical precepts—call them rules if you must—are available to help you harness their power once you've properly regressed.

So whereby we, the people, seek to recapture the hope, faith, and innocence of childhood, and whereby we strive diligently for purity of thought and freshness of idea, we hereby hold the following truths to be self-evident, the first being:

Fun Is Fundamental!

There's no way around it. You absolutely must have fun. Without fun, there's no enthusiasm. Without enthusiasm, there's no energy. Without energy, there are only shades of gray. It's a law of creativity physics.

> *If it isn't fun, why do it?*
> JERRY GREENFIELD
> cofounder of Ben & Jerry's Ice Cream,
> *Rolling Stone* magazine, July 9, 1992

You might as well try surviving for a week without oxygen as create without fun. Creative ideas are a natural by-product of exhilaration. Not of tedium. This isn't an exam. This isn't school. It's recess. No—it's a field trip to the fun house.

> *Kids have more ideas because they play with toys. Playing with toys makes ideas come to you. It's fun, too.*
> KRISTYN HALL

Hard-core academic research underscores the link between creativity and fun. Alice Isen of the University of Maryland made the point in an article she wrote for *The Journal of Personality and Social Psychology*. She described a study in which two groups of college students were shown two different videotapes, then given a range of creative problems to solve. The first group saw a five-minute clip of bloopers lifted from *Gunsmoke*, *Have Gun, Will Travel*, and *The Red Skelton Show*. The students in the second group watched a math video entitled *Area Under a Curve*. I've never seen this production myself, but I imagine it is every bit as gripping as the title makes it sound.

Guess what? The students in the first group—the ones who'd been laughing and were in a good mood when they took the test—were found to be 300 to 500 percent more likely to come up with successful solutions to the problems they were given.

Stop. Think. Look how easy this is. You can increase your brain power three- to fivefold simply by laughing and having fun before working on a problem.

Fun fuels your brain.
RICHARD SAUNDERS

A key element to the success of Richard Saunders International has been our knack for generating big-time media support. We've done this, basically, by pitching ourselves as fun, and maybe even slightly deranged, people. The media likes to do stories about fun people. Deranged ones, too.

Early on, I tried to put a provocative, memorable, clippable spin on myself with eccentric media mailings. At one point, I introduced a board game with a packet announcing a company I called HaHa!, complete with the new game and a sampling of my other games, a card proclaiming myself the King of the Elves, and a photo of myself dressed in forest green tights and shoes with pointy toes that curled upward. *Entertainment Tonight* turned it into a story that paid dividends long afterward.

After leaving Procter & Gamble, I ran across a reporter at the *Wall Street Journal* who remembered the King of the Elves mailing. She was so amused by the photo that she'd kept it.

I thought, this guy has some spirit. Not many people mail out pictures of themselves in tights. And there were the games. But the thing I admired was that the cover letter said that if I wasn't interested in writing about HaHa! I should donate the games to a hospital or a charity, and that hit a positive chord, too. Because I thought, OK, this guy's out there hawking his goods. But he also has a soul.

ALECIA SWASY,
Wall Street Journal staff reporter

I began mailing Alecia, along with other journalists at various publications, subscriptions to AcuPOLL Reports, our newsletter on consumers' reactions to new products. At the same time, I offered to provide reporters a spirited, humorous quote whenever they needed one. Whenever I spoke with reporters, I had some sort of funny insight into marketplace trends or the state of new products. Among the subjects that I pitched to reporters: the trend toward ugly foods and blue foods, the evils of neck tourniquets and new products that I didn't understand, including Oil-Free Oil of Olay, Low Salt Mr. Salty Pretzels, Caffeine-Free Mountain Dew, Aspirin-Free Bayer, non-ivory-colored Ivory Clear dish detergent and Ziploc vegetable bags with holes in them.

A few months later, a brief item about our services appeared in the *Wall Street Journal*'s marketing column, written by Alecia. My telephone lines nearly melted from the heat of the hundreds of calls I received in response.

Alecia seemed to have a well-developed sense of humor. To thank her, I took a chance and sent her an old wooden bedpost with a notch carved in it for every phone call I'd received during the first week after the story appeared. When Alecia called to tell me it had arrived, she was still laughing. Six months later, she wrote a lengthy feature story on Richard Saunders International. The way I see it, fun was fundamental in gaining that exposure.

The process of fun begins down in the gut with a good belly laugh. Here are a few methods for mining belly laughter from your everyday routine:

1. Check out a country music karaoke night at any Holiday Inn near any Japanese auto plant in the Midwest.

2. Dig through your past for your most embarrassing moments as a child, as a youth—the ones that, despite the passage of time, still make your toes curl under with self-incrimination. Trade them with your friends. You go first.

3. Distribute a couple dozen whoopee cushions to your fellow passengers the next time you take a bus, a plane, or the Staten Island Ferry. Encourage them to use them. There is something about that sound. It is so ... so

4. Give your boss a wedgie—or, as it's referred to in some parts of the country, a snuggie. A wedgie is what happens when you sneak up behind someone, grab the waistband of their trousers or underpants, and yank it upward so that the seat of the aforementioned garment becomes wedged snugly between the cheeks of your victim's nethermost region.

5. Rent a stack of old-time comedy flicks. For inspired lunacy, you can't go wrong with the Three Stooges, the Marx Brothers, or the Little Rascals. If you think you have it bad, spend a half hour watching Laurel and Hardy trying to move a piano up eight zillion flights of stairs in east L.A.

6. The next time you and your friends go out to eat, let food dribble out your mouth and down your chin. Pretend not to notice. *"What?!? What!?! What are you looking at?!?"*

7. Tickle somebody. A good place to start is at the knee. Squeeze it. Pretty soon, you'll be laughing, too.

8. Peruse most any issue of the *Weekly World News*. Believe it or don't.

9. Turn down the sound on a really bad 1950s vintage grade C science fiction flick and supply your own dialogue.

10. Wrap your arms and legs in aluminum foil. Wrap a football helmet in foil and put it on your head. Attach two aluminum pie pans side by side and wear them as a chest protector. Fashion a shield and sword from cardboard and wrap them in foil, too. Walk up and down the sidewalk in front of your house or apartment, brandishing the sword. Watch your neighbors' faces.

With the possible exception of No. 4, you'll find that laughter uncoils tension, relaxes invisible guards, and opens minds to new thoughts. When you're feeling fun, you open the doors to your whole brain. When you're having fun, you open the floodgates to bold, ridiculous, original thoughts. Original thoughts don't seem so absurd as they do when you're not having fun.

Consider how often you laugh on a typical day. Chic Thompson, author of *What a Great Idea!*, told me that the average five-year-old guffaws about 110 times a day. As the years pass, our laughs-per-diem quotient drops until, by the age of forty-four, we typically yuk it up only eleven times daily.

Given the natural order of things, the human mind is at its creative peak at the age of five. It's also quite easily amused. The correlation is as direct as it can be.

By the age of forty-four, we're bogged down with obligations. Our shoulders are slumped, our brows are furrowed, and we have a hard time mustering a grin. Which means we have less fun. Which makes us less creative.

Joel Goodman, founder and director of The Humor Project, Inc., in Saratoga Springs, N.Y., is convinced that humor and creativity are inextricably linked. He points out that both offer new perspectives on old realities, that both generate energy for solving problems and taking on challenges.

> *Humor and creativity are kissing cousins. If you want to develop your sense of humor, invite more creativity into your life—and vice versa. In the presence of humor, new creative perspectives naturally occur. You can't stop them.*
>
> JOEL GOODMAN

Goodman differentiates between two types of laughter. One type is a tool for enhancing creativity. The other has the opposite effect. One is laughing with; the other, laughing at. A chart borrowed from *Laughing Matters* magazine, edited by Goodman and published by The Humor Project, Inc., lays it out in the following manner:

Laughing WITH Others	Laughing AT Others
1. Going for the jocular vein	1. Going for the jugular vein
2. Based on caring and empathy	2. Based on contempt and insensitivity
3. Builds confidence	3. Destroys confidence
4. Involves people in the fun	4. Excludes some people
5. A person chooses to be the "butt" of the joke	5. A person does not have a choice in being made the "butt" of the joke
6. Amusing, invites people to laugh	6. Abusing, offends people
7. Supportive	7. Sarcastic
8. Brings people closer	8. Divides people
9. Leads to positive repartee	9. Leads to one-downman-ship cycle
10. Pokes fun at universal human foibles	10. Reinforces stereotypes
11. Nourishing	11. Toxic
12. Icebreaker	12. Ice maker

For a free information packet on the positive power of humor and creativity, send a self-addressed envelope with four first class stamps on it to: The HUMOR Project, Inc., Dept. EUREKA!, 110 Spring Street, Saratoga Springs, NY 12866 or call (518) 587-8770.

It's a principle of humor logic. Take two companies that put out exactly the same product. At Company A, people are having fun. They work together, they laugh together. They arrive early and stay late. They're so absorbed in their work, they lose track of time. It's not a job, it's a passion.

At Company B, fun is a four-letter word. The spines of Company B personnel are permanently bent from the burdens they carry.

You tell me—at which company do you suppose employees are opening their mouths and minds to new thoughts? Which company would be able to weather a cyclical downturn; which could take advantage of an upturn in business? You don't need a Ph.D. from MIT to know the answer.

Not only does fun affect working pleasure, it also has an impact on your potential to get a job in the first place. Consider:

> *A recent survey found that 98 percent of 737 chief executives would hire a candidate with a good sense of humor over a solemn competitor.*
>
> *Sky Magazine,*
> August 1992

Another virtue of fun is that it reduces stress levels. Stress smothers the mental process. It may help you summon enormous energy and physical power, but it shrivels brain power. Not only does it reduce your ability to think clearly, scientists say it actually kills brain cells.

> *Brain cells create ideas. Stress kills brain cells. Stress is not a good idea.*
>
> RICHARD SAUNDERS

I advocate juggling as a way to de-stress. Because it demands single-minded concentration, juggling is just the ticket for sweeping cobwebs from a tired brain. When you're juggling, you can't be thinking about anything else. If your mind wanders, you're liable to get beaned with a ball, ring, or club. The process also induces laughter. Finally, juggling can be profitable. I juggled my way through the University of Maine.

As a life member of the International Jugglers Association, I'm sworn to pass the art along to as many nonjugglers as humanly possible. What follows is the method I used to teach it to thousands of folks of all ages while kicking around New England as Merwyn the Magician.

Merwyn's Juggling Method

(Read entire instructions before starting. If you're left-handed, I'm sorry, but you'll have to reverse these instructions.)

Step 1: Find three tennis balls. Better yet, get three beanbags. They don't roll as far. To minimize spinal stress from excessive bending over, practice over a bed. Or, to minimize runaway tennis balls, situate yourself in a sandbox, on a beach, or in the middle of the Sahara Desert.

Step 2: Hold one ball in your right hand with your arms bent at a ninety-degree angle as if you're carrying a tray. Slide your right hand to the center of your body, right about where your belly button is. **Open your hand and pop the ball up and across to your left,** to a spot just above your left ear.

Step 3: Catch the ball in your left hand. Then slide your left hand to the center of your body and **pop the ball up and across to your right,** to a spot just above your right ear.

Step 4: Practice **slide, pop, catch** until you can do it without thinking. The ball should follow a sideways figure-eight trajectory. Pop the ball with your wrist up and across your body. Don't use your arm. Your elbows should not move. A common beginners' mistake is known in juggling circles as the "stiff-wristed roll-off." Instead of popping the ball across their body, they roll it off their fingertips, causing it to go forward instead of across.

Step 5: Put a ball in each hand. With your right hand, **slide and pop up and across.** When the ball reaches its peak, **slide**

and pop the ball in your left hand **up, across, and under the ball in the air.** Continue practicing RIGHT • LEFT • STOP • RIGHT • LEFT • STOP. Now do it the other way—LEFT • RIGHT • STOP • LEFT • RIGHT • STOP. Remember this tempo. When you're juggling three balls, the rhythm is the same.

Step 6: Now it's time for partner juggling. Recruit an assistant, lovely or otherwise. Stand side by side. Put your adjacent, inside arms behind your backs or, if you and your assistant are on intimate terms, around each other.
  • The person to the right puts two balls in his or her right hand and makes the first toss up and across to the left.
  • As ball #1 reaches its peak, the person on the left tosses ball #2 up, across, and back to the right.
  • As ball #2 ball reaches its peak, the person on the right tosses ball #3 across and back to the left, etc., etc., etc.
  • Continue popping back and forth until you establish a rhythm.

Step 7: Juggle solo. Put two balls in your right hand and one in your left. Remember to pop each ball **up, across, and underneath** the ball that preceded it. Always use your wrists.

Relax. Don't watch one ball at a time. Concentrate on the three moving parts as a whole. Picture yourself as the nucleus of an atom, the balls orbiting around you like electrons. Don't rush—gravity controls the speed of the balls. Get a feeling for the speed of gravity. Once you understand the tempo, you'll have it made.

If you have problems with tossing balls forward instead of up and across, practice in front of a wall. The balls will hit the wall, then they'll hit you. After you've been clunked in the noggin a few dozen times, you'll learn to **pop up and across**.

The International Juggling Association is a wicked good organization. To learn more, write to Box 443, Davidson, North Carolina 28036.

The second self-evident Eureka! truth addresses the neonatal stage of creativity, that being:

Respect the Newborn!!

You need to take care of a baby. Babies need lots of loving.
TORI HALL,
Age 3

Be glad for what you get with babies. I wanted a sister, but I got a brother. It wasn't what I wanted, but he's really great.
KRISTYN HALL,
Age 5

Act I: Brain Training: Welcome

fjFkiv ivj m VV ZZZZ ZZZZZ ZBNM 5 VN VDH
GFHJH HHH bvchy fff ktfjo tist

> Brad Hall's typed response,
> in the interest of equal time,
> age 1

Ideas, when they first occur, aren't full-blown finished products. They aren't born one second, then standing up and walking the next. Thomas Edison didn't conceive of the lightbulb on Monday morning, then flip the switch that afternoon.

Newborn ideas are fragile, like babies. They need nurturing, protecting, patience, loving, commitment. They require you to sit up with them at night, fret over their futures, watch them grow. And like babies, they can't be hurried. They unfurl and blossom in their own time.

The problem most adults have with the creation process is that they're too quick to kill the newborns. Adults are so accustomed to censoring themselves that censoring a newborn idea is almost an involuntary action. Like blinking. "That will never work," they say with an air of knowing authority. "It's not reasonable, it's not practical, it's not possible."

Admittedly, like babies, newborn ideas are sometimes mud ugly. They may appear to be wretched little mutants that ought to be strangled in the cradle.

Don't.

Let's face it. Birth is a traumatic experience—both for the child and its parents. You've seen pictures of newborn babies on coworkers' desks and in the billfolds of family members. Many times these babies are, well, ugly. They have little red, blotchy, bulldog faces; their mouths hang open; their eyes are crossed and their misshapen heads are hairless. But you keep your feelings to yourself, because you know the first impression is not the finished product.

So it is with baby ideas. Newborn ideas seldom arrive as completed entities. How many gawky Little Leaguers have grown up to hit home runs in all-star games? How many former finger painters have created works that hang in the world's great art museums? You get the picture.

You'll increase your creative potential once you begin to value your own thoughts.

RICHARD SAUNDERS

Give your newborns room to grow. "I thought of that" doesn't count. Thoughts are cheap. It takes courage to bring a real new-to-the-world idea out into the light of day—because you're going where no one else has been.

I was fortunate enough to have been involved with the creation of Crystal Pepsi. Since then, at conferences and client meetings, I've heard at least two dozen marketing experts claim that, at one time or another, they'd conceived of a colorless cola.

I would ask them what happened to the idea. Aaaahhhh, they'd say. They'd decided to put the brakes on it. They didn't trust it. It was too different, too impractical, too something. They filled in the adjectives of their choice.

I'd say, to myself, that all they'd really had was the illusion of an idea. A figment. It's not an idea unless you're willing to take action on it.

Don't make the same mistake. Give your newborns a quiet place in the sun where they can be protected from the whims of ruthless Real World Adults. If you, your team, your company, or your family is too ready to kill a newborn idea, try this:

When an idea sprouts in your mind, write it down on a scrap of paper. Then put it in a newborn incubator. This can be a folder, a shoebox, or an empty mayonnaise jar—any safe, quiet place where your idea can have a chance to grow straight and true. Add other newborns as they occur to you.

At the same time, tuck your ideas away for refinement in the soft, warm folds of your subconscious. Then, after a few days or weeks, go back to your newborn incubator and sort through the occupants.

Every idea that travels through your cranium has some merit, even those of a seemingly hopelessly harebrained nature. But it often takes time to discern their value. If you give them room to incubate, you'll be amazed at their potential.

Which leads me to the third self-evident truth:

Breakthroughs Contradict History!!!

Great ideas shake the world. They deny precedent and redefine the world. An idea has to break rules to be wicked good. If it doesn't, it's been done before.

> *Inventing is the great theatrical art of "what if."*
> RICHARD SAUNDERS

AcuPOLL tests of tens of thousands of new products bears this out: As an idea becomes more new and different, it's more likely to be either terrific or terrible.

On the flip side, as an idea becomes less new and different, it moves more toward the essence of average. It becomes safe. Safe is all right for the brain dead; safe means they can't screw up. It also means they can't be great.

Consider the following chart:

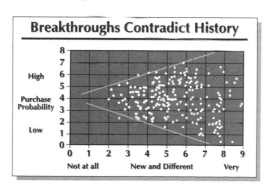

Breakthroughs Contradict History

Steven Spielberg and George Lucas created two of the most boffo box-office hits of all time—*Star Wars* and *Raiders of the Lost Ark*. Both rated high on the scale of new and different. Both took risks.

George Lucas knew he was rolling the dice. He said as much in a 1994 interview with the *Wall Street Journal*:

> *Listen, a lot of the films that I've made have been off-beat, really high-risk movies.* Star Wars *was a complete-ly high-risk, nobody-out-there-understands-it kind of movie. Once it came out, it was a big hit because it was so fresh and different. Because it was so high-risk.*

Then Spielberg and Lucas turned around and did *1941* and *Howard the Duck*, which ended up on the list of all-time stink-eroos. Again, both movies were new and different. Twenty years hence, *Star Wars* and *Raiders of the Lost Ark* will be remembered. The other two will have been long forgotten.

When an idea is not new and different, it's just another face in the crowd. When a number of companies sell the same product or service, they're dealing in a commodity market. Commodities sell for commodity prices; that is, they don't sell for much. New and different is where the money is.

The same principle applies when the product is yourself. When I was interviewing for jobs fresh from the University of Maine, I sought to stand out from the crowd. Where my classmates carried textbook-perfect one-page resumes, I presented a scrapbook of my business ventures and copies of my press clippings. I performed a magic trick I called Merwyn's Magic Bunnies and gave the interviewer a set of sponge bunnies for his very own. Despite an academic record of the C-plus variety, I landed as many job offers as my AAA competitors.

A prime example of a product that contradicts history is Clearly Canadian—a clear, carbonated fruit beverage in a teardrop glass bottle. Nincompoops created Clearly Canadian. No question about it.

Anyone who has ever conducted any market research on the soft drink industry will tell you that a fruit beverage has to be colored. Otherwise, consumers won't know it's a fruit beverage.

Secondly, the idiots at Clearly Canadian priced their stuff at twice the going rate for standard soft drinks.

On the third hand, Clearly Canadian came out with glass containers at a time when all the studies said the smart money was on aluminum cans.

Obviously, the dolts at Clearly Canadian didn't know what they were doing. Who would have guessed they would pioneer the entire billion-dollar New Age segment of the beverage industry?

> *In today's sailing races, they have all these rules that restrict you. They tell you how to set every one of your ropes. I think I should be able to do whatever I can to win, no matter how dumb it may seem to those young folks, as long as I don't have an engine or a larger boat or sail.*
>
> WILLIAM H. HOLDER,
> my great-grandfather

It's human nature to discourage the new and different. Human nature relies on history but forgets to learn the lesson history teaches—namely, that it's the breakthroughs that change the world. I'm all for respecting history, but I also believe in creating it.

That brings us to the fourth self-evident Eureka! truth, to wit:

Reality Is Not Relevant!!!!

> *Of course it's impossible. That's why you should do it, and that's why you'll make money.*
>
> RICHARD SAUNDERS

When inventing ideas, ignore reality—at least during the invention process. You'll have time enough for reality later. It has a way of imposing its values in self-fulfilling ways.

Reality is relative. Current reality rejects new ideas in favor of conventional wisdom. With original thinking, it's possible to define new realities, change entire system, and create a new balance of constraints and opportunities.

> *Wee Willie Winkie runs through the town,*
> *Upstairs and downstairs, acting like a clown,*
> *Rapping at the window, laughing at the flock,*
> *What's relevant's irrelevant, and history's a crock.*
> RICHARD SAUNDERS

What's relevant is perception. What counts is what people think it is, not what it is. Perception is the only reality customers will spend their money on. It's the only reality that will compel them to switch to your business or contribute money to your charity. If you want to jump-start your thinking, forget about truth, reality, and fact. Deal instead with the world of perceptions, feelings, and gut instincts.

A legend at Procter & Gamble illustrates the power of perception. It's the legend of Ben, the new brand manager.

There was this guy, Ben, and he was getting ready to go to his first budget meeting. In those days, it didn't take much for these annual meetings to degenerate into public executions for brand managers as senior management types challenged them to justify marketing budget requests for the upcoming year.

Ben decided that wouldn't happen to him. He resolved to fight intimidation with intimidation. Just before leaving for the meeting, a formal affair where jackets were required, Ben asked his assistant for two thousand sheets of paper. He divided them into stacks of twenty to thirty sheets each, piled each stack crosswise, one atop the other, and slapped a real business fact sheet on the top of this pile. All of the other sheets in the pile were blank.

Ben entered the meeting room with the largest stack of material in the history of budget meetings. The meeting went well for Ben. While no one can say for sure, it's generally believed that Ben's tower of paper created among management types the perception that he had the answers to any question they could possibly ask.

College graduates can have a hard time dealing with perception when they enter the Real World. They're used to dealing with numeric test scores and specific letter grades.

The Real World is filled with abstraction. It's built on shifting sands, with an entirely different set of priorities and measurements. In the Real World, a fresh college grad cries foul if he or she is passed over for a promotion or a raise he or she thinks is deserved simply because he or she has fulfilled the requirements of his or her position. Their problem is that, quite often, they don't know how to keep score in the Real World. They're under the impression that it's enough to do their job properly.

It's more important that the boss thinks they're doing a good job. This is not a veiled endorsement for brownnosing. Not at all. Brownnosing, kissing butt, or playing politics is the work of those without brains enough to accomplish something of substance.

> *It's not boasting when you deliver.*
> RICHARD SAUNDERS

Perception is about marketing yourself. It's about selling your substance, skills, and abilities. Muhammad Ali was arguably the greatest sports promoter of all time. His mouth generated record worldwide attention. But more importantly, Ali delivered on his boasts in the ring. You either loved him or you hated him. But in his prime, no one doubted his ability as a boxer.

In the Real World, one must always remember to deal with how one is perceived.

Are you seen as industrious, committed, passionate about your work? Do you show up early every day? Are your reports on time? Do you anticipate problems or react to them?

> *Life, like love, is not logical. Life is a three-dimensional sensory perception.*
>
> RICHARD SAUNDERS

Franklin addresses the importance of perception in his autobiography. When he was starting out in the newspaper business, he occasionally had to borrow money. To that end, he'd make a great show of hauling the metal type from his press back and forth from his home to his print shop in a rickety wheelbarrow—particularly when passing by the tavern, where he knew the bankers would be drinking and discussing the issues of the day.

The clanking, clattering wheelbarrow drew the bankers' attention night after night. Before long, they formed an impression.

That young Franklin, they'd say, certainly is an industrious type. A real go-getter.

In fact, he was. But the bankers wouldn't have discovered it for themselves as quickly as they did had he not created the proper impression.

With that, we have arrived at the fifth self-evident Eureka! truth, namely:

You Have to Swing a Lot to Hit Home Runs!!!!!

You remember Reggie Jackson, don't you? The baseball player? Man, that guy could hit home runs. He knocked 563 balls into the seats during his twenty-one-year major-league career, which is good for sixth place on the all-time home run hitter list.

It turns out Jackson was No. 1 on another all-time list. He struck out more times than anybody—2,597 times in all. The No.

2 guy on that list, Willie Stargell, wasn't even close with 1,936. Then again, Stargell only hit 475 homers, which tied him for sixteenth place on the home run roster.

Indeed, the top ten home run hitters in big-league history took about fifty-four swings for every home run they hit. But swinging is more than just making the effort. It also involves risking and accepting failure. The greatest home run hitters of all time made, on average, eleven outs for every home run they hit.

In your life, how would you deal with eleven failures for every success? Would you continue to swing for the fence or would you start declining your at bats?

> *Being alive is about playing to win. Being brain dead is when you play not to lose.*
>
> RICHARD SAUNDERS

In that sense, ideas are like home runs. It takes a lot of whiffs to knock one out of the park. The June 28, 1993, issue of *Newsweek* reported these findings by Dean Keith Simonton of the University of California, Davis:

> *In a study of 2,036 scientists throughout history, Simonton found that the most respected produced not only more great works, but also more "bad" ones. They produced. Period.*

The same article addressed the importance of trying:

> *The creative geniuses of art and science work obsessively. They do not lounge under apple trees waiting for fruit to fall or lightning to strike. "When inspiration does not come to me," Freud once said, "I go halfway to meet it." Bach wrote a cantata every week, even when he was sick or exhausted.*

How hard you try is rooted to how often you try. I'm frequently approached by people who are looking for a job or have an idea to sell. The first question I usually ask is how many doors have been slammed in their faces. If they haven't already succeeded, a dozen doors isn't nearly enough. Not if they believe in themselves or in their ideas.

> *It's to be expected that you make mistakes when you're breaking new ground.*
> JERRY GREENFIELD,
> cofounder Ben & Jerry's Ice Cream,
> *Rolling Stone* magazine, July 9, 1992

> *Every shot you don't take is a guaranteed miss.*
> RICHARD SAUNDERS

There's no way around it. You have to keep trying until you're convinced you're all tried out. And then you have to try some more. Because one more try is often all it takes. Look at it this way:

STANDARD   FAILURES BEFORE GIVING UP

If you're as good as the top home run hitters	54
If you're half as good as the top home run hitters	108
If you're 10 percent as good as the top home run hitters	540

Similarly, the more ideas you generate, the more good ideas you'll have. And your good ideas will be of a higher caliber. Quantity is the shortest possible distance to quality. And more quantity is a straight line to better quality.

> *The more ideas you generate, the greater the odds a high-quality solution will result.*
> DR. ARTHUR VANGUNDY
> *Idea Power*

This was the finding of a series of experiments conducted in the fairly sanitary confines of the Richard Saunders International laboratories. We assembled groups of ordinary people and asked them to invent ideas for new eyeglasses. We told the groups we were looking for ideas that were related to new eyeglass products, promotions, or marketing strategies. Each group's ideas were typed and tabulated.

An independent panel then reviewed the ideas, rating each for how "wicked good" it was. Stat man Mike Kosinski advises me that he can say with 96 percent statistical confidence that quantity of ideas is directly related to quality. Mike modeled the data and found the following relationship between quantity and quality:

# OF RAW IDEAS	# OF WICKED GOOD IDEAS
100	19
200	36
300	51
500	84
1,000	163

So there you have my self-evident Eureka! truths, in no particular order. One more time, but in short form, they look like this:

- **Fun Is Fundamental** (if you're not laughing, you're not doing it right)
- **Reality Is Not Relevant** (think of perceptions, feelings, tastes, sights, sounds, smells)
- **Breakthroughs Contradict History** (cut against the grain)
- **Respect the Newborns** (write down every idea, no matter how wild)
- **You Have to Swing a Lot to Hit Home Runs** (go for quantity)

CHAPTER 105

The Birth of Eureka! Stimulus Response

You know the feeling. You're faced with a desperate situation that cries out for a creative solution. Maybe you have to squeeze a six-foot davenport through a three-foot door. Or your significant other has developed an allergy to your beloved chihuahua. Or a million-dollar-a-year client has given you an ultimatum to come up with a concept that will make the competition's blood run cold.

You sit and think and scratch your head. You ponder the problem and you scratch some more. Maybe lightning strikes and an idea magically presents itself.

More likely, it doesn't.

You have to make it happen. And when it comes to creating solutions to everyday problems, you have two choices.

BRAINDRAINING

This is the method of idea generation that comes into play 99 and 44/100's percent of the time on this good earth. In Braindraining, you sit and think about what to do. You suck, stew, drain, fret, and bleed ideas from our skulls, hoping something great will ooze out. The brain is the sole source of inspiration.

Typically, these sessions revolve around a dozen or so humans seated around a table in a locked room, each one of them trying to squeeze, suck, and otherwise siphon ideas from their heads. It's a draining experience. The picture is further complicated by the fact that when these groups of humans assemble, it's usually in an incestuous gathering—be it a family, a team, a club, or a work detail. The result is, they're so close to the roots, they can't see the tree.

> *When familiar people try to solve familiar problems,*
> *they tend to develop familiar solutions.*
>
> RICHARD SAUNDERS

Someone at the head of the table details the mission, casts a baleful glance at each of the humans, and says, "OK, be creative."

The humans do their best to oblige. They groan, grunt, and sweat from every pore. They hack away at a series of tired "how to" and "I wish" exercises. And they may as well be trying to hatch dinosaur eggs.

Early in my career, having been dubbed a creative type, I was regularly called upon to participate in these death marches. Invariably, these sessions suffered from a serious lack of fun. As a result, new-to-the-world ideas were as rare at Braindrainings as duck lips.

Usually there was a ridiculous surplus of justification, self-censorship, defensiveness, and counterproductive debate on technicalities and feasibilities. The process was a mental skeet shoot. Someone hollered, "Pull!" Someone else squeezed off an idea. And someone else shot it down.

These sessions produced precious little in the way of creativity. Participants quickly learned to prejudge their newborn ideas until only the safest, most restrained, least threatening-to-the-world-as-they-knew-it were allowed to emerge.

Time after time, corporate CEOs complain to me about the lack of creativity in their organizations. The fault, my friends, is not in the people. Most people want to be creative. The fault lies with the approach. Nonetheless, Braindraining is the standard approach used every day in corporate meeting rooms throughout America.

But wait! It's possible to improve your productive creativity by more than 500 percent. How's that, you ask?

EUREKA! STIMULUS RESPONSE: CREATIVITY, THE NEXT GENERATION

In creating thousands of ideas for client corporations, I've tried dozens of different approaches. Some delivered, others didn't. The obvious question was, Why? I found the beginnings of the answer in my background in chemical engineering at the University of Maine.

New ideas often arise from the associations of two or more established ideas. New ideas tend to be transformations that occur when basic everyday elements are brought together. Just as water is a combination of one part oxygen and two parts hydrogen. Just as two parts nitrogen attached to one part oxygen produces laughing gas.

When it comes to chemical reactions, other factors come into play. Sometimes the application of, say, heat or pressure causes a reaction—not unlike when the boss tells you that, if you don't come up with a solution, you're history.

A less painful and more efficient method of creating a chemical reaction is to use a catalyst. A catalyst is a little item that, when introduced into a chemical equation, speeds the reaction, sometimes with explosive force. A catalyst is a stimulus.

I thought, if it happens in chemistry, could it be possible to provide people with stimuli to make them better able to create new ideas? If we treated the process of creating ideas as if it were a chemical reaction, a catalytic process, could we be more effective?

Thousands of hours of experimentation, research, and development lead to the creation of the process I call Eureka! Stimulus Response.

With Eureka! Stimulus Response, your brain is used as if it were a stimuli-processing computer, not a reference source. Instead of looking inside your mind for solutions, you react to stimuli to create new associations, new connections, new solutions. Stimuli act like fertilizer for your brain.

As outlined in the introduction, it all comes down to a simple equation:

$$\mathcal{E} = (S + \textbf{B.O.S.})^{F}$$

Or in greater detail:

$$\textit{Eureka!} = \left(\textit{Stimulus} + \begin{array}{l}\textbf{B}\text{rain}\\\textbf{O}\text{perating}\\\textbf{S}\text{ystem}\end{array} \right)^{\textbf{Fun}}$$

The big idea comes from allowing your Brain Operating System—B.O.S., for short—to react to stimuli in an environment of fun.

When stimuli enter your senses, they set off a chain reaction, so that one thought provokes new thoughts, ideas, and inspirations. You experience a rush of new combinations of thoughts and ideas. Let's chew on a stimulus right now.

Lollipop!

Your brain immediately begins sparking connections: *sweet, sticky, on a stick, round, shiny, hard.* As the seconds tick, more tangential thoughts emerge: *wrapper, playground, friendship, mmmm-good, smaller and smaller, tongue, licking, Halloween, giving to the needy, food stamps.*

A great thing about stimuli is the multiplicative impact of them. When new stimuli enter the brain, a new set of multiple thought patterns unfurls, like waves rippling across the ocean. As these waves of thought crash into each other, powerful tidal waves of wicked good ideas begin to gather momentum.

The amount of stimulation is up to you. It can be a simple matter of leafing through a collection of books or magazines, walking through a mall with your eyes wide open, talking to the ice cream man, or putting yourself in an entirely new and alien environment for a few hours. The more varied the stimuli, the more quickly your mind will click—but even a small dose can jump-start your brain dramatically.

Throughout time, stimuli of one sort or another have led directly to all kinds of famous breakthroughs. A few examples:

Harley Procter was stuck for a name for his company's new floating white soap. At the time, his was one of dozens of companies that were selling white soap. He tried *Roget's Thesaurus* and pored over lists of soaps manufactured in foreign markets. But he couldn't come up with the right name!

Then, one Sunday in 1879, at the Mount Auburn Episcopal church in Cincinnati, Ohio, he was listening as the minister read a verse from Psalms:

"All thy garments smell of myrrh and aloes and cassia, out of the ivory palaces whereby they have made thee glad."

Eureka! Thus came the inspiration for the name of what would become America's #1 selling soap—pure, clean, fresh Ivory Soap.

Samuel Morse, the inventor of the telegraph, was looking for a way to keep his telegraph signal flowing strong over great distances. No matter how much "power" he pumped into the line, the signal would fade in proportion to the distance it traveled.

One day when traveling on a stagecoach from New York to Baltimore, he was struck by the stimuli of his immediate surroundings. His Brain Operating System connected his problem with the fact that the stage company periodically harnessed new teams of horses to the coach to keep it running on schedule. In a like manner, he realized he could create relay stations to keep his telegraph signal running strong.

In 1873, Chester Greenwood was trying out a new pair of skates. The setting was Farmington, Maine, and it was pretty cold outdoors. Chester nearly froze his ears off.

Legend has it that, in an effort to reduce the likelihood of freezer burn, he held his mittens over his ears. "Hmmmmm," Chester thought, or words to that effect. "Mittens over one's ears keep them warm, but it is rather inconvenient."

Chester asked his mother to sew pieces of fur to two ear-size loops of wire. Four years later Chester was granted patent #188,292 for earmuffs.

In 1887, back when bicycles still had hard rubber tires, John Boyd Dunlop found it very uncomfortable to ride his bicycle over cobblestone streets. The stimulus of a garden hose pulsing with water gave him an idea. He wrapped a hollow rubber tube around the rims of his two-wheeler and pumped them full of air, thus inventing the pneumatic tire.

Back in the early 70s, University of Oregon track coach Bill Bowerman was searching for a design for a new kind of track shoe for his star runners. Legend has it that one morning while he was mulling ideas for a high-performance sole, his wife served him a plate of waffles for breakfast. Suddenly, he envisioned a slab of rubber pressed in a waffle iron.

Thus was the creation of the famous waffle-pattern sole, which in turn became the initial spark for the world's greatest sports footware and apparel corporation—Nike. To this day, Mrs. Bowerman's rubberized waffle iron is displayed prominently at the Nike Town superstore/museum in Chicago.

You probably don't realize it, but you routinely use a form of Stimulus Response to solve problems in your everyday life. In my lectures, I challenge my audience with a series of questions:

What do you do when you're stuck for a word? The folks in my audience tell me they look for stimuli in a thesaurus or dictionary, in conversations with anyone who happens to be nearby, or in magazines, many of which are filled with words.

What do you do when you need ideas for a birthday gift for Great Aunt Agnes? They tell me that they'll stimulate their imaginations by strolling around in a mall, browsing through a catalog, or talking to people who know Great Aunt Agnes, as well as to people who don't.

What if you need an idea for a theme for your company picnic? Typically, my listeners would look for stimuli at a party store, in the imaginations of coworkers, or in the pages of books and magazines about the art of partying.

To help you further understand the distinctions between Braindraining and the Eureka! Stimulus Response method, let's walk through another example.

Your task: To come up with ideas for summer vacation destinations.

Braindraining: You begin listing all the ideas you can think of—where you've been, where you might like to go, places others have told you about. Before long, your stream of consciousness slows to a trickle and eventually dries up altogether.

Eureka! Stimulus Response: You array before you a multiplicity of mental stimulus triggers, stimuli that will lubricate the contents of your cranium. These might include:

- A map of the United States or a topographical globe
- Vacation brochures, travel magazines
- Articles about bicycling, waterskiing, art museums
- *New York Times* travel sections on musical productions, summer fairs, and amusement parks
- A book on country inns
- A Robin Leach videotape of *Lifestyles of the Rich and Famous*
- Stepping outside the four walls of your normal environment, talking with other folks who will push and prod you with off-the-wall suggestions
- Going to a place that can stimulate the mind with vacation ideas—a zoo, a mall, a travel agency, a sporting goods store, a bookstore, a museum, a store that features foods from around the world

Can you feel the ideas for your next vacation welling up inside you?

Which method do you think will get you more ideas? Which method will get you better ideas? Seems obvious, doesn't it? It is.

I hear you. Some of you are complaining it's unfair to have all that stimuli to create ideas. These are the people who also think it's fun to push an elephant with diarrhea uphill.

You're rewarded for the quality of your ideas, not the pain it took to create them. Sure, it's macho to tough it out when it comes to ideas. But why bother when you can think quicker, better, faster with stimulus-activated thinking?

The Eureka! Stimulus Response method works. It opens the mind and quickens the soul. And it's light years more fun than Braindraining. More importantly, it consistently produces wicked good results. At the typical Eureka! Stimulus Response session, ideas fly like bees to a hive, like sparks from a grinding wheel, like snowflakes in a blizzard.

Still not convinced? Try the following test. It'll take just ten minutes.

Task #1:
The joy buzzer factory is for sale and you have the option to buy it, but you have to justify the purchase to your investors. You have ten minutes to come up with ideas for maximizing the plant's capacity. Use as much paper as you need. Knock yourself out.

Task #2:
The largest whoopee cushion manufacturing facility in the world is for sale and you have the option to own it. Once again, you have to justify the purchase to your investors. You have ten minutes to come up with ideas to maximize the factory's capacity. Number your ideas as you go along. Use as much paper as you need. But this time, use any or all of the following words, selected at random from a recent issue of *USA Today*, to stimulate your thinking:

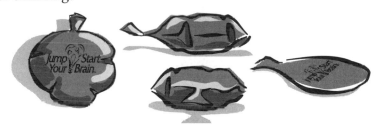

- Aladdin
- Brewers
- Weight lifting
- Assault
- Championship
- Edison
- Pillows
- Sailing
- Harmony
- Coffee
- Cowboy
- Lobster
- Aviation
- Packaging
- Gossip
- Candid
- U.S. Postal Service
- Bully
- Hospital
- Kite
- Sandwich
- Beer
- Tennis
- Defense
- Sledgehammer
- Armageddon
- Heritage
- Innocence
- Insects
- Montana
- Viper
- Air bags

Remember the Eureka! Stimulus Response truths we hold self-evident:

- **Fun Is Fundamental** (if you're not laughing, you're not doing it right)
- **Reality Is Not Relevant** (think of perceptions, feelings, tastes, sights, sounds, smells)
- **Breakthroughs Contradict History** (cut against the grain)
- **Respect the Newborns** (write down every idea, no matter how wild)
- **You Have to Swing a Lot to Hit Home Runs** (go for quantity)

Ready? Count the number of ideas you created with either approach. When I do this exercise in a Jump Start Your Brain seminar setting, I usually collect at least twice as many ideas with stimuli versus without. When the allotted time is extended from five minutes to thirty minutes, to three hours and on to a full eight-hour day, the difference between Braindraining and Eureka! Stimulus Response becomes disproportionately greater.

Dr. Arthur VanGundy of the University of Oklahoma, an internationally known authority in the field of creativity, compared the effectiveness of Braindraining, Eureka! Stimulus Response, and a wide range of other creativity techniques in a series of experiments early in 1993.

More Ideas!

Dr. VanGundy randomly recruited college students, assembled them into sets of six groups of four, and gave each group forty-five minutes to invent ideas for new snack products. The participants in the six Braindraining test groups were given no special guidance and no special direction. They were simply asked to come up with ideas for new snacks: chips, pretzels, that sort of thing.

After their brains were drained, VanGundy counted an average of 29.7 ideas per group. That's a shade better than one idea every two minutes. At that rate, it would take more than thirty-three hours to come up with a thousand ideas, not allowing for potty breaks.

Then VanGundy let similar groups of college students use the Eureka! Stimulus Response approach. He blended such stimuli as product samples and magazine photos with divergent Trained Brains and divergent Brain Operating Systems in a fun, spontaneous environment with loud music, good food, and Nerf guns. These groups churned out, on an average, 310.8 snack food ideas in forty-five minutes. That's better than ten times what the groups using the traditional Braindraining method were able to muster.

IDEA GENERATION OUTPUT: SNACK FOOD IDEAS IN 45 MINUTES

Dr. VanGundy, University of Oklahoma
(Average per group of 4 people)

Braindraining	29.7
Eureka! Stimulus Response	310.8

More Wicked Good Ideas!

But the difference in quantity is only part of the story. You've already seen how quantity breeds quality, that the more times you swing, the more home runs you're going to hit. VanGundy collected all the ideas from all the groups he tested, then had them evaluated by a trio of real-world new product gurus—two directly from the Frito-Lay company and one outside new product expert. The ideas had been shuffled and scrambled, using a random number generator, so that the evaluators would be unable to identify the sources of the ideas.

The real-world evaluators scored each idea on a scale of 1 to 5, based on the marketplace potential they felt each idea had. The lists were unscrambled and the votes tallied.

The results? Let me just say that a trumpet fanfare, a twenty-one-gun salute, or, at the very least, a drumroll would be appropriate here. Scientific analysis of the output from the research of

Braindraining and Eureka! Stimulus Response found that an average group using the Eureka! Stimulus Response method generated 36.3 ideas per group with wicked good marketplace potential, as opposed to 6.5 via Braindraining.

This means that, according to an objective independent panel, Eureka! Stimulus Response generated 558 percent more wicked good ideas than the creative method used by most people, most of the time.

"Wicked Good" Idea Output: Snack Food Ideas in 45 minutes

Dr. VanGundy, University of Oklahoma
(Average per group of 4 people)

Braindraining	6.5
Eureka! Stimulus Response	36.3

More ideas is a great result. More **GREAT IDEAS** is even better.

Greater Personal Satisfaction!

An even more exciting part of the VanGundy study was the impact on the people. Each of the participants in VanGundy's experiment was asked a series of questions following the research. They were asked to rate their satisfaction with the process they utilized:

1. To what extent did you feel free to participate and contribute your ideas?
2. How satisfied are you with the quantity of ideas generated by your group?
3. How satisfied are you with the quality of ideas generated by your group?
4. In general, how satisfied were you with the process used by your group?

The results for each question were tabulated and summed together on a 100-point scale, with 0 scraping bottom and 100 knocking on heaven's door.

Braindraining scored a 64.8. In school, that gets you an F on your report card. Eureka! Stimulus Response scored a 96.8. In school, that's called an A!

Wow! Not only does Eureka! Stimulus Response generate more wicked good ideas. It also builds self-confidence, self-esteem, spirit, and enthusiasm!

When I saw Dr. VanGundy's validation numbers, I felt like running outdoors and climbing a tree in celebration, pounding joyously on a tom-tom and howling at the moon. Instead, I celebrated by calling a holiday.

PARTICIPANT SATISFACTION WITH IDEA GENERATION METHODS

Dr. VanGundy, University of Oklahoma
(100-point satisfaction scale)

Braindraining	64.8
Eureka! Stimulus Response	96.8

Eureka! Stimulus Response thinking has proven itself in the academic community and with clients in the marketplace. Scientific evidence further indicates the method is in line with the way the lump of soft tissue between your ears works.

Consider the humble rat. Consider, too, the rat's humble brain. In a famous study on the effects of stimuli with these creatures, University of California, Berkeley, psychology professor Mark Rosenzweig put a dozen lab rats in a roomy, three-by-three-foot cage full of toys—ladders, running wheels, lightbulbs, Ping-Pong balls, and an assortment of other bright, colorful items that he supposed might amuse a rat. This he called an "enriched environment."

Into smaller cages, about one foot wide by eight inches deep, furnished only with a food dish and a water supply, Rosenzweig would put a single rat. He called this an "impoverished environment."

You can find similar impoverished environments in most major American corporations, usually occupied by midlevel managers.

From the late 1950s and into the early 70s, Rosenzweig compared the rats in either setting as to their abilities to solve problems.

The rats in the stimulus-rich environment turned out to be a lot better at it—a result, Rosenzweig concluded, of a combination of social interaction with other rats and their ready access to objects de fun, a.k.a. objects de stimuli.

He also found that the brains of the rats in the enriched environment were more developed; indeed, that certain cognitive parts of their brains weighed up to 10 percent more than those of the lonesome rats in solitary confinement. (Yuck.)

> *Later on, we took cross-sections from the brain and measured the thickness of the cerebral cortex, which controls memory storage and information processing. We found the cortex was thicker because, in the enriched environment, the nerve cells had branched out and made more connections. We concluded ... that complex interaction with the environment leads to a significant increase in the development of the brain and a significant improvement in the ability to solve problems.*
> Dr. Mark Rosenzweig
> University of California, Berkeley

In fact, Rosenzweig's rat studies are the reason why many of today's infant toys are so brightly colored.

At the far end of the creative stimulus landscape are the Eureka! Stimulus Response invention sessions we conduct for clients who are looking for new products or services to take to the marketplace. These sessions are loaded with stimuli you can see, touch, smell, and taste. They stretch stimulus thinking to the extreme and, if the occasion calls for it, absurd lengths—my feeling being that more is better, unless you're on a diet.

A little brain with imagination makes your brain bigger.
KRISTYN HALL

Kristyn's comment is more insightful than it might at first seem. The number of brain cells is not the relevant factor when it comes to jump-starting your brain. What counts is the number of connections between them. When your brain is exposed to a stimulus, it creates new wiring connections. As more connections are completed, your brain becomes bigger, heavier, smarter.

It's a short hop to the inevitable conclusion: The more stimuli you use, the more powerful your brain becomes.

Think of your brain as a vast series of electrical circuits. Each of us is born with about 100 billion brain cells, which is roughly equivalent to the number of stars in the Milky Way. Each cell communicates with other cells at a rate of 100 million electrochemical impulses per second across a network of brain wiring. That may sound like a lot, but the total wattage of these impulses is barely powerful enough to light a night-light. In that sense, even Einstein could be considered a dim bulb.

The more connections your brain cells share, the more efficiently and effectively your brain works. Scientific proof abounds. Brain scans of people with higher IQs indicate that less of their brain is active when they are solving a problem then those with lower IQs. Because their brains have built more connections, it takes less work for them to solve problems, draw associations, and invent new ideas.

The more you exercise your brain with stimuli, the greater the number of connections in your brain. Remember when you first learned to play tennis, golf, or ice-skate, you were intensely aware of every basic movement. With practice, you became more acquainted with the process. As you became skilled, you seemed to be operating on automatic pilot.

Experience with the task opened your mind to new plateaus of performance. You were able to think in terms of top spin, back spin, or triple axel.

In the same way, brain workouts generate brain efficiency. The reason we can invent ideas as quickly as we do at Richard Saunders is that we've already written oceans of ideas. Ideas beget more ideas. The more you invent, the better you get at inventing.

From time to time, I find myself suffering from inventor's block. In most every case, the reason is that I've gotten lazy in the care and feeding of my mental food processor. I've drained my brain. I need to refill, recharge, refresh the contents of my cranium. I need to get up, move my feet, and feed my brain some stimuli.

> *Always taking out of the meal tub, and never putting in, one soon comes to the bottom.*
> BEN FRANKLIN

On a recent flight to Florida from Cincinnati, I was trying to create names for a new breakfast product. The hour was late and I was tired—so tired that I fell into the trap of Braindraining. I took a sheet and started listing ideas. An hour later, I looked at the paper on my lap and found nothing but a collection of doodles.

What I needed were stimuli. But how? Where? The airline magazines! I lunged for the pocket of Delta Travel Vacations, *Delta* magazine, even the airline emergency card that tells you what to do when an engine catches fire and those little yellow oxygen masks drop down from the ceiling. Thumbing through these materials, I began to think of fun names, international names, funky names, sensory names, rational names, image-laden names. Inside of thirty minutes, I had three dozen viable alternatives. I wrote them down and faxed them to the client upon arrival at my hotel. Shortly before this book was released, a new breakfast product was being introduced with a name that was inspired from the pages of *Delta* magazine. I wish I could tell you the name, but as of this writing, I am bound by my contract with the client to keep it a secret.

Gathering stimuli can be a simple matter of talking to other people about the challenge, strolling through a supermarket, watching MTV, leafing through the latest copy of *Boy's Life* magazine, flipping on a Three Stooges video, watching Wile E. Coyote employ another Acme product in hopes of finally catching the Roadrunner, playing with a client's latest thingamabob, or violating the speed limit on the interstate with the stereo turned all the way up. Wherever you are, you can find stimuli.

> *WHEN I NEED TO JUMP START MY BRAIN I go to a baseball stadium with real grass, sit in the sun, and let my mind wander. Or maybe I crank up some early Clash and drive at high speed. I recommend "Clampdown" or "Safe European Home."*
>
> Page Thompson,
> Marketing Manager

An idea stimulus can be anything that takes you out of your normal frame of reference and, if only for a moment, opens your eyes a little wider.

In summary, the Stimulus Response approach is the best way I know of to turbocharge your mind. It's a jet pack for your brain. The result is a whole new chain reaction of ideas—each of which can be built upon, blown out, and otherwise molded into an idea with the potential to make history.

In that sense, a good idea is like a string of firecrackers. You can light just one, and the explosions will echo long afterward.

CHAPTER 106

Welcome to the Mansion

You've been assigned to come up with an idea that will leave your competition selling No. 2 lead pencils on skid row. You sit in your office blinking at a blank sheet of paper. Or you gather your creative team around a conference table in a meeting room on the thirty-fourth floor. The room has a window, but the only way to open it is with a brick.

You explain that they aren't here to have fun—they're here to produce. You warn them you're prepared to create straight through until midnight if necessary, so they'll be expected to perform. To ensure positive results, you have arranged to have large mounds of cold cuts on hand should anyone get hungry.

What's wrong with this picture?

Everything. Unless, of course, you're trying to invent a way to grind creativity to a bloody nub.

And yet, every day throughout corporate America, Braindraining brainstorming sessions take place under strikingly similar circumstances.

It's unimaginable. The truth is, the proper setting is as vital to generating genuine creativity as the process you use and the people you choose.

I've worked hard to make the Eureka! Mansion a haven for free and original thought. It's a cozy place in the country where even the stiffest, staunchest, starchiest RWA (Real World Adult) can uncoil without suffering withdrawal symptoms.

My clients have come to think of it as a "corporate detox center."

It's like that secret place you had as a kid, where you could say whatever bubbled into your mind and not worry what anyone thought. Maybe it was on top of the monkey bars, out behind the barn, or in a private corner of the attic where you and your imagination would go to explore the farthest reaches of the universe.

When you went to your secret place, you had no fear. Try to remember the worlds you created there. Try to recall the heroic roles you invented for yourself, the demons that fell before you, the villains you vanquished.

Today, your enemy is sameness. The villain is Real World status quo. You need to rediscover your secret place. You need a Eureka! room of your own.

> *The first step for me is to get into a environment where creativity can take place. And that doesn't happen sitting in an office, behind a desk with phone calls coming in from a billion different people. I have to break away and get back to being "me." I have a room in my house that is my "sports central." It's got a cardboard Michael Jordan in a corner with Bugs Bunny from the Nike commercial. It's got basketball pictures everywhere, memorabilia stuff from my college days, and a lot of historical stuff to remind me of where I've been. Most of my great ideas come in that room....*
> ERIC SCHULZ,
> Walt Disney Company

This chapter is intended as a suggested blueprint for creating a secret place of your own. In many cases, I have scientific evidence to support my suggestions. In others, the lack of scientific evidence in no way hinders me from drawing conclusions. In those instances, I draw on experience and opinions—my own and those of my companions in creativity, the Richard Saunders Trained Brains.

My blueprint may not be your ideal. Your tastes may differ from my own. You may, for example, be allergic to Maine lobster. You'll probably have some ideas of your own. That's fine.

The point is that every element in your secret place is, in one way or another, a potential stimulus for ideas. This is simply how I've done it. And I've had happy results using the environmental elements cited here with some of the world's largest and most successful corporations.

FOOD AND DRINK

The role of food and drink in the creative process is a controversial one. I find two polar points of view—among the Trained Brains, at least. I can see advantages to both sides.

Nature Babies:

Their bodies are temples, not to be sullied with calories, fat, cholesterol, or artificial sugars. In terms of liquid refreshment, their preferences run to spring water and fruit juices. Given a choice

between a sticky bun or a carrot stick, they'll behave like a wild hare.

They believe the fuel provided by high-fat, sugar-caked foods burns out quickly and leads to premature crashing. And to the extent that scientific studies show that animals on low-cal diets live longer and healthier, Nature Babies make good sense.

As a serious eater of fine junk foods myself, I find this position more than mildly disconcerting. But I can testify to the impact of a reduced caloric intake. When I eat light, my energy level is generally greater. In the process of writing this book, I found that my pages-per-hour output increased by nearly a third when I was eating lighter meals. When the belly is glutted with heavy grub, it seems your body spends so much energy processing the food that the brain is shortchanged.

> *If thou art dull and heavy after a meal, it's a sign thou has exceeded the due Measure; for meat and drink ought to refresh the body, and make it cheerful, and not to dull and oppress it.*
>
> BEN FRANKLIN

Nature Babies eschew fat in particular, leaning instead toward chicken and shellfish. The connection between creativity and ultra low-fat, high-protein foods has some basis in scientific fact. Indeed, numerous scientific studies indicate shellfish is the highest of all high-octane brain foods.

> *Shellfish, low in fat and carbohydrates, and almost pure protein, delivers large supplies of an amino acid called tyrosine to the brain, which then converts into the two mentally energizing brain chemicals, dopamine and norepinephrine.... Extensive research with both animals and humans proves that when the brain produces [these chemicals], mood and energy pick up. You tend to think and react more quickly, be more attentive, motivated and mentally energetic.*
>
> JEAN CARPER,
> *The Food Pharmacy*

One point to keep in mind when ripping into your shellfish: Avoid butter, bread, potatoes, and deep-frying. Researchers tell us that loading up on fat or carbohydrates can dull the mind.

Of course, oysters, clams, crabs, and shrimp are fine. But in my totally biased and unfounded opinion, the best brain food in the world is the Maine lobster. The fact that I was born and schooled in the great state of Maine is coincidental.

Fat and Sassy Hedonists:
Their bodies are temples of doom, at least from the perspective of pure physical health concerns. They like their food rich, exotic, and in great steaming heaps. Like Jimmy Buffett and my son, Brad, Fat and Sassy Hedonists believe the first item on the menu in paradise is a cheeseburger.

> *I always hated going to focus groups where all they had to eat were cold cuts. I mean, it was "gag me," and I shut down. But give me something exotic to eat and my mind gets exotic.*
>
> DIANE ISEMAN,
> Trained Brain

Fat and Sassy Hedonists argue that the supreme fluid for jump-starting a brain is coffee. While the debate over coffee's benefits has raged for centuries, I stand firmly behind the brown bean. Here's why:

- Coffee is 100 percent natural, with no chemicals or preservatives.
- Coffee contains no calories.
- A cup of hot joe costs less than a nickel a cup when you brew it fresh.
- Ounce for ounce, a cup of brewed coffee contains five times the caffeine of colas.

Throughout history, such great creatives as Franklin, Voltaire, Twain, Bach, Beethoven, and Brahms have heaped praise on coffee. The brew itself is dark, but its power is clear.

Caffeine results in a clearer and more rapid flow of thought [and an] allaying of drowsiness and fatigue. After taking caffeine, one is capable of a greater sustained intellectual effort and a more perfect association of ideas. There is also a keener appreciation of sensory stimuli, and reaction time is appreciably diminished. In addition, motor activity is increased: typists, for example, work faster and with fewer errors.
The Pharmacological Basis of Therapeutics

Caffeine boosted [test subjects'] performances on every single one of the mental tests.... [It] stirred the brain to improve mental functioning, reaction speed, concentration and accuracy.

JEAN CARPER,
The Food Pharmacy

More than 200 years ago in parts of Europe, distribution of the bean was restricted because it was thought to be responsible for stirring rebellion among the masses. The coffeehouses of the day, not the taverns, were forums for hotheaded radicals spouting doctrines of revolution.

One of the most interesting facts in the history of coffee drinks is that wherever it has been introduced, it has spelled revolution. It has been the world's most radical drink in that its function has always been to make people think. And when the people began to think, they became dangerous to tyrants and to foes of liberty, of thoughts and of action.

WILLIAM UKERS,
All About Coffee

Medical opinions vary on the benefits and risks of consuming coffee by the bucketful. For every coffee-related study that cites a potential negative health effect on the human physiology, there's another study to the contrary.

The mystical, magical properties, of the wondrous,
*   marvelous bean,*
will get you rolling in the morning, and thinking swift
*   and clean.*
The power of this incredi-brew is almost too great to
*   conceive.*
Through morning, noon, and night, it will help you to
*   achieve.*
RICHARD SAUNDERS

So strong is my faith in the brew that I've developed a custom blend called Eureka! Mansion Brain Brew, a mix of some of the world's greatest coffees—java from Java, pure Colombian, high-grown Guatemalan, and exotic Tanzanian peaberry—that can jump-start brain cells morning, noon, and night.

Of the store-bought brands, Maxwell House is said to be good to the last drop and Chock Full O' Nuts purports to be heavenly. But Folgers is, bar none, the best part of waking up (note here how I inserted a blatant endorsement for a client).

This book was fueled with Brain Brew; my coauthor, David Wecker, and I consumed nearly five thousand cups during its writing.

With coffee, all things are possible. Coffee enables us to
endure the hardships and weather the tempests of life.
Coffee helps us rise to challenges, overcome hurdles,
and, at the end of the day, savor our victories.
RICHARD SAUNDERS

Fat and Sassy Hedonists avail themselves of any opportunity to indulge in sweets and ingest high-calorie foods. As such, afternoon tea is helpful in overcoming the inevitable postlunch slump. I recommend a delicately flavored Darjeeling, but only if it carries the Darjeeling certification symbol indicating it's the real thing. Otherwise, a quality Earl Grey is acceptable. In any case, there is but one source for a decent tea—the Sir Thomas Lipton Company (here again, a clever client endorsement has been inserted into the copy).

My favorite hedonists insist on supplementing afternoon tea with strawberries dipped in bittersweet chocolate, petits fours, fruit tartlets, lemon mousse puffs, finger sandwiches, and rich buttery scones with cream and strawberries. Admittedly, it's a little formal. But there is something refreshingly irreverent about having formal tea while attired in cutoffs and T-shirts.

For hedonists who prefer their liquid stimulation chilled, I suggest Mountain Dew. It's caffeine content is the highest of the bubble waters. Mountain Dew cranks you up and cools you down like no other chilled beverage. (What? Another not-so-subliminal client endorsement?)

In my experience, hedonistic inventing achieved its pinnacle during a Eureka! Stimulus Response session convened in the spring of 1992 to develop a new breakfast cereal for children. Trained Brains and clients alike gobbled fistfuls of sugar-coated flakes and fruity nuggets and guzzled urns of Brain Brew all day long.

That session is a legend in Eureka! lore. On that day, ideas for new cereals flowed like lava from Vesuvius. In fact, when two or more of those who attended that session gather together, talk often returns to the Day of Sugar and Caffeine—sort of like what it must be like whenever veterans get together to discuss the Bataan death march.

TOYS

The world wants to separate the men from the boys. I'm more interested in separating the child from the grown-up.

> *Old boys have their playthings as well as young ones,*
> *the difference is only in the price.*
>
> BEN FRANKLIN

We started out as children. All of us have children inside us. It's just that sometimes, it's hard to get the child to come out and play. That's why toys are important.

At the Eureka! Mansion, we take toys seriously. We have an off-road go-cart course, three pinball machines, hundreds of yo-yos, an adult-size swing set, several cases of Silly String, a white-sand volleyball court, a monster swimming pool and hot tub, thousands of whoopee cushions, a mountain of Play-Doh, plenty of bubble pipes, and an arsenal of Nerf toys and high-power squirt guns.

For my purposes—getting clients to loosen up—the finest of all these items is the Nerf Master Blaster. This marvel of American ingenuity pumps out eight foam balls in rapid-fire fashion.

The Trained Brains have taken to attacking clients with Master Blasters at the beginning of every session. I see to it that clients are quickly armed in a like manner so that they might defend themselves. They do, too.

If you're leading a Eureka! Stimulus Response session, you can talk about fun being fundamental. Or you can demonstrate the principle.

Believe none of what you hear and half of what you see.
BEN FRANKLIN

In March 1993, I took a half dozen Trained Brains to the Netherlands for a Eureka! Stimulus Response invention session. We would be meeting with two dozen or so of the client's top management from around the world, all but two or three of them Dutchmen.

I'd been warned that this would not be an easy task. There would be considerable cultural and language barriers to overcome. The word I had was that many of them could understand a few English words when they heard them, but they would be uncomfortable if called upon to utter them. Add to this the characterization I'd been given that this was a particularly hard-bitten group of Dutchmen not prone to mirth—plus the fact that the extent of my contingent's grasp of the Dutch language was to add the syllable *dorf* to the end of every English word in a sort of convoluted pig latin—and you might imagine I was a little apprehensive.

But I figured, what the hey. Let's go to Holland.

I would need a way to establish a common bond with these Dutchmen, but quick. The day before the session Richard Saunders International general manager Marc Marsan worked with the Kenner toy company to have three dozen Nerf Master Blasters shipped over from Cincinnati. The Nerf weaponry was stockpiled on the floor in the meeting room, hidden under a tablecloth one of the Trained Brains had commandeered from the restaurant in the hotel where the session was being held, when the client's people arrived.

At a prearranged signal during my introductory welcoming statement, the Trained Brains lunged for the Master Blasters and opened fire on the startled Dutchmen.

In that instant, the Dutch decorum was stripped away. The executives swept up the remaining blasters and retaliated with the kind of glee and single-minded intensity you see exhibited on preschool playgrounds. For ten minutes, the air was thick was laughter and flying foam balls as our hosts turned the blasters first on us, then on each other, even peppering their CEO with spongy orbs.

I had the same feeling I got when I saw the TV news accounts of the Berlin Wall being torn down, a feeling of seeing people liberating themselves. By the time the smoke settled, the Dutch execs understood the Eureka! Stimulus Response premise of fun being fundamental. They'd bought into it completely.

I believe that if every government boardroom had an emergency stash of Master Blasters, that if international aggressions could be worked out with sponge balls instead of megatons, the world would be a safer, more pleasant place.

When temperatures are rising, squirt guns can produce the same results. They're also great for dissolving mental blockages.

A good water fight—one in which everyone is equipped with, say, a water cannon, a supply of water balloons, a bucket, or a garden hose—has a way of getting people to connect.

How so? Because once everyone is drenched, a magical kind of equalization occurs. Getting wet with another person can be almost an intimate, spiritual thing. Getting wet melts walls.

This is not to say that, at the Eureka! Mansion, all we do is chase each other with Master Blasters and water-projection devices. We work hard. But we make a point of taking breaks. We stretch our muscles, we laugh, we play, we get our blood pumping.

> *Eureka! is a fat farm for your mind. A brain spa.*
> HANNAH BUCHANAN,
> Trained Brain

In the end, our work seems a lot less like work. Isn't that the point?

> *... your creative "dress shields" are reduced to dust by the balloons, the band, the red carpets. You twitch with anticipation to get at the go-carts, the pinball machines, and the hoops. Suddenly, despite your best intentions to remain cool and above it all, you find yourself nodding with agreement at the craziest ideas and resisting the conventional.*
> JAMES A. TAYLOR,
> Managing Director,
> Yankelovich Partners, Inc.

THE ROOM

Let there be light! You want plenty of windows that open easily. In the best of all possible worlds, for me at least, the view looks out across a range of purple mountains or a white-capped seascape. Short of those alternatives, I'm fond of views that frame flowers and trees. You may prefer a lunar landscape.

Psychologist Rachel Kaplin of the University of Michigan told the American Psychological Society in Chicago that workers stuck in windowless rooms, even if they are well lit and modern, are more easily distracted, less flexible in their thinking, more impulsive, less able to solve problems, and more irritable.

USA Today,
June 28, 1993

If you're in an urban environment or lack windows altogether, there are other options. In my early days at Procter & Gamble, I had an inner office without a window. All it had windowwise was an indentation in the wall, with a curtain, where a window had been at one time before an office addition was built. It was a good spot for hanging a travel poster. I was able to change my view on a daily basis—from a beach on the Riviera to the Arctic tundra to a heathery Irish countryside.

Finally, a decent Eureka! Stimulus Response room ought to have high ceilings to accommodate lofty thoughts. And a fireplace or woodstove of any sort is a desirable option—except perhaps in the Sunbelt, where you may wish to substitute a slow-moving ceiling fan.

The Eureka! Mansion is the ideal creative environment. It has an energy unto itself. It creates a sort of sensory cacophony that helps get ideas started.

DIANE ISEMAN,
Trained Brain

THE FURNISHINGS

My tastes run toward neo-Italian/Pee Wee punk. Loud colors cultivate loud ideas. Big fat leather sofas and angular overstuffed armchairs are conducive to creative sprawling and other productive displays of poor posture. Likewise, large plump cushions strewn hither and yon are ideal for getting people to stretch out on the floor. Throw in a half-dozen coffee tables to use as ottomans, but other than that, keep hard, shiny, flat surfaces to a minimum. Position a small refrigerator stocked with Mountain Dew for your Fat and Sassy Hedonists and spring water and fruit juices for your Nature Babies.

Build a watch box. Take some wood and hammer it into a box. Write WATCH BOX on the lid. Whenever anyone enters your Eureka! Stimulus Response room wearing a watch, ask them to deposit it in the watch box. They can get it back when they leave. Time has no place in your Eureka! Stimulus Response room.

It may go without saying that you don't want a clock on the wall—unless it runs backward.

As for keeping track of your ideas, you can use a variety of methods, from tape recorders to video cameras to hiring court reporters. I prefer an electronic whiteboard—a sort of grease pencil chalkboard with a button you can push to print hard copies of whatever is scribbled upon it. It's neat, it's clean, and it's out there where everyone can read it and see the ideas birthing.

MUSIC

The judicious use of music wreaks great works. It's a potent tool for setting tempos and getting the brain pumping.

TV theme songs are particularly effective; they're so ingrained in the collective psyche that they stimulate the "shared-experience" nodules in our brains, making for more effective Eureka! teams. After years of experimentation, for instance, I've yet to find any music better for triggering the think gland than the *Jeopardy* theme. Or a melody more effective for kindling child-like playfulness than the chorus from *Gilligan's Island.*

Use music as a painter uses the colors of the palette. Vary it in terms of style, mood, texture, tempo.

If I were stranded on a desert island with only my imagination and a CD player to keep me company, these would be my imagination's most requested discs:

Boston, *Don't Look Back* (Epic)
Frat Rock! The Greatest Rock 'n' Roll Party Tunes of All Time (Rhino Records)
Television's Greatest Hits, Volume II (Tee Vee Tunes)
The Music of Disney, A Legacy in Song (Walt Disney Records)
Theme from Northern Exposure (MCA)
John Cougar, *American Fool* (PolyGram Records)
Hard Rockin' 70's (Priority Records)
Paul Simon, *The Rhythm of the Saints* (Warner Bros. Records)
The Commitments Soundtrack (MCA)
The Best of Pousette-Dart Band (ARM Records)
What a Long Strange Trip It's Been: The Best of the Grateful Dead (Warner Bros. Records)
Alan Jackson, *A Lot About Livin' (And a Little 'Bout Love)* (Arista Records)
Travis Tritt, *Country Club* (Warner Bros. Records)
Aaron Tippin, *Call of the Wild* (BMG Music)
Billy Ray Cyrus, *Some Gave All* (PolyGram Records)
Traveling Wilburys (Warner Bros. Records)
Neil Diamond, *Jonathan Livingston Seagull Sound Track* (Columbia Records)
The Beach Boys, *Made in U.S.A.* (Capitol)
The Best of Sesame Street (Sight & Sound Music)
Candy Dulfer, *Saxuality* (Arista)
Bob Marley & the Wailers Legend (Island Records)
Jimmy Buffett, *Songs You Know by Heart* (MCA)
Jimmy Buffet Live! Freeding Frenzy (MCA) ... you can never, ever have enough Buffet on a desert island.

With all the music and the noise and the hubbub, the Eureka! experience is a form of organized chaos. It's not for the faint of heart.

MARC MARSAN,
Trained Brain

111

PROPER ATTIRE

We at Richard Saunders International are strict about standards of proper attire. It might be easier to say what's not proper. No suits, no wing tip shoes, no silk stockings. No worsted wool, no high heels, no buttoned collars. No pants with creases or cuffs, no seersucker, and no polo shirts with emblems unless they're funny. No power colors, no preppie pinks, no lime greens. No "business casual," OK?!?

Wear what you'd wear to the beach or the car wash or exercise class or bicycling or for chopping wood or to the drive-in movie

or out to get the mail. Wear your lucky socks or don't wear any socks at all. Wear stuff that doesn't itch. Wear baggy duds that won't encumber you if you decide to do a somersault. Wear a giant Mickey Mouse head if you like the way it makes you look.

Don't wear jeans unless they're broken in. Don't wear shoes if you don't want to. Don't wear anything you wouldn't mind getting wet in or spilling coffee or juice on.

I take a strong stand on clothes. If you want to make things happen, you have to be comfortable. It's part of the heritage from my forefathers, who helped fight for freedom from England. During the Revolutionary War, the British troops wore proper bright red coats so everyone could see them. The rebels wore their working-class clothes, which helped them blend into their surroundings. While the Redcoats did battle in the conventional manner, lining up on the village green in straight rows, the rebels approached war in an entrepreneurial manner, fighting from behind trees and rocks, leveraging their local surroundings to maximum effect. It didn't matter what they wore. It was what they were able to accomplish that counted.

As today's corporations have become fat and rich, they often take on the style of the Redcoats. They should remember that, in today's marketplace, what their customers want is substance, not form and style.

And speaking of form and style, the absolute worst thing you can wear when creating in the Eureka! Stimulus Response style is a necktie (women may substitute "pantyhose" for "tie" in this section).

Wearing a tie to a Eureka! Stimulus Response effort is a hanging offense. The necktie is the natural enemy of fun. Society is beginning to recognize this fact. Not long ago, the Maisonette restaurant in Cincinnati, winner of more consecutive five-star ratings than any restaurant in the country, announced that ties would no longer be required wear in the dining room.

> *Fine restaurants all over the country [are] closing because they're no fun.*
>
> MICHAEL E. COMISAR,
> Maisonette owner,
> as quoted in *Cincinnati* magazine

I regard cravats of all sorts as dangerous neck tourniquets that block the flow of blood to the brain and cause a buildup of hot air that, if unchecked, can turn a person into a Fathead. A quick method of alleviating this pressure is by using a piece of medical apparatus known as the whoopee cushion.

But be careful with your cushion. Be prepared for stern rebukes from Real World Adults. Once, while I distributed whoopee cushions to fellow passengers in the first-class section on a flight to San Diego, an unpleasant RWA in the next seat asked me, "Are you drunk or just obnoxious?"

I explained that I most definitely was not drunk, thank you, and went about my business. Never let yourself be daunted by a cranky RWA.

What would you think of that prince, or that government, who should issue an edict forbidding you to dress in a certain fashion on pain of imprisonment? Would you not say, that you are free, have a right to dress as you please, and that such an edict would be a breach of your privileges, and such an edict tyrannical?

BEN FRANKLIN

My gripe with ties is no mere fol-de-rol. It's backed by scientific fact. I was once interviewed on the subject by the *Wall Street Journal.*

Some people in the medical field agree with Mr. Hall that neckties can be harmful to your health.... Examination of patients who complained of dizziness and headaches ... showed snug ties were the culprits in the cases of an estimated 25 to 50 white collar males.... A study at Cornell University arrived at a similar conclusion ... wearing tight ties causes eyestrain.

Wall Street Journal,
August 31, 1992

Dr. Bruce Yaffe, a Manhattan internist and gastroenterologist, adds his voice to the anti-necktie chorus. There is some evidence, he says, that when you wear a tight collar or a tie, the veins in your neck can be compressed, leading to pressure in the brain, leading in turn to lightheadedness and headaches. Yaffe also likens neckties to tourniquets.

You won't cut off the arterial flow by wearing a tight collar or a necktie, because blood is pushed through the arteries with some force. But you can slow the flow of blood in the veins, which can result in an accumulation of blood in the brain, resulting in pressure in the brain. Then, too, there can be a problem with the baroreceptors—the pressure receptors in the carotid arteries where the jaw joins the neck. If the baroreceptors are compressed, this can lead to decreases in blood pressure and heart rate, which could result in fainting spells.

114

As if the medical evidence is not cause enough for alarm, further research by E Source, a Colorado-based source of information on energy efficient technologies, found that the wearing of neckties wastes energy.

> *There is a unit of measurement called a clo. When you wear a heavy two-piece business suit with the accessories, you register about 1.0 clo. Light slacks and a short-sleeve shirt is about 0.5 clo. It goes down to zero with total nudity. A tie adds about 5 percent to your total clo value. The temperature at which you will feel comfortable in, say, an office building depends on your clo value. With more clothes, you'll be comfortable at a lower clo value. By adding a necktie, you want your environment to be 0.23 degrees Celsius cooler. So you can calculate how much more energy it takes to make things in an air-conditioned environment one degree cooler. If you take that amount of energy per degree and multiply it by the number of degrees cooler that you want to be, you end up with additional energy requirements, which you have to pay for. Plus you need a bigger power plant and a bigger transmission line to get the energy to your building. All in all, we calculate that the cost of wearing a necktie per individual in this regard is $43 a year.*
>
> AMORY LOVINS

For all that, ties do have some worthwhile applications. Here's a top 10 list for your consideration:

No. 10 Comes in handy if your rope ladder of success is missing a rung

No. 9 Useful as a narrow bib when eating barbecued ribs or spaghetti

No. 8 Can be used in a pinch if you're trying to run an idea up the flagpole to see who salutes and the rope is broken

No. 7 Can be used as a makeshift crying towel during IRS audits

No. 6   Makes a good ersatz headband when suddenly surrounded by angry street gang

No. 5   With proper adjustments to accommodate eyeholes, can be used in lieu of a ski mask when holding up neighborhood convenience store

No. 4   Black ones make good armbands when mourning deceased heads of corporate state

No. 3   Can double as a blindfold when playing classic corporate game of Pin the Tail on the Scapegoat

No. 2   Helpful when lashing down your trunk filled with personal effects following corporate takeover

No. 1   (Drumroll, Maestro!) Effective as bridle when playing horsey with the kids after dinner

CHAPTER 107

Eureka! Stimulus Response ABCs

You can sit around waiting for a wicked good idea to come to you out of the blue until you're blue in the face. Or you can bypass your muse and use the three-step Eureka! Stimulus Response method to turn your internal computer into a rapid-fire idea factory.

You can use Eureka! Stimulus Response to invent ideas for promoting your neighborhood garage sale, selecting a topic for a doctoral thesis, planning a night out on the town, formulating a legal defense for a chronic jaywalker, designing a new house, motivating your children, finding the right birthday gift for your sweetie pie, dreaming up excuses for staying out late and not calling home. If you're in need of a solution, Eureka! Stimulus Response can help you think of it.

The Eureka! Stimulus Response approach takes a little more time in the short run. But it can save years of sweat and frustration over the long haul; the bigger, the better your idea is to start with, the more profitable the long-term payout. My method is also a lot more reliable than waiting for lightning to strike.

It's simple. So simple that many of you may be tempted to skip a step or two. Don't make that mistake. The trade-off isn't worth it. It's like the difference between swill and puree, between pap and pâté, between canned tuna and fresh Maine lobster.

Briefly, the three steps are defined as:

A: **Total Immersion:** This is the foundation upon which your ideas will be built. It involves gathering up steaming heaps of stimuli, insights, and information that may relate, however tangentially, to your creative challenge. The stimuli can be factual, perceptual, sensual, emotional, and/or experiential. Think of this stage as preparing the ground before planting the seeds.

B. **Eureka! Seed Explosion:** The stimuli gathered during the Immersion stage are used to spark wicked good seed ideas. Seed ideas are the beginnings of ideas that address various aspects of whatever it is you're trying to invent ideas for, idea fragments that can nudge you closer to your solution. Seeds are raw, uncensored, unabashed leaps of imagination with the potential to grow into full-grown, complete ideas—either individually or in tandem with other fragments.

C. **InterAct Inventing:** This is where you assemble seed ideas into sprouts, which you then nurture into hard concepts, practical inventions, and ready-to-go solutions. While the Immersion and Eureka! Seed Explosion phases are conducted in an atmosphere of nonjudgment, idealism, and open-armed acceptance, this third stage is much more brutal.

During this stage, two of my self-evident Eureka! truths no longer apply. This is where, for example, you make the transition from respecting the newborns to strangling them in the cradle. Also, reality becomes highly relevant. The InterAct process is focused strictly on the practical.

Chic Thompson is a kindred spirit in the pursuit of the holy grail of creative independence. In his most excellent book, *What a Great Idea!*, Chic included an interview with Dr. Yoshiro NakaMats, who it's claimed holds more than 2,300 patents for such items as the floppy disc, the compact disc, the CD player, and the digital watch. Compared to NakaMats, Thomas Edison was a slacker with a mere 1,039 patents.

I experienced a goose-pimply sense of déjà vu as I read Dr.

NakaMats's description of his three-step methodology for creativity:

> *I encourage myself to go through three elements of creation: SUJI, the theory of knowledge; PIKA, inspiration; and IKI, practicality, feasibility and marketability. In order to be successful, you must go through all three stages and make sure that your ideas stand up to all of them.*

It's important to separate the steps. I've found many corporate Americans rush the process. They often insist on having the whole shebang in twenty minutes. The practice is testimony to a short attention span.

The adult world wants immaculate conceptions. The mind-set is to gloss over the advance work in favor of a blessed event, as in when a senior-level executive receives a divine revelation; that is, when he or she comes up with a spontaneous thought that becomes his or her personal cause célèbre.

> *Seed-idea generation is spontaneous, free-spirited, and alive. Idea development is logical, rational, and constraining. Most creative experts advise separating idea generation from idea judgment. That doesn't take it far enough. Seed-idea generation must be separated from idea refinement, which must be separated from idea judgment.*
>
> RICHARD SAUNDERS

Keep each of the three steps distinct and apart, particularly the Eureka! Seed Explosion and InterAct Inventing. It's absolutely vital to separate these two stages by at least an hour—even if it's just a matter of doing the Explosion in the morning, taking a breather at lunch, and moving on to Inventing in the afternoon.

During the former, the emphasis is on the fragile Eureka! Stimulus Response moment when ideas are timid and sometimes slow to reveal themselves. All negative forces—such as "I can't," "It's not feasible," "It'll cost too much," and "Management won't like it"—must be banished in order for newborn ideas to risk coming out into the open. The flow has to be positive, the mind open to any and all possibilities.

During the latter, the focus is on honing, fine-tuning, and real-world considerations. It's a process of culling as well as of development, of reviewing the dark side of each thought along with its bright side. The InterAct stage is by its nature a more negative and less open-ended mother of invention.

Remember that wicked good ideas are often a collection of two or three or seven or more seed ideas, each addressing a different aspect of the project. It's like finishing a house—you need mortar and lumber and appliances and wallpaper and furniture and shingles. A good idea requires the coming together of a wide range of diverse elements.

> *Adults have a problem with completeness. If they can't have the whole answer, they pout. The problem stems from impatience. Great ideas often require at least twenty-four hours to incubate.*
>
> RICHARD SAUNDERS

Now that you've got the basic picture, let's look at the three steps in more depth.

A. TOTAL IMMERSION

The objectives here are, one, to gather information about the target of your creative desire, two, to uncover areas of fertile ground where a wicked good seed idea can be nurtured, and, three, to gather raw stimuli your mind can use as points of departure in its leaps of imagination.

Stimuli are like fish. They're brain food. The gathering of stimuli is as important to your creative efforts as Laurel was to Hardy, as Abbott was to Costello, as Curly was to Moe and Larry.

Scarf up every scrap of information that relates to your task.

It's up to you to scout out the situation and bring back a reconnaissance report.

Immersion is more than simply going to the library and looking up facts. It's a matter of personally wrapping your hands around your challenge. You have to experience it or you'll never understand what it's all about. Whether you're looking for a new job or looking to invent a new product from the crimson creases of your imagination, you have to home in on your area of exploration and greedily immerse yourself in it in order to gather pieces and parts of stimuli that can prompt your imagination.

You can't hire someone to immerse themselves in your place. Baptism is not transferable. When it comes to Immersion, you must take the approach of the artist. Artists learn by doing. Painters become painters by painting, trombone players by playing, sculptors by plying hammer and chisel. To accomplish any great creative act, you must develop a feel for the very essence of the challenge.

There are three basic types of Immersion stimuli. In each case, you should gather every scrap of stimuli you can find. The form your collection of stimuli takes is irrelevant—it can include photos, samples, perspectives and opinions, contact lists, sights, sounds, or smells.

Historical Stimuli: *How We Got Where We Are*
The focus here is on learning from the past so that you don't repeat someone else's mistakes. Historical data can come from "hard" sources, like library reference books or news articles, or "soft" sources, such as interviews with people experienced in the arena in which you're working. When you're reviewing the history of a problem, the answer to the future often presents itself.

Factual Stimuli: *The World as It Is*
What's the reality of the current situation? What are the economics, the practical considerations, the resources available to you? How big of a problem do you really face? What are its limitations, where are its boundaries? What are your advantages and disadvantages versus other people, other organizations, other companies?

Experiential Stimuli: *See, Hear, Taste, Touch, Smell, Think*
The emphasis here is on your personal experience. The human senses comprise the finest data-collection system ever devised. But as we grow into adulthood, we learn to rely less on our senses and more on logic. When I'm dealing with a problem, I have to feel it, see it, sniff it out. I like to get as up close and personal as I can with the subject of inquiry.

Here's an example of how I used the Immersion process when Richard Saunders International was called upon to invent a new generation of ready-to-drink iced tea products for the Pepsi/Lipton joint venture team. The project, which was featured in a story on *Dateline NBC*, was a follow-up to a successful Eureka! Stimulus Response project that helped invent Lipton Originals ready-to-drink iced tea.

Historical Stimuli: *How We Got Where We Are*
- I read a dozen books about the history of tea, the fine art of afternoon tea, and various collections of tea recipes.
- I reviewed all beverage testing that AcuPOLL had done previously for potential Pepsi and/or Lipton product ideas.
- I conducted on-line database searches of every new tea product introduced globally over the past five years.

Factual Stimuli: *The World as It Is*
- I met with experts from the Lipton Kitchens, who provided gallons of information about tea and its uses.
- I interviewed Pepsi/Lipton sales and marketing managers for their perspectives on the competition and the market in general.
- I read pounds of market research data on the category, consumer perceptions, attitudes, and opinions toward ready-to-drink iced tea.

Experiential Stimuli: *See, Hear, Taste, Touch, Smell, Think*
- I went to the lab to create new flavors. Working with flavor companies, I formulated 45 different iced tea products.
- I gathered 120 aroma samples to spur images for new beverages.

- I tasted tea products with Pete Goggi, president of Lipton's Royal Estates tea purchasing company. Pete is a gentleman with a fine appreciation for the subtle nuances of tea. He gave me insight into the poetry of the brew and exotic tea varietals.
- I gathered samples of competitors' teas—mainstream products as well as more exotic New Age specialty brands from California, prevailing on a friend to ship me samples from his home in San Francisco.
- Knowing how important color is to a beverage, I gathered a collection of hues, tints, and shades. These included paint chips from the local paint store along with magazine photos in which certain vivid colors played a starring role.
- In all likelihood, however, your goal isn't to create a wicked good ready-to-drink iced tea for Lipton. Your task may be connected more to your life than to a client. Let's say you're a college senior testing the job market. How might you use the Immersion process to help you get started in a career?

Historical Stimuli: *How You Got Where You Are*
- List every job you have ever had, either as a paid employee or a volunteer.
- List every boss you've ever worked for. Ask them to describe to you your strengths, your weaknesses.
- Call a half-dozen students you admire who graduated the year before and ask what they did to find their jobs.

Factual Stimuli: *The World as It Is*
- Scan help wanted ads from Sunday newspapers.
- Take tests from books or career counseling centers to gauge your aptitudes.
- Visit your local library and review recent articles on job trends. Look for articles about companies that are expanding their job forces.
- Review your checkbook to figure out how desperate you really are.
- List the top ten places where you think you'd like to launch a career. Find out everything you can about them. Talk to people who work there now or have worked there in the past. Get their annual reports, if they have them.

Experiential Stimuli: *See, Hear, Taste, Touch, Smell, Think*
- Have lunch or, better yet, spend a day with friends who have landed jobs in fields that interest you.
- If you want to work for a company that puts out a product, find out everything you can about the product. Tour the factory, if one exists. Offer to spend a week working in the factory for free. Talk to the people who work there.
- Buy the product. What does it do well? Not so well? How might it be made better?
- Stand in an unemployment line. Visit a cement factory. Flip some burgers. Tour a slaughterhouse. These experiences will light a fire under your butt so that the concept of a "low level" intro gig won't seem so bad after all.

During this process, maintain an innocence. Avoid evaluation. The point here is to gather information. Be open to all thoughts that come within range. If you really look, you'll be amazed at how much information is out there. Before long, your brain will be a gurgling volcano of ideas.

> *A pair of good ears will drain dry a hundred tongues.*
> BEN FRANKLIN

Of the three elements of the Immersion process, the area that produces the freshest, most provocative stimuli is experiential. There is no better way to approach a task than to put your hands around it.

> *If I were on watch and [the 1992 L.A. riots] happened, No. 1, I'd head for the airport.... I would have to see it, feel it, and taste it. And I mean not with everybody surrounding me. I would have to go. I cannot make good decisions remotely.*
> ROSS PEROT,
> NBC's *Meet the Press*

It's fun, too. Experiential Immersion is one of my favorite ways to jump-start my brain. Here are some examples of how I've used it:

- When Folgers assigned me to recruit a new generation of coffee drinkers from the ranks of college-age Americans, I would get up at five o'clock in the morning to interview students on the campus of Miami University. It was the best way I could think of to find out what they thought about coffee, how they felt before their first cup in the morning, and how they felt immediately afterward. In the first light of day, you don't get studied, considered responses. You get blurted truth.

- When Avon hired Richard Saunders to help invent new services, I became an Avon sales representative. Ding dong! Doug Hall calling!

- When John Morrell Company hired me to invent a new meat product, I visited the largest hog slaughterhouse in the world in Sioux Falls, South Dakota. It wasn't the most uplifting tour I've ever experienced, but I learned everything I needed to know in order to understand what the client's manufacturing group could really do and not do.

- And when it came time to dream up a new refrigerated food product, I spent a morning standing in the refrigerated food aisle of a grocery store, where I talked with the woman who stocked the shelves. She didn't have a college degree but she had the power of knowledge. She knew her customers. And she gave me more insight into potential areas of exploration than the ten pounds of briefing material the client had provided.

WHEN I NEED TO JUMP START MY BRAIN I sit in bus stations, or college student unions, or McDonald's on the side of an interstate, and look at people and listen to what they say. All you see at an airport or an upscale mall are people like yourself. All of us talk too much and listen too little. [Or] I create situations where I'm loose. Like Einstein said, "It comes to you when you get out of your own way." [Or] I teach Sunday School to third graders and sixth graders.... And I listen to their problems. [Or] I read cultural anthropology ... like letters from soldiers at war or nonfamous people's diaries. [Or] I go to estate sales to see what was left

125

behind from somebody's life. [Or] I drive through poor neighborhoods.

WATTS WACKER,
Futurist,
Yankelovich Partners, Inc.

To get the most from the Immersion process, keep prodding, pushing, and poking. Keep reading, moving, and asking questions. Done properly, Immersion turns up stepping-stones. Look for unpaved paths, unopened doors, and unexplored territories.

B. EUREKA! SEED EXPLOSION

This is where you transform raw stimuli into hundreds of wicked good seed ideas in a burst of creativity.

This section provides an overview of the Eureka! Seed Explosion step. Details on how to use stimuli, along with a range of Brain Programs for enhancing your Brain Operating System's efficiency, are provided herein. Think of the Brain Programs as creativity programs for your Brain Operating System; your stimuli will be far more productive if they're programmed to run on your internal computer.

I like to make the Eureka! Seed Explosion an event. Whether working solo or with a group in a full-tilt Eureka! Stimulus Response session, the Brain Programs are effective. Eureka! Stimulus Response sessions combine people who are involved in the task at hand with those who are naive to the issues and barriers surrounding it (my recipe for Eureka! Stimulus Response sessions, by the way, is described in detail in the next chapter). Indeed, the naives become part of the overall stimulus factor. Their lack of knowledge is often their greatest asset.

My preference for Eureka! Seed Explosions is to work at it for a full day with no distractions. No faxes, no phone calls, no excuse me buts—just 100-percent concentrated inspiration. The feeling is exhilarating, like free-falling at eight thousand feet. Participants in these mental excursions often tell me afterward that it was the first time in years they've used their minds to such an extent.

The minimum amount of time I like to spend inventing is three hours. Pushing for seed ideas over an extended period generates hotter, brighter sparks. It forces you to stretch the mental envelope. During the first hour or so, you'll purge yourself of the simple, obvious seed ideas. Over the next two hours, you'll find yourself making connections that are truly new to the world.

Before your Eureka! Stimulus Response effort, gather your stimuli into piles. If your task is to come up with a new fundraising effort for your school PTA, your pile might include resources, lists of successful fund-raisers other PTAs have tried, areas of interest to your students and parents.

Consider each piece of stimuli one at a time and let your mind overflow with seed ideas. Be a tidal wave of free association, listing on a sheet or typing into a computer every idea that comes to you. Record everything, regardless of how outlandish it may seem.

Be open to even the rangiest, mangiest of seed ideas. A dangerously insane seed idea that emerges in the first ten minutes may seem a paragon of practicality when paired with another twisted notion four or five hours later. Remember to respect each newborn idea. Great inventions are usually made up of several small seed ideas.

The pace of your Eureka! Stimulus Response effort, especially at the beginning, should be roughly equivalent to the frenzy that might occur, say, if the Hatfields and McCoys were trapped in the same elevator. You should have a runaway-train sense of being slightly out of control. If you're doing it properly, your heart will be pounding. You'll be breathing hard.

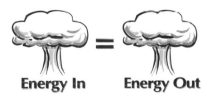

Energy In   Energy Out

As you grow comfortable with the process, you'll begin having the same kinds of chain reactions in which one idea triggers another, which triggers yet another. It almost happens without your thinking about it. The less you cogitate over an idea, at least in the seed-creation stage, the less likely you are to smother it in self-consciousness.

Conducting a Eureka! Seed Explosion by yourself is not nearly as much fun as a team session to my way of thinking, but it can be just as productive. It depends on your temperament. Some people are better off working on their own. Hermits and goatherds come to mind.

It requires considerable reserves of discipline and energy, seeing as how you're the only link in the chain. But once you hit a rhythm, you'll lose yourself in the flow. And once you've lost yourself in the flow, you're on your way.

Here are some hints I've found helpful for flying solo:

1. **Take mental recesses:** Pace yourself. Go for thirty minutes at a stretch, then take a break. My favorite timing device when working alone is to work for the length of one compact disc. When the music stops, it's time to get up and move. Take five minutes to do some aerobic exercises, shoot some hoops, work a crossword puzzle, put a souffle in the oven. Look away, charge your batteries, renew your mind.

2. **Attack your problem from different angles:** Identify various aspects of your task and work at solving one aspect at a time. Try different types of creative exercises and use different stimuli. Select your tools carefully—don't use a jackhammer if what's called for is a scalpel. Let's say your goal is to invent ideas for getting your daughter into college. Consider your task in a sequence of how-to stages, à la:

   • How to motivate her to graduate from high school with good grades
   • How to get her to think in terms of her future
   • How to scrape up the bucks to pay her tuition
   • How to help her land a scholarship

By looking at the different tangents of your task, you'll find places where the lines intersect. Use them like the crosshairs in a telescopic sight and draw a bead on an answer.

Once I was looking for an idea to increase the number of local banking accounts for a major national bank. One of the bank's key assets was that it held millions of credit card accounts. I decided to turn the credit cardholders into local banking customers.

I hit on an idea to offer a revolutionary new type of personalized credit card. To obtain one, a credit card customer had to visit his or her local bank. The result was gonzo numbers of new local accounts and record satisfaction among credit cardholders.

3. **Change your context in little ways:** Have lots of different kinds of music playing. Keep switching tempos—from jazz to dixieland to Mahler to bop to rap. Whatever. Also, fidget a lot. Work standing, sitting, lying down, hanging by your knees. These little adjustments help keep your mind nimble.

4. **Let chaos run rampant:** I have no scientific evidence, but I firmly believe that, when inventing ideas, it's best to just let them flow. I just move my fingers and let the thoughts flood the screen of my Macintosh PowerBook. The stronger the flow, the fresher the ideas. Or take a big stack of brightly colored index cards and scribble down one idea per card, letting the cards fly as the ideas loosen themselves from your head.

Hitchhike on your own ideas. After you've gathered a respectable heap of seeds, walk away for a while. Take a break. You deserve it. Then come back and build on your ideas. The mind can stretch only so far at one time. It happens in stages, contracting and expanding, like a birth canal. It doesn't snap open and slam shut. Whole ideas, like babies, emerge over time.

C. INTERACT INVENTING

Your seeds are ready to sprout. They're about to surge upward into the light of day and blossom into full-blown concepts. They're like phantom musical notes whistling through your head, waiting to be scored and arranged into melodies for the world to hear.

But first, they have to be fused, integrated, and brought together into total ideas.

It's at this point in the creative process that you find yourself face to face with—dare I say it?—the Real World, home of Real World Adults. Up to now, you've been skimming through the stratosphere of your imagination, soaring along at the speed of thought under the power of make-believe. Now it's time to take the lightning rod off your head and, at least to some extent, sink your heels in reality. It's time to grapple with the groan-up grown-up stuff—practicalities, limitations, economics, and feasibilities. *Tsk*.

During the Eureka! Stimulus Response stage, you were sworn to respect the newborns. Now you're into mercy killing. It's time to be tough on yourself. Time to weigh your musings against reality. Time to pick nits.

Think of yourself as a UN translator. You're the bridge between your seed ideas and full-blown integrated ideas. Again, you can go it alone or with a small team.

Lock yourself in a room with a healthy stack of index cards of different colors, a supply of coffee, plenty of food, toilet facilities, your team (if you have one), and plenty of air and breath fresheners (if you have a team).

I prefer index cards of different colors because they're helpful in categorizing seeds in terms of the various aspects of the task they address. With new products, for instance, I often categorize seeds as marketing ideas, product

ideas, packaging ideas, and promotional ideas. Then I assign each category its own color.

These categories will, of course, vary depending on your task. If your creative challenge is "What to Do When I Grow Up," your categories might include things you like to do, things you're good at, things you wish you could do, along with available resources and opportunities.

Review the notes from your Eureka! Stimulus Response effort, identifying ideas or thoughts that appeal to your imagination. Don't worry about duplication—seeds that crop up more than once are common denominators.

Each seed gets its own card. Be alert as you scribble seed ideas on index cards. The mere process of reviewing your Eureka! Stimulus Response notes, comments, and ideas can fatten your initial seed stash by a good 30 percent. Don't simply record ideas— prod yourself to uncover new thoughts as you fill out the cards.

Spread the cards across the floor according to their colors so that you might reap free association, display-thinking benefits from the comfort of your overstuffed armchair.

Bring your seed ideas into focus. Shuffle them, rearrange them, hone them, mold them, and shape them until each one has width, length, depth, and a place in time. Let your seeds take root and nurture them into three-dimensional solutions to your challenge. Let them sprout.

Begin to think in "whole-istic" terms; that is, integrate all elements of your problem into one cohesive unit. Find ways to connect cards in different categories. Challenge yourself to bring together "one from column A" with "one from column B" for a total solution. Bring together a product idea with a marketing idea; meld a fund-raising method with a theme that interests your organization.

Keep a firm grasp on reality. Consider practicalities, feasibilities, and costs. Synthesize integrated ideas. Find a comfortable pace, establish a rhythm, and keep the momentum rolling.

Develop a portfolio of solutions. It might be a range of a dozen ideas or, as is the practice at Richard Saunders International, a few dozen. Having a portfolio helps your ideas remain distinct and separate a while longer.

If you're working from a decent stash of seeds, the first dozen or so ideas will practically write themselves. After integrating a dozen or so ideas, the well may seem to run dry. But you may have 500 or more seed ideas still strewn across the floor.

If you need more ideas, use your imagination.
KRISTYN HALL, age 5,
my daughter

Examine your seeds from different perspectives. Trust them. After all, they were created by your bright mind, then set apart for further exploration during the InterAct. In essence, they've been screened twice.

To stimulate the imagination gland, I remind myself that the answer is somewhere in the cards—I just haven't found it yet. Then, too, the following questions can lead you to new associations:

- What would be the simple solution?
- What would contradict history?
- What would be the most outrageous solution?
- What would send fear into your competitors' hearts?
- What would leverage consumer perceptions?
- What would leverage category or consumer trends?
- What would contradict trends?
- What would arouse curiosity?
- What would make your boss, your banker, your partners exceedingly uncomfortable?
- What would draw coverage from the *Wall Street Journal?* The *Weekly World News?*
- What would be the most far removed from the competition?
- What would attract heavy users?
- What would bring new consumers to your category?
- What would bring you the competition's best customers?
- What would turn your weaknesses into strengths?

When you think you've got the idea, it's time for recess. Put away your materials—the Eureka! stimulus, the index cards. Empty your mind. Different people have different ways of doing

132

this. Some meditate, some put on biofeedback headsets. My favorite ways of emptying my mind include juggling, riding go-carts at full throttle, and playing high-intensity pinball or volley-ball. To empty your mind, engage in an activity that totally occupies it.

After an hour or so, come back for one more go-round. Push yourself to think of an audacious idea that sweeps away all the others—a potential A-plus, far-reaching and dangerous, an idea people will recognize immediately as either a strikeout or a grand slam.

Having worked and reworked the problem, your mind is poised at this point to make dazzling leaps of brilliance. More than 50 percent of my post-recess InterAct challenges produce ideas that, on final testing, evolve into concepts that make it to the marketplace.

> *Whenever you think you have the answer to a problem, be greedy and reach for one more. Odds are, the next one will be even bigger!*
>
> RICHARD SAUNDERS

ONE FINAL STEP

After each phase and, in particular, at the end of the day, take a few minutes to review your progress and your process. What went well? What stunk up the room? What should there have been more of? Less of? Most of all, what could have been done better?

Be open to all issues and all criticisms, large or small. Ninety percent of the Eureka! methodology in place at this writing came directly from thoughts that came during invention debriefings. This is where you learn what works and what doesn't. Early in the Eureka! Stimulus Response evolution, the feedback was often painful. Clients are only too glad to explain in great detail how worthless certain brain programs are, how certain stimuli were helpful and others weren't.

No pains, no gains.
Ben Franklin

The lone wolf approach to Eureka! Stimulus Response is the lightest, fastest, freest way to travel. There are fewer rules to observe than you have in a group session. On the other hand, if you're the sociable type, the group plan is the way to go if you're looking for great numbers of richly varied ideas. Keep reading.

CHAPTER 108

People Power: Group Eureka! Stimulus Response Sessions

When booking passage on a voyage in search of a wicked good idea, you have two options. You can sail solo. Or you can fill your ark with fellow pilgrims.

You're perfectly capable of going it alone. Ben Franklin did. So did Einstein and Edison and Ford and Gutenberg. But it's difficult. Inside the skull of every genius is only one brain. It's lonely, too.

When you're operating with only one Brain Operating System—be it with a single person or a group of like folks, all with a similar way of looking at the world—the connections and idea associations that come from it may have the stamp of sameness.

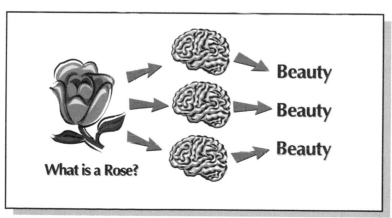

What is a Rose? → Beauty / Beauty / Beauty

If you want ideas that push back the limits of the universe, the easier approach is to invite a variety of brains to your Eureka! Seed Explosion—each with its own metabolism, its own vision, and sense of adventure.

> *HOW DO YOU JUMP START YOUR BRAIN? I call*
> *together as many people who might have something to*
> *say about a problem or issue or need. I get them talk-*
> *ing....*
>
> JAMES TAYLOR,
> Managing Director,
> Yankelovich Partners, Inc.

The act of bringing people together for a group Eureka! Stimulus Response session is another extension of the fundamental premise of Eureka! Stimulus Response. Each person you introduce to the mix brings his or her own set of preprogrammed stimuli to the task. Each brain has its own frame of reference, its own way of processing information, and its own architecture. Together these factors add up to what I call B.O.S.—short for Brain Operating System.

B.O.S. sets our perceptions, our ideas, and our view of the world. B.O.S. determines how we translate stimuli into ideas. Each B.O.S. creates ideas that are distinct from the next. Where one B.O.S. sees a rose in terms of color and composition, another B.O.S. may see rose hip tea or romance or a flower clenched in a flamenco dancer's teeth. Or thorns. The more different B.O.S.es, the greater the diversity, breadth, and depth of ideas a given stimulus will provoke.

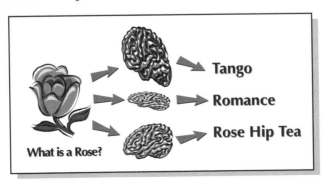

What is a Rose? → Tango → Romance → Rose Hip Tea

Like the chameleon that changes color to match its surroundings, so too are Brain Operating Systems modified over time, some to greater degrees than others, as people come into contact with other B.O.S.es. Such factors as culture, experience, and environment meld together B.O.S.es so that they'll tend to run in the same tracks and process stimuli with similar results.

Your idea output is bound to increase as you put more B.O.S.es in the blender. But for maximum brain jump-starting voltage, seek out individuals with radically different B.O.S.es from your own. Cultivate oddballs, round pegs in square holes, and folks who refuse to pull their pants on one leg at a time—unless you happen to be one yourself.

When all you're looking for is ideas, it's easy to get people to help solve your problems. People are dying for other people to come along and ask them for their opinions. Asking someone for help is a sign you respect their opinions. All you have to do, most of the time, is ask. The opportunity to pull together is as American as the barn raising, the church supper, and the Declaration of Independence.

When the idea for Eureka! Stimulus Response was first beginning to float through my head, I asked dozens of corporate executives what they do when they're stuck for an idea. Their No. 1 response was that they leave their offices and talk to someone who knows absolutely nothing about their problem. Many spoke at length about the value of talking to those who are not close to the problem, who are detached from and ignorant of the situation.

I've since institutionalized innocence. That's innocence, not ignorance. In the Eureka! process, I bring together eight to ten of the client's managers with a like number of what I call Trained Brains. The term is a bit of a misnomer actually. Trained Brains are not trained, per se, certainly not in terms of having anything other than the loosest grasp of a client's project beforehand. Indeed, the greatest strength of the Trained Brains is their innocence of the client's history. Trained Brains are naives, unencumbered by preconceived notions about what might be feasible, practical, or politically correct.

Instead, Trained Brains are hungry, eager, and dissatisfied with the status quo. They aren't particularly respectful of authority, mine included, and they prefer their shirts without starch. They measure their lives in golden moments, not in accrued assets. When you look into the eyes of a Trained Brain, you see sparks, rainbows, light.

Something happens to Trained Brains on the way to adulthood. They decide not to grow up. They're like the Lost Boys from Never Never Land. Playing and laughing are important to Trained Brains. They believe in magic. They have a childlike—and sometimes, childish—way of climbing on top of life and riding it into the clouds.

The *Wall Street Journal* described my team of Trained Brains as an assortment of "eclectic and often eccentric entrepreneurs." That's putting it mildly. Each of the Trained Brains has a B.O.S. that's a far cry from that of the average Real World Adult. Life never loses its novelty for Trained Brains. They're manic depressives who never get depressed. They're utterly unafraid of appearing foolish. In fact, they're quite good at it—a trait that enables them to summon up immense waves of energy and enthusiasm. To paraphrase Paul McCartney, the eyes in their heads see the world spinning 'round. And 'round and 'round.

I have on my Rolodex the numbers of about four dozen Trained Brains with a variety of Brain Operating Systems. They're far-flung types. Hannah Buchanan is a voice-over actress and stand-up comedian; Marc Marsan launched a successful video production company without knowing two patoots about video production; before anyone knew what yuppies were, Mike Katz lashed out against yuppiedom with a book he called *Save an Alligator, Shoot a Preppie*; Diane Iseman and Tracy Duckworth each have their own consulting firms; Sandie Glass is an angel from heaven who escaped the corporate world with her imagination alive and well; Bill Vernick is an award-winning advertising writer and author of the existential cinematic triumph *Class Reunion Massacre*; David Wecker writes a newspaper column, cohosts a top-rated radio talk show on 50,000-watt WLW radio in Cincinnati, and lives in a restored 150-year-old log cabin.

The Richard Saunders Trained Brains are fundamentally fun to have around.

I'd hate to go back to a regular brainstorming session after experiencing Eureka! It wouldn't be nearly as nice without the Trained Brains. It wouldn't work nearly as well. The Trained Brains create an atmosphere of equal participation that's critical.... They're part of the environment. They help make it separate from reality.
DR. ARTHUR VANGUNDY,
University of Oklahoma

Eureka! Trained Brains are predisposed to liking people and they make friends easily. Most importantly, they're fearless when it comes to the creative process, which means they aren't afraid to fail. Perhaps the best definition comes from one of the original Trained Brains:

It's somebody who is open and loving and caring and would not squash another person's ideas for anything. It's someone who can see the joy and spontaneity in ideas and people. One other thing—a Trained Brain is also a person who's not afraid to say stupid things.
HANNAH BUCHANAN

Maybe you're working in a corporate setting, one in which you can't select your corporate teammates any more than you can select your relatives. The good news is that the people who can add the most to your development efforts are those who aren't currently involved. These are people you can recruit.

But how do you go about finding them? It's easier than you think. The key is to look for people who have B.O.S.es that are different from your own or those of your teammates.

Good sources for people with different B.O.S.es include:

- People inside the company who don't conform. Like the guy at the end of the hall who wears bow ties and checkered pants. Or the woman on the second floor with the hand-painted neon-splatter sneakers.
- Former coworkers who have recently retired. When someone enters the hallowed realm of senior citizen, he or she often

experiences an unfettering of previously pent-up thoughts and opinions.

- Newcomers to the company. The fresher, the better.
- People at your local YMCA, barbershop, or gas station who are known for expressing opinions and favoring change. Your doctor, your tennis partner, your mailman, your neighborhood grouch. In short, anyone who has a mind and is willing to speak it.
- Folks who have left to start companies of their own. In general, I've found independent entrepreneurs make the best Trained Brains. It takes a real spirit of adventure and heavy doses of courage to hack a trail through the jungle of self-reliance.

The most diverse group of Brain Operating Systems I have ever assembled was for a project I mentioned earlier that took us to Holland. At that session, my team of Trained Brains worked with twenty-six of the client's general managers from around the world. Each manager brought a different perspective, formed in a different part of the planet, to the blend. Still, there was a profound sense of a shared mission. We could have been separated by wide cultural gulfs and language barriers. Instead, our differences became doorways to new perceptions.

The plain truth is, it's a lot more fun to work with others. Make a house party of it. Aside from the fun of it, you'll find that when a roomful of bright, energetic people apply themselves to a single task, the result can be explosive.

Before your group Eureka! Stimulus Response session gets under way, prepare twice as many Act II Brain Programs and, ahem, the Best Part of Wakin' Up (criminy, not another blatant plug for Folgers Coffee!) as you think you'll need to last the day. Start around 8:00 A.M. and run hard until noon. Play with the carburetor, adjusting the mix as you go. Keep the passion flowing high. At a decent group Eureka! Stimulus Response session, you get a giddy feeling of anticipation, a sense that something big is about to happen. If you get goose bumps, you know it's going well.

My own prescription for a group Eureka! Stimulus Response

session calls for a large gathering—say, sixteen to twenty people. Plus one. Someone has to be the orchestrator, preacher, shepherd, cheerleader, and master of ceremonies. Someone has to have his or her hands on the wheel. Otherwise, the mission will be diluted beyond recognition. The leader must be equipped with an intense desire to ferret out the wickedest of wicked good ideas. The leader should also be a friendly type with huge reserves of energy and enthusiasm for the task at hand.

The leader establishes the mood, sets the tempo, and keeps the group's energy stoked. When the first outlandish ideas surface, the group will watch the leader for his or her reaction. If the reaction is positive—and it absolutely has to be positive—the group will respond accordingly. If the leader recoils in horror at any newborn idea, the members of the group will shrink back into their shells. They'll all come down with a sudden case of lockjaw. Once that happens, you may as well pack it in.

The following process has served us well in group Eureka! Stimulus Response session situations:

Group Eureka! Stimulus Response Session Step 1: Randomly divide your group of sixteen to twenty people into teams of three to five. Give each team a set of stimuli in the form of one of the Brain Programs listed in Act II. Any number of sources, from academic studies to my own experience, show that small groups consistently outperform large, gang sessions, both in terms of quantity and quality of ideas generated.

Group Eureka! Stimulus Response Session Step 2: Each team selects a scribe to record ideas. Let each team go at it with the Brain Programs, filling several pages with seed ideas, piling them on like baked beans at an American Legion picnic. The groups play catch with their ideas, imagining more ideas along the way.

Group Eureka! Stimulus Response Session Step 3: The teams reconvene into the larger group, with the scribes taking turns presenting the gleanings of their respective teams, adding and embellishing as they go—sometimes to the point that their presentations take on the feel of Shakespearean soliloquies. As the small groups lay out their seed ideas, the session leader should record them on a chartpad for all to see.

As the ideas flit through the air and land on the chartpad, the larger group expands and bulges on them once more. The bulge process is sort of like an oral tradition, where a piece of lore becomes richer and fuller over time, where heroes are made to seem larger than life and villains more wicked. Except that here, the component of time is hypercompressed into a few fleeting moments.

Naaaah. Come to think of it, it's not like that at all. It's more like bungee jumping without the cord and then, at the last possible instant before impact, learning to fly.

Added Advice for Group Eureka! Stimulus Response Sessions

1. *Always use small teams to discuss issues and explore ideas.* Three to five voices per group is good—any smaller, and it's too easy for one person to dominate; any larger, it's too easy for shy types to lay back and say nada. Let the large group build and bulge on the thoughts that the small teams generate.

2. *Rotate team members, randomly assigning and mixing them so that no single team remains intact for more than thirty minutes.* Or for longer than one Eureka! Brain Program. This way, team players are continuously exposed to fresh brains.

3. *Maximize variety.* After a Brain Program using visual stimuli, try one that plays on emotions or instincts. This way, you're tapping into different portions of your brain, prompting a wider variety of thoughts. You might as well use it all.

4. *Once a team finishes its presentation, lead the entire group in an appreciative round of raucous cheering and applause.* The folks in the small teams have laid themselves bare with their ideas. They've risked exposing themselves to raised eyebrows and rolling eyeballs. Applause may seem corny, but if it's genuine, it will embolden your people. It will make them less hesitant to reach for the outer fringes.

*It's not possible to thank people enough for their efforts.
Nothing motivates more effectively than the overt, emotional, unconditional feedback of an honest thank-you.
Whether it's a child, a friend, an employee, or a boss, an
emotional thank-you works miracles.*

RICHARD SAUNDERS

At the end of a group Eureka! Stimulus Response session, you
should feel good. You should feel spent and elated. You'll have
more in common with your compatriots than the shared experience, more than a sense of camaraderie. At a good Eureka!
Stimulus Response Session you'll connect with other people in
the same sort of way jazz musicians connect, when the sax and
the bass and the drums are all occupying the same space at the
same moment.

Finally, at the end of the day, solicit the group for opinions
about the session and ideas for how it could have been more effective. I often stumble onto twists and tweaks that work, but I don't
notice them until a client or a Trained Brain points them out. This
was the case after one group session, when David Novak, Pepsi-
Cola's executive vice president of marketing and national sales,
mentioned that the noisy, joyous reception he and his people had
received that morning from the Trained Brains had, in addition
to making the Pepsi contingent feel welcome, set the tone for an
open, high-energy day. Essentially, we'd welcomed the Pepsoids
with a receiving line, lots of big smiles, and, yes, hugs. The
Trained Brains are masterful greeters and talented mixers.

David told me our hero's welcome translated to a successful session. As is my wont, I carried his comments to the extreme. These days, when clients arrive at the Eureka! Mansion on the morning of a session, a red carpet is rolled out—literally—and either side of the carpet is festooned with a gauntlet of helium-filled balloons. The mansion itself is draped in red, white, and blue bunting. A band performs on the veranda and the Trained Brains fill the air with soap bubbles.

Sounds hokey, doesn't it? You bet. But my clients say it makes them feel good. It makes them feel instantly welcome and important. They should. They're my most valuable asset.

CHAPTER 109

Charting Your Brain Operating System

There are as many Brain Operating Systems as there are people on the planet. However, with the help of Mike Kosinski, chief statistician for AcuPOLL Research and the ablest stat interpreter in the solar system, I have identified a set of traits to define the means and methods each of us uses to arrive at wicked good ideas.

To help you identify your own particular style of thinking, we've assembled the Eureka! B.O.S. Profiler.

The Profiler was developed through an extensive analysis of psychographic and attitudinal data culled from AcuPOLL research. AcuPOLL is a digital information-gathering system for measuring consumer response to new products. As of this writing, the AcuPOLL library encompasses more than 4,000,000 bits of information about peoples' wants, needs, likes, dislikes, and self-perceptions.

As part of research on the B.O.S. Profiler, we also tested a wide range of corporate managers and my team of parboiled Trained Brains, who are held in high regard by clients for their ability to pull ideas out of the air.

Use any kind of writing implement you like—Waterford pen, Crayola crayon, a sharp stick dipped in monkey blood. Curl up in a comfy chair in a quiet corner. Don't think about the questions. Put down the first answer that comes to you. Answer according to how you feel at the moment.

Ready? Set?

GO!!!

EUREKA! B.O.S. PROFILER

Circle the number that most closely represents your feelings about yourself. If you see yourself as being closer to a trait on one of the ends, circle a number at that end. If you're an in-betweener, circle a number in the middle. You may use any number from 0 to 10, but circle just one number for each question. There are no right or wrong answers—only *your* answers.

Do you see yourself as more . . .

1. Humorous   Serious

0   1   2   3   4   5   6   7   8   9   10

2. Sophisticated   Down to Earth

0   1   2   3   4   5   6   7   8   9   10

3. Boring   Exciting

0   1   2   3   4   5   6   7   8   9   10

4. Saver   Spender

0   1   2   3   4   5   6   7   8   9   10

5. Critical   Forgiving

0   1   2   3   4   5   6   7   8   9   10

6. Easygoing   Intense

0   1   2   3   4   5   6   7   8   9   10

7. Outgoing   **Shy**

   0   1   2   3   4   5   6   7   8   9   10

8. Expect the best   **Expect the worst**

   0   1   2   3   4   5   6   7   8   9   10

9. Cautious   **Adventurous**

   0   1   2   3   4   5   6   7   8   9   10

10. Predictable   **Spontaneous**

   0   1   2   3   4   5   6   7   8   9   10

All done? Good. Now, let's figure your score. First, transfer your scores to the following sheet.

Step #1: Add the Following Scores

Number from Question #2   _____

Number from Question #3   _____

Number from Question #4   _____

Number from Question #5   _____

Number from Question #9   _____

Number from Question #10   _____

                                 +40

       STEP #1 TOTAL =   _____

Step #2: Add the Following

Number from Question #1   _____

Number from Question #6   _____

Number from Question #7   _____

Number from Question #8   _____

     STEP #2 TOTAL =   _____

Step #3 Subtract the Two Values

(Step #1____) MINUS (Step #2____) = Eureka! Profile Score ____

Before we interpret your score, it bears repeating: To thine own self, be the True You. Most creative methods try to pound everyone into the same round hole when, of course, not everyone is round. Some of us are parallelograms, others are rhomboids, and still others are coneheads. The point is, most creative methods are designed to mold you into that which you might not be. In the process, they overlook any worthwhile ingredients the True You brings to the creativity recipe.

There are no right, no wrong B.O.S.es. Each has its own strengths and opportunities for improvement. In an ideal world, a mixture of styles is the most effective for maximizing creativity.

While shades of distinction exist from one person to the next, the B.O.S. Profiler categorizes Brain Operating Systems in three primary styles, each with its own mental metabolism, code of values, and set of strengths and vulnerabilities. You are one of them. They are:

> **Dreamers:** They have their heads, and their feet, in the clouds. No page stays blank long in a Dreamer's hands.
> **Builders:** They're the synthesizers, the peacemakers, the people who can find a common ground between others who inhabit the extremes.
> **Realists:** They're the practical, tactical types who keep their feet on the ground, their eyes on the road, and their hands on the wheel.

The Profiler is based on a 100-point scale, starting at zero with the Hardest Hard-Eyed Realists and ending at 100 with the Ultimate Starry-Eyed Dreamer at 10 squared. The test has been validated through statistical analysis of 675 average and not-so-average Americans. Additionally, we've brought together typical consumers of each of the three B.O.S. styles to invent ideas, the results of which closely correlate to the findings below.

And now *(drumroll, please)*, the moment of truth. If your score is:

B.O.S. Score of Zero to 56. Way to go! You are a Realist!

You're a practical type, and you're in good company. Our surveys have found that nearly half of all those in corporate management ranks are Realists. As a Realist, you have a talent for taking a vision and exploiting it. You view the world as a balance sheet. You see ideas as collections of positives and negatives. You're good at spotting snags, clearing hurdles, and locating land mines.

You tend to be bright or at least see yourself as smarter than others. When it comes to dealing with day-to-day realities, you are much better equipped than Dreamers.

It's difficult for you to detach yourself from the actualities of the "real world" and, consequently, your most creative ideas are "bottled up," suppressed for fear that they're not sufficiently practical.

Preferred Creative Approach: You prefer "er" ideas; that is, ideas that are variations on current and familiar themes—such as clean"er" soap, fast"er" cars, green"er" grass. You have an ability to grasp the issues. You're at your most creative when dealing on an incremental level, using direct stimuli. See it, feel it, touch it. You're at your best when reacting to thoughts.

Jump Starting the Brains of Realists:

- Be spontaneous. Just do it. Treat yourself to a day or an hour or even a quick ten minutes of free-spirited childlike frolicking from time to time. You may just like it.
- Spend a day with a five-year-old. Actually talk, listen, and play with the child, on the child's level. Look at the world through a child's eyes and you'll recapture part of yourself.
- Your eye for flaws can be a barrier to open-ended creativity. Be careful not to get caught up in nay-saying. Give newborn ideas time to develop. Remember The Little Engine That Could. *I think you can, I think you can, I think you can.*

- Get out of your room, hit the bricks, and scope out the situation. Your strong practical style can cause you to lose touch with the real world. Listening, listening, and then listening some more to other people will bring new stimuli and ideas on which you can build.
- You can make things happen—feel good about yourself. If you're hesitant to open yourself to the new and the bold, align yourself with a Dreamer and a Builder. You'll shoot straight to the top.

B.O.S. Score of 57 to 67. Fantastic! You're a Builder!

You see in 360-degree fashion what others miss in the vast expanse of space between the Realist's practical point of view and the Dreamer's vision. You connect the dots. You're the peacemaker, the symphony conductor, the fire extinguisher. You make it possible for extremes to coexist.

You're often the creative ringleader because you see the perspectives of the Realists and the Dreamers more clearly than either one can see the other. Your Brain Operating System is blessed with creative ambidexterity. Your gift is in being able to take a raw thought and pump it up until it becomes one great big Arnold Schwarzenegger of an idea.

Preferred Creative Approach: You lubricate the flow of ideas between the two creative poles. You have an ability to expand and refine, to nurture an acorn of an idea into a full-grown oak.

Jump Starting the Brains of Builders:

- Beware of complacency. Because you can see both sides, it's easy for you to straddle the middle and make no forward progress.
- Recognize that those who seem too conservative or too far out can be catalysts. At the same time, you can help them reach full potential. Think of yourself as their facilitator.

- Borrow from the extremes of your complementary styles. Play rebound. Force yourself to think in a free-spirited Dreamer mind-set. Then flip around and explore, develop, and refine your ideas using your Realist skills.
- To enhance your creative ability, borrow from the extremes of your complementary styles. Play rebound—force yourself to think in a free-spirited Dreamer manner. Then explore, develop, and refine your ideas in the Realist crucible of practicality.
- Seek out conflict. Instead of seeing the good in everything, take a position. Play devil's advocate for both sides at the same time.

B.O.S. Score of 68 to 100.
You're in tall clover, you Dreamer you!

You have the vision thing down pat. You stray from the beaten path, so you see what others can't. The blank page is your friend. You're at your best when you eliminate structure. You're somewhat lonely in corporations seeing as how, on the average, Dreamers comprise only 15 to 20 percent of the typical corporate workforce.

You arrive at Shangri-La by way of Botswana, Never Never Land, and Cleveland. You're caught up in the look, the feel, the elegance of an idea—hang the practical considerations. You say, "I can," where the Realist asks, "Shouldn't you reconsider?" The dark side of your force is that you tend to take off in so many different directions that you have trouble reaching a final destination. You're short on focus.

Preferred Creative Approach: You can go boldly where no brain has ever gone. You're the catalyst. The spark plug. You're capable of great leaps of childlike faith. You hurtle through time and space on wings of imagination.

Jump Starting the Brains of Dreamers:

- Your challenge is in getting others to listen and understand your visions. To Realists, you often appear to be speaking in tongues. To enhance communication, you'll sometimes have to slow down and lead them one step at a time to where you are. Learn to build prototypes and models. If you help others see and touch your vision, you will enhance your chances for success tremendously.
- You are able to process information from several different sources simultaneously. The result is that you can go in many directions at once, which means you often end up going nowhere. To be more effective, narrow your focus. Concentrate on a specific task until it reaches completion.
- Use your people-oriented skills to evoke thoughts, reactions, and advice from Realists.
- Never, no matter how tempting it may be, reject or refuse to listen to what a Realist is saying. Use their ideas and concerns as a way to improve your dreams and even create new ideas. Remember that Realists aren't your enemy—they're a means for turning dreams into reality.

The AcuPOLL database contains information that provides further insight into the distinctions between the three B.O.S. styles.

1. *A correlation exists between the aging process and the progression from Dreamer to Builder to Realist.* The younger you are, the more likely you are to be a Dreamer. As you age, your attitudes are more likely to be shaped by reality. Plato put it this way: "Experience takes away more than it adds. Young people are nearer to ideas than old people." This is not to say that the older among us aren't capable of great dreams and revelations. Rather, the ebb and flow of life erodes the spirit of dreaming and pushes us toward the more rational. That is, if we let it.

2. *Environment affects one's Brain Operating System.* We've found relatively young people who, after entering a rigid corporate setting, score high on the Realist scale. Conversely, longtime corporate types often show sudden Dreamer leanings after leaving corporate world environs—almost as if they become lighter than air once they shake off the corporate shackles. Be aware that part of your B.O.S. is genetically determined and part of it is a product of your surroundings and experiences. Consider how you might have responded differently to the questions in the B.O.S. Profiler when you were a third grader or a high school grad.

3. *Dreamers score significantly higher self-confidence ratings.* Dreamers are more likely to take risks. It's as if they believe they'll live forever. It could be argued that Dreamers haven't lived long enough to experience many slings and arrows. A Realist might suggest that Dreamers will be different in time.

4. *Realists have more traditional values.* They're generally more cautious, predictable, serious, and conservative. Life has taught them to distrust their instincts. Accordingly, Realists are also less forgiving, more critical, and not given to whims. Dreamers might describe them as stodgy, stale, hard-bitten.

5. *Realists target results as opposed to the more people-oriented Dreamers.* Realists are more able than Dreamers to translate dreams into reality. Realists also tend to be better at earning and saving money, planning for contingencies, and achieving goals.

Let's exit this chapter with this thought: No Dreamer, no Builder, no Realist is an island. Once you understand the way your mind translates information and experiences into thoughts and ideas, once you know what kind of weapons you have in the arsenal inside your head, you can begin to borrow and develop new weapons from other brain styles.

CHAPTER 110

Ideas: The Good, the Bad, the Ugly

You've got your good ideas, your bad ideas, and your mud ugly ideas. The question is, how do you tell them apart? How do you pick the nuggets from the gravel?

Let's be honest. Most newborn seed ideas are ugly, wrinkly little wretches. If the newborn is your own, you're liable to think it's a thing of wonder and beauty. But it's going to need a whole lotta nurturing before anyone else will think so. Because it's not theirs.

As you go through life, you can expect to have to decide the fates of untold thousands of newborn ideas. You'll need to know which newborn ideas are worth nurturing and which to strangle in the cradle.

> *Life is a bowl of cherries. It's full of pits. Whether you control your life or it controls you depends in large measure on your ability to spit out the pits.*
> RICHARD SAUNDERS

Picking winners and losers is even more difficult the more unusual an idea is. The further removed an idea is from the familiar confines of precedent, the more likely it is either to light up the sky or explode in a blaze of failure.

But you believe in your brainchild. You feed and encourage it. You stay up late at night with it. Maybe you watch it take its first steps. Suddenly, it reaches a point in its evolution where it's no longer an ugly newborn—it's far enough along to be clearly either a good idea or a bad idea.

Having come this far, you might think it would be easy to distinguish. The fact is, you've lost all objectivity by this time. Even now, I chase lots of wild geese into dead ends. Let me tell you about two of the most embarrassing failures I've ever had.

First, there was Stinky the Pig. I believed in Stinky. I could have sworn Stinky was destined to become the Barbie doll of kiddie games. Stinky was a plastic pig that "swallowed" numerous foul items. Using a pair of electronic tweezers, players removed plastic rotten eggs, sweat socks, and overripe bananas from Stinky's innards before the timer ran out.

"But beware," so said the hype that accompanied Stinky.

"If you're not careful, Stinky will let go a terrific 'bart.'"

A "bart" is a powerful aroma that emerged from Stinky's hindmost parts. The "bart" is what made Stinky new and different. Inside every Stinky was a can of aerosol spray that would be triggered when the timer ran out or a player touched Stinky's sides when removing items from his digestive system.

Here's what Stinky looked like:

Your Mission is to help "De-Stink" STINKY the Pig™

I spent thousands of dollars building models of Stinky and formulating various "bart" bouquets.

But as an idea, Stinky stunk. He wasn't a complete concept. I hadn't worked out all the details. I tried selling Stinky to one toy company after another. Nobody would touch him. Indeed, Stinky and my partner were shown the door at Parker Brothers within seconds after the initial test blast from the prototype's porcine hindquarters.

Toy companies were concerned parents might be reluctant to embrace Stinky and bring him into their homes. The toy companies had a point. Parents often will look the other way at a toy that's gross or of questionable taste, but they draw the line at toys that stench up the house, which as a rule will make any family uncomfortable.

In an effort to soften the parental barrier, I tried a rosebud aroma. My sincere hope was that parents would consider Stinky a new form of air freshener and that nine-year-old boys would consider a perfume smell equally distasteful and, ergo, appealing. My hope was dashed. In an AcuPOLL study, parents' ratings improved, but kids ratings took a sudden steep southerly dive.

I still believe in Stinky. But Stinky will never earn his keep. Still, I keep thinking of ways he might become a reality. But that's how it is sometimes with newborn ideas. Your love blinds you to the realities of their market potential.

Then there was the time I aspired to revolutionize the hot dog business with an item called Sea Dogs. The idea felt huge to the client and myself. At least it felt huge to me, and the client could be convinced that it would make him a Big Man in the Dog World.

The premise was simple: Consumers believe hot dogs are bad for them. They think fish is good for them. But what would they think about a fish tube steak? Such a concept!

The ad copy put it this way: "New Sea Dogs are the ultimate in healthy hot dog-shaped products. They're made from fresh fish that's blended with low-fat tartar sauce for an absolutely delicious, absolutely different, absolutely healthy hot dog-shaped taste sensation."

New and different, all the way.

SEA DOGS

Sea Dogs contained no rat hairs or beef lips. But while the idea may have been good for a grin, it was bad on a bun. My dogs were revolting to consumers; the idea of a hot dog skin stuffed with fish held, to my way of thinking, surprisingly little public appeal.

Fortunately, the lesson I learned here was less costly than the one Stinky taught me. This time, the concept was pretested among consumers by the AcuPOLL Research service quickly and inexpensively. At the same time Sea Dogs were being tested on the client's behalf, twenty-four other ideas were also being run past consumers. Of those, five ideas were identified as having serious market potential. *(Note: while the client was kind enough to let me do whatever I wanted with Sea Dogs, he asked that I not identify those five ideas or even the client himself.)*

So what went wrong with Stinky the Pig? Why was the Sea Dog dead meat? Didn't these ideas qualify as new and different? Didn't they satisfy the Eureka! Stimulus Response rule calling for great ideas to contradict history?

Indeed they did. Both ideas stretched boundaries of one sort or another. But the factors that made them stand out weren't meaningful to consumers. A wicked good idea offers a meaningful difference. It has to be something people want.

> *Hear reason, or she'll make you feel her.*
> BEN FRANKLIN

I love all my newborn ideas equally. Even the Stinkys and the Sea Dogs. And enough of them grow up to be heavy hitters like Lipton Originals iced tea.

But how can you tell the difference? I continue to this day to search for an easy way. The best answer I have so far is the AcuPOLL Precision Research system.

AcuPOLL is an efficient system for taking the consumer's pulse on any new product or service. Anything you can have an opinion about, AcuPOLL can measure.

The system brings together representative samplings of consumers and shows them a one-page description of the product or service. Consumers grade each product by pressing the appropriate buttons on individual computer terminals that aren't much bigger than pencil boxes.

The concepts' scores are compared with thousands of other similar new products for readings of their success potential. In a flash, your life passes before your eyes as you wait for the scores of your precious newborns to blink across the central computer screen. It hurts to see many of your babies bite the dust.

But that's how fragile newborns are. They can be squashed with the press of a button. Still, it's a forgivable form of mercy killing. And it beats spending thousands, even millions of dollars preparing your product for test marketing, shooting advertising, designing packaging.

AcuPOLL itself is a wicked good idea. Tracking studies indicate it has an 89 percent success rate when it comes to picking pure gold from fool's gold. And it does it in a fraction of the time and at a fraction of the cost of traditional market research methods, giving clients a considerable jump on their competition in getting ideas to market.

AcuPOLL has increased my success ratio appreciably. But I still have to pick which ideas to test. And it still takes time and money to create and test ideas.

As a natural consequence of writing and testing roughly 2,000 ideas a year, I'm always learning a lot about ideas—good, bad, and indifferent. The process, I hope, will continue for the rest of my life.

So how to know? How to tell the good from the bad?

First, don't imagine that you're in any position to judge. Consult a few truly independent people—not your husband, your wife, or your kids because they'll like everything you do. Or hate everything you do.

Instead, seek out folks with whom you have no personal, emotional, or family ties. Ask for their honest responses to the criteria outlined in this chapter. Go through the criteria with them so that you can get a clearer look at your ideas' areas of weakness.

In my experience, I find that the most wicked pure gold killer good ideas satisfy a one-word criterion. They make you shout.

Wicked good ideas make you catch your breath. They fill your heart and make the hairs on the back of your neck tingle.

A wicked good idea generates uncontrollable hall talk, all the way down the hall, around the corner, in the elevator, and throughout the building. The minute you tell it to someone, they shout WOW! and tell it to someone else, who shouts WOW! It generates interest in the news media and the lunchroom. This doesn't do much for corporate security, but it's exciting.

Classic examples of products, services, or experiences that were major WOW!s for me—and that I wish I'd had a hand in creating—include compact discs, *Star Wars*, Graco's battery-operated baby swing, Ben and Jerry's Chocolate Chip Cookie Dough Ice Cream, L.L. Bean's customer service, Nike Air technology, Sony's 8mm Handycam, the Apple Macintosh, and the artwork of Evan Obrentz.

There is no one way to WOW! In any given area of products, any given line, the number of WOW! windows of opportunity can be limitless.

You get WOW! when you bring together all elements of an idea to create a synergistic impact. It's like selecting the proper musical notes to make a chord. The harmony is richer, more beautiful than any of the single notes alone. The harmony makes you gasp, stirs you both emotionally and rationally.

Ideas that generate a WOW! use beauty, simplicity, and elegance to appeal to the emotions.

Ideas that generate a WOW! offer logical, tangible superiority.

Just as the twelve notes of the chromatic scale can be arranged into an infinite number of melodies or the twenty-six letters of the Arabic alphabet can be combined to form an infinite number of books, so is there no limit to the WOW!s that can be extracted from any creative problem you may face.

The key is to stake your claim—define your area of excellence, then muster all your efforts into delivering that singular point of excellence.

WOW! ideas are the best at whatever it is they are. They identify a particular area of expertise and establish their entry as the ultimate in its class. Procter & Gamble is a master of defining areas of expertise. It paints Top Job as the best there is for greasy kitchen dirt, Mr. Clean as the Cadillac of shiny surface cleansers, and Spic & Span as the Godzilla of the no-wax floor. Ours is a society of specialists.

So you might have a better understanding of WOW! both in terms of its impact and its diversity, take a Saturday afternoon and test-drive four different automobiles. The cars I'd suggest you test have been broadly recognized as adventurous pioneering vehicles that defined new WOW!s in driving. They range in price from $10,000 to more than $50,000. Each offers different benefits, features, and different WOW! factors.

(Note: The cars I'm suggesting are built by foreign car companies. This is not to imply there are no American vehicles with WOW! There are a number of them, and the number is increasing rapidly. Two of the most exceptional American WOW!s

defined new experiences: the Jeep Cherokee, the coolest of the off-road vehicles, and the Chrysler Minivan, the world's greatest kid mover.)

First stop at a Mazda Dealer. Drive a Miata with the top down. This car provokes emotional reactions. It's a romantic, head-turning flirt. I bought one of the first ones. I remember driving along, having entire construction crews watch me go by. I'm not a shapely blond woman; I'm a short, bald guy in glasses. I'm pretty sure the construction guys were looking at the car. The WOW! here is focused on looks.

Next go to a Honda Dealer. Drive a Civic Si. Check out the sticker price. The WOW! this car offers is in driving excitement per dollar. For the money, this car offers more driving fun, better handling, and better acceleration than anything on the market today. It's not as pretty as the Miata, but it's more fun to drive.

Then head to a BMW Dealer. Drive a 325i. Push it when you drive it. It's too bad the BMW became synonymous with yuppies in the 80s. This is a serious driving machine that lets you feel the road like no other. The cost is three times that of the Honda, but the thrust is markedly different. The WOW! is its driving ability.

Your last stop should be the Lexus Dealer. Drive an LS400 and enter a different world. Luxury with a capital LUX. While exalting in the comfort, space, and sheer pleasure of the car's environment, feel the driving. You won't feel much. But the lack of "road feel" is not the lure here that it is with the 325i. Here, the WOW! is the splendor of it.

Each of these cars is considered by most road magazines to be among the ten best automobiles in the world. Here's what they have in common:

- Each offers a complete experience.
- Each offers an original experience.
- Each offers an experience you can see, feel, and understand in an instant.
- Each has a magic spark that sets it apart from the others.

I spell WOW! like this:

Whole Idea

Originality

Wicked Easy to Understand

! Be magic

WHOLE IDEA

A wicked good idea is complete. It sweats the details. If it's a new product, it has a balance of marketing, packaging, and advertising that leaves you panting in anticipation. And once you actually experience the product, it surpasses your expectations.

Few experiences are worse than getting all worked up over a new product, service, restaurant, amusement park ride, or blind date only to have it fall short of your expectations. You feel conned, like you might if you were to purchase the Brooklyn Bridge or swampland in Florida.

If it's any consolation, your feelings of disappointment don't come close to the emotional upheaval of the folks who create these ideas. It pains me whenever I see certain products or services I helped create that, for whatever reason, lack completeness. Sometimes we invent both the idea and the product. Other times we invent just the idea. There are a number of highly publicized products on supermarket shelves today where the product development efforts don't live up to the expectations of the idea that we had created. I cringe when I see these products. Or my stomach turns when I see the advertising for them.

Each of the four automobiles you took for a test drive represents a whole idea. The whole idea is not hidden. It's out there where consumers can easily identify it.

An analysis of the AcuPOLL database and a range of academic studies shows how important it is to have a whole idea; that is, both a superior product and a strong marketing approach. Products or marketing strategies that are significantly more appealing than what is currently available are registered below as Outstanding. If they're significantly worse than what's already out there, they show up as Terrible.

Success Rate
Outstanding Product + Outstanding Marketing Idea = 90%
Outstanding Product + Terrible Marketing Idea = 10%
Terrible Product + Outstanding Marketing Idea = 5%

How to Tell When Your Idea Is a WHOLE IDEA!

First, break your idea down into its components. On index cards, list your idea's key elements—product, packaging, name, experience, feeling, and function, as well as any sensory sights, sounds, and smells it may offer. Sort your idea pieces into Yes/No piles.

- *Does the element contribute to the whole idea?* Does it reinforce and add to the customer's overall experience? Is the seed idea generic, something that anyone could do, or is it exclusive to your idea? If it's the latter, put it in your Yes pile.

  If it's not, it goes in the No pile. These are your Achilles' heels. These are the places where your competition can take advantage of you. At the same time, they're places where you have opportunities to improve your idea.

  Sort the cards from your Yes pile into Yes/No piles again.
- *Is the idea as suggested by the seed feasible?* Can it be made on this planet at a fair price? Can the name be trademarked? Can the product, service, packaging elements be produced? Can they be produced cost effectively? If so, it goes in the Yes pile.

  Look at your No pile. These are your barriers to greatness. These are the hornets that will come back to sting you if you don't deal with them. These are the objections your boss, investors, and/or teammates will raise when you're trying to sell them your vision. Deal with these issues now. The more you anticipate their objections, the greater the chances that they won't have any.

• If you've been through the piles and your newborn idea is still pumping with excitement, party on. If not, then return to Go and do not collect $200.

ORIGINALITY

Ideas must be original to be wicked good. Same old, same old doesn't cut it. You have to offer something that's original, new, and different to get consumers to change their buying patterns.

> *New & Different sat on a wall,*
> *New & Different had a great fall.*
> *All the King's horses*
> *And all the King's men*
> *Proceeded to put them together again.*
> *Giving New a new tweak, starting Different from seed,*
> *Doing the New and the Different is how you succeed.*
> RICHARD SAUNDERS

Wicked good ideas offer benefits that haven't already been experienced and appreciated. They chart new courses and explore new ground. Alternatively, they are the first on their block to eliminate the key negatives. They offer sports car handling at a Civic Si price.

Original ideas generate their own excitement and awareness. Everyone knows Neil Armstrong was the first man on the moon. But can you name two other Apollo astronauts who also set foot on the lunar surface? I doubt it, unless you're related to one of them. Being the first, the original, sets you apart. Being the first is newsworthy. It makes people stop and take notice. It's the pioneers who reap the benefits of fame, publicity, and profits. A study of AcuPOLL data shows that, on average, pioneers generate 2.7 times the market share of copycats.

A survey reported in the *Harvard Business Review* (March–April 1976) quantified the value of originality and uniqueness to profitable success. It looks like this:

	PROFITABLE SUCCESS RATE
Dramatically new and different products	69%
Similar or marginally different products	31%

You double your odds of success when you stick out your neck and do something different.

RICHARD SAUNDERS

Look closely at your idea. Is it truly different? And can that difference be articulated simply and concisely? If your customers don't buy your idea, is there another they would? What do they give up in your collection of benefits? What do they gain from your harmony of attributes?

Originality leads. The same old stuff follows. It takes courage to lead. Franklin, Jefferson, Washington, and Adams had it. The folks who stayed in England didn't. It's always much easier to stay in England. All you have to do is sit there.

How to Tell if Your Idea Is a Grade-A Original!

List the alternatives to your idea, your mission. If your customer doesn't like your idea, what are their options? If your boss doesn't go with your idea, what's her alternative? If your children don't like your spinach and liver soufflé, what choices do they have? If the nice lady who answers the door isn't interested in your Girl Scout cookies, what would interest her?

These alternatives are the competitors to your idea.

For each of the key alternatives, take the following steps:

1. On index cards, list every factor, be it rational or emotional, that sets you apart.
2. Sort the cards into three piles. In the first pile, put the cards listing differences that give you a meaningful advantage. In

the second, put the differences that give your competition a meaningful advantage. In the third, put the differences that aren't significant one way or the other.

3. Spread the piles out on a table and look at them as honestly and objectively as you can. You are looking at the reasons why you will either fail or succeed. Would you buy what you're selling? If you wouldn't now, your boss or your children or the nice lady who answers the door won't later. If you would, move forward. If not, go directly to jail, do not pass Go, do not collect $200.

Wicked easy to understand

A wicked good idea is simple. It's easily defined. At first glance, you "get it." If it takes more than ten seconds to grasp or ten words to explain an idea, it's probably not wicked good.

It doesn't matter if your challenge is a high-tech computer, a hydrocarbon chemical, a sugar water soda pop, or sliced bread. Complicated ideas never work. Complicated ideas are a sign of hazy thinking.

Nothing delivers the kiss of death more quickly than an idea that is unclear, complex, or obtuse. If your customer or your boss or your banker don't understand, you lose. You are the only one who will give your idea the benefit of the doubt.

I emphasize name and packaging for the sake of simplicity. I want people to get my ideas immediately, if not sooner. I want them to see them as I see them.

Maybe you're simply looking for ideas for a PTA fund-raiser. It's still important to name it and package it properly. Unless you live in a bubble, any idea you want to develop has to be communicated to others.

The success of your idea will lean heavily on your ability to involve others in your mission. They can't wax enthusiastic about your vision if they don't know what it is. Martin Luther King, Jr.'s vision was simple. "I have a dream," he said. John F. Kennedy's vision was simple. "Ask not what your country can do for you; ask what you can do for your country," he said. People understood. And they responded.

Simple ideas are self-evident. In the hypercluttered Information Age, there is no other kind. Self-evident products make you want to pick them up when you see the name and the front of the package—no additional communication required.

Simplicity engenders impulse purchases. Complexity generates contemplation. You lose when your consumer has to contemplate your idea. In the process of all that contemplating, they start looking at other options.

Sometimes people are put off by simplicity. They get the idea that if an idea is simple, it's not worthwhile. They might think it lacks depth. I disagree.

> *Simplicity is the essence of brilliance.*
> RICHARD SAUNDERS

History's great geniuses are remembered for finding simple order in chaos. Albert Einstein, for instance, boiled the universe down to $e = mc^2$.

How to Find Out if Your Idea Qualifies as Wicked Easy to Understand!

Describe your idea in fifty words. Then describe it in twenty-five words. Then cut it down to a dozen.

Look at what's left.

If your idea is too complex now to capsulize in a dozen words, it will only grow more muddled later. Or if you find that, in the process of paring down from fifty to a dozen words, your idea has been drained of its excitement, you know what to do. Go directly to jail, do not pass Go, do not collect $200.

! HAVE MAGIC

This is the least tangible, most ephemeral element of the WOW! factor. It is also the most difficult to create. It's the spark that lights the fuse that sends ideas hurtling off into the stratosphere. It's what makes people want to stand in line and pay higher prices than they know they should.

Once upon a time, the market was saturated with dozens of board games that centered on the theme of trivia. Then a handful of Canadians came along. They gambled their lives, homes, and sanity to develop a game they called Trivial Pursuit. It took off like a rocket, setting unheard-of sales records. It also sold for an unheard-of price.

But Trivial Pursuit was magic. It touched off a craze in the world of board games that wasn't rational, one that in a million years could never have been predicted. It just happened.

Magic comes about from the right mix of function and design. I see it in the Macintosh PowerBook, Swatch watches, L.L. Bean boots, and Ben and Jerry's Ice Cream. Magic also is a function of timing, of being in the right place at the right instant. The Chrysler Minivan came out at a time when baby boomers were trying to figure out how to haul their baby boomlets to soccer practice. Rap music emerged when a new generation was looking for its own identity, separate and apart from the rock 'n' roll rhythms of their baby boomer parents.

How to Tell When Your Idea Has Magic!

Magic is the most difficult of all elements to measure. For the most part, it's more a function of emotion, art, and feeling than it is of an engineered benefit. I know of no way to know objectively if an idea is endowed with magic. But here are a few ways to tell it might:

- Your idea runs continuously through your head. You can't turn it off. It's all-consuming.

- Other people have tried to steal it. Or take credit for it.
- It has multiple dimensions. It has onion-peeling depth. When you describe it to someone else, they immediately have thoughts and suggestions.
- Write your core idea in the middle of a sheet of paper. Attach thoughts, free associations, and applications to it, like spokes from a hub. The more new thoughts and opportunities a core idea sparks, the greater the likelihood that you really do have magic on your hands.

If you don't think you have it, don't give up. More runs are scored with singles and doubles than grand slams. But in those rare opportunities when magic strikes, grab it and hold on tight.

When it comes to evaluating ideas, you have to be willing to walk away. There's a fundamental truth in the idea business, that being, if you can create one, you can create many. You need to know when to hold them, when to fold them, and when to go on to something else altogether.

On an average project for an average client, I find myself walking away from more than 100 ideas for every idea I pursue. Of course, it's much easier to be selective when you have plenty of options.

Each year, I create and test thousands of my own newborn ideas. I love them all, but if I had to select my pets—not necessarily the best-selling, mind you—the following would make the list:

- *Merwyn's Magic Bunnies:* This was a simplified version of a classic magic trick in which mommy and daddy sponge rabbits disappear and reappear with a spongy bundle of baby bunnies. I was twelve years old when I developed Merwyn's Magic Bunnies. I sold them at country fairs for $1 a bag, using a nickel's worth of material. As I demonstrated the trick, my future wife assembled bunny kits for sale. It was a fun product, plied in a fun environment, and it helped me pay my way through college.
- *Lipton Originals:* This ready-to-drink iced tea was the first project I did for Pepsi-Cola. What makes the concept special to me is its simplicity. It's made through real brewing; the

world's largest tea bag is lowered into a giant pot of hot water, and the tea is brewed. Other tea products use reconstituted chemical concentrates and call it brewing.

- *Spic & Span Diamond Promotion:* This one broke a lot of rules. It's also one of the most widely copied ideas I've ever created. During my stretch at Procter & Gamble, I was responsible for the national introduction of Spic & Span Pine Cleaner. So I wanted to kick up a ruckus that would have the competition trembling with fear.

Through a happy coincidence, it turned out that Spic & Span was about to celebrate its seventy-fifth birthday, an occasion that translated into a diamond anniversary. About that same time, I happened to hear from a friend about cubic zirconiums—man-made diamonds. These separate pieces of information came together in a promotion where a diamond—some of them real, most of them man-made—was placed in every box and bottle of Spic & Span.

The idea had another dimension. The campaign was tied in with the Jewelers Association of America, which agreed to place signs in the windows of its stores identifying them as "Diamond Validation Centers." These were places where you could have your diamond checked to see if you had a cubic zirconium worth $5.00 or a real one-third-carat diamond worth $600.

Finally, the program was launched in February around Valentine's Day. The whole shebang linked Spic & Span's seventy-fifth anniversary, Valentine's Day, and diamonds. In my mind, the slogan "Buy your honey a box of Spic & Span for Valentine's" was a wicked neat twist on an old theme.

I was promoted shortly after creating the idea and setting it in motion. The marketing event garnered millions of dollars' worth of free exposure—from *Good Morning America* to the *Wall Street Journal*. More importantly, it generated record sales for Spic & Span and helped Spic & Span Pine become one of the most successful new product launches in Procter & Gamble's history.

CHAPTER 111

The Courage to Face Fear

I hear you. You're saying:

"OK, Doug, let's see if I've got this straight—contradict history, be original, change the world, chase dreams. But it's tough out here, man! The economy is tight, the competition is brutal. Companies are laying off people left and right. Are you out of your mind, Doug?"

Of course I am.

I admit it. I love trampling on the established ways of doing things. I love to shake it up.

But then again, what choice is there? If you do something, anything, there is a chance you will fail. There is also a chance you will succeed.

Most everyone wants to live on the edge. Maybe the feeling is deep down, but it's there. Most everyone would like to be out front, the very best. But the only way to know for sure you're on the edge is to slip over it. You can't inch your way to it and peek over. You have to step out front and fall a few times. Success doesn't happen without failure.

Maxime Faget, NASA's chief designer for more than twenty years, put it this way in an interview in the book *Inventors at Work*:

> *No one felt like every test had to be a success, like it is now in NASA.... A test is supposed to find out if some-*

thing works, not prove that it works.... We had some-thing like twenty different tests of the Mercury capsule without men, and six or seven of them were failures.... We'd have a failure, and then a few months later, we'd have a success. If we had a failure, we didn't shut every-thing down for a couple of years and put our tails between our legs and hide. We just kept going ... [We] learned what was wrong as well as what was right.

Do not labor under the assumption that the safe way is to do nothing. In today's marketplace, if you're not moving forward, the competition is passing you by. Standing still is not a realistic option. You can't afford to maintain the status quo.

There's no escaping change or risk.

It's as risky to maintain the status quo as it is to reach for the new and bold. In the first case, you can get run over. In the second, you have a chance to swing for the fence.

RICHARD SAUNDERS

If you want to change your life, your job, or your business, you'll have to change the way you do things. You can't wish your way there. You have to take action.

The only way to get a significantly different result is to do something significantly different.

RICHARD SAUNDERS

I see a lot of fear. I see it in clients at high levels and low lev-els. Maybe they're fearing for their jobs. Maybe they work for companies where reorganization is a seasonal event, companies where a lack of leadership at the top trickles down to pain and suffering in the ranks below.

I've gotten so I can smell fear. Within ten minutes of entering a client's office, if it's there, I can smell it. It casts a shadow over the conversation. These people are not hopeless cases. Most of the time, all they need is a jolt of entrepreneurial enthusiasm.

Top 10 Ways to Identify Scaredy-Cats

1. They regard whoopee cushions as a potential form of sexual harassment.
2. The veins in their temples look like interstate road maps.
3. They shuffle papers faster than 99 percent of the blackjack dealers in Vegas.
4. They walk with a limp because their toes are permanently curled under.
5. They have honed political correctness to a fine art.
6. They know the names, ages, and dispositions of all their pharmacist's children.
7. They have whiplash from looking over their shoulders so often.
8. They update their résumés on a weekly basis.
9. They become intimidated when forced to choose between today's specials at lunch.
10. They are not in the least bit amused when you sneak up behind them and yell BOO!

Clients who are paralyzed with fear are exceedingly difficult to help. They can barely make a decision. When we face such a client, we handle with care. Sometimes a game of killer volleyball or a spin on the go-carts or a *Nerf* Master Blaster free-for-all will loosen them up to the point where they can be productive. But when all else fails, we seek to protect them—we assume the responsibility for the project ourselves.

We present scaredy-cat clients with a minimal number of decisions. We do as much of the deciding as we can. Sometimes the best way to help clients save their jobs is to protect them from themselves.

Where does fear come from? What does it look like? On the belief that, once we know where fear comes from, we can start to deal with it, I've identified the High 5 of fears. Here they are, along with the five best ways I know for finding the remedy—courage!

HIGH 5 OF FEARS

1. FEAR of Being Laughed At

This is one of the most basic of all fears. It starts at an early age. When we are young, we're insecure about our abilities. We're still learning what we can and cannot do, pull, and/or get away with. The sad truth is that we often try to mask our own insecurities by laughing at others.

The fear of ridicule causes us to build walls between ourselves and the world. It prevents us from asking questions so we won't appear foolish. It keeps us from taking on new and different pursuits because we might fall on our faces. It discourages us from reaching out and revealing our true selves because we might be rejected. It ties our hands, clamps our mouths shut, and closes our minds.

We fear being laughed at because of a phenomenon called WAWPAT, which is short for Worrying About What People Are Thinking. WAWPAT saps our energy, drains our self-respect, and makes us choke up on our swing.

I sometimes get caught in this trap myself. When making presentations to corporations or giving lectures, I always wear jeans or shorts and sneakers or sandals. I believe in looking the part of the entrepreneur since that's what I'm selling. Besides, it's more comfortable. But there are times my surroundings compel me to rethink my position.

Like the time I delivered my Jump Start Your Brain lecture to a group of company presidents and their spouses at a castle in The Hague, Netherlands. A cocktail reception was held beforehand. The ambience was a bit intimidating—waiters in black tie, a huge coat of arms hanging over the fireplace, upper-level executives in outfits worth more than my entire wardrobe. Even the janitor wore a tux.

I was in my customary bare feet, jeans, and T-shirt, laced up tight in my canvas and leather-trimmed straitjacket. I had in my bags about 120 whoopee cushions. I can't say for sure, but I think it was the first time anyone had brought whoopee cushions to this place.

The stark contrast between myself and the general atmosphere of old-money formality nearly affected my brain. I made a tentative start on the lecture. Instead of throwing myself into it, I pulled back on the jokes. Instead of playing to win, I played not to lose.

I was in the death grip of WAWPAT. After about ten minutes, it became painfully apparent to me that it was not going at all well. The whoopee cushion gag was coming up, but I was going down in flames. At that moment, I looked over and saw Liam Killeen, an Irish gentleman who had arranged my series of lectures on that day. Liam is a dream to work with. He works and plays hard, like few clients I've ever had.

In the haze of my panic, I saw Liam hoist his beer glass in my direction, his grin as wide as his face. In an instant, I regained my composure, turned on the jets, and let the enthusiasm fly. Some of my points seemed to hit, others didn't. But the energy in the room increased a couple of notches. My formal audience actually guffawed out loud at the whoopee cushion gag.

To my surprise, I was mobbed at the end of the presentation. An animated ring formed around me. They told me they needed to hear more messages like my own, that they needed to learn how to open their minds, have fun, kick back, and relax. "To be more like you wild Americans!"

Since the Holland trip, I've made it a point to crank up the energy for every lecture. At the first hint of WAWPAT, I think of Holland and of Liam raising his glass, grinning at me like a skunk.

If you're not careful, you can let a lot of energy evaporate while you're looking over your shoulder. Don't think about WAWPAT. Put it out of your head. Instead, concentrate on swinging through the ball and give it your best shot.

> *Being laughed at is a sign of potential genius. Think of Franklin in a thunderstorm, the Wright brothers on the beach at Kitty Hawk, Edison with his lightbulbs, Ted Turner with his Cable News Network.*
> RICHARD SAUNDERS

My great-grandfather, William Holder, didn't suffer from WAWPAT. His father, George, ran a sail-making shop in the New Brunswick, Canada, harbor town of St. John. It was one of a number of shops on the bay that handcrafted sails for the tall ships. The process was a long, arduous one, and my great-grandfather decided there had to be a better way.

He talked his father into buying a couple of sewing machines as an experiment. It was the first time anyone had ever seen sewing machines in a Canadian sail loft. The men who worked with him didn't take kindly to the machines, and young Will Holder came to be known as the Petticoat Sailmaker. He was the laughingstock of the harbor.

But he paid extra to any man who was willing to work on his machines. And while the old-timers were laughing at him, he was taking their business. More than a century has passed, and the

George E. Holder & Son sign still hangs over the bay in St. John; it's the only one of the original sailmakers still in business.

2. FEAR of Losing What You Have

I built my reputation at P&G solving the unsolvable. From Spic & Span to Folgers Coffee, I developed solutions to seemingly hopeless challenges. I thrived on it. In fact, it's almost easier to solve the unsolvable. When a problem seems unsolvable, people are more likely to muster the courage for bold and sometimes bizarre solutions.

The fear of change, of losing what one has, is at its most profound in the middle. It's when you are neither succeeding nor failing dramatically, when you have more than nothing to lose but not so much that you're willing to risk any of it.

Highly successful people think they're bulletproof. They believe they have the Midas touch. Fear is difficult for them to fathom. Conversely, when people have hit rock bottom, when they have nothing to lose, they have nothing to fear. And they are more willing to accept significant change.

The people in the middle are trying to coast. They often play not to lose instead of playing to win. They are the ostriches of the human race. They create elaborate justifications for their lack of action and forward motion.

The result is disillusionment. Which leads to twisting in the wind, which in turn leads to certain death.

If you hang on too long, you are most assuredly going to get yourself hanged.

RICHARD SAUNDERS

3. FEAR of Rejection

It can be pretty intense in high school. You can stew for months over a certain dreamy and unapproachable someone, over how to break the ice with just the right words that will ensure that the two of you live happily ever after in Tahiti. But you never find the words that suit you. Or if you do, you bite your tongue when the moment arrives because you couldn't bear what you're sure would be a withering glare from that certain someone. So you never do get to Tahiti.

The fear of rejection grows stronger as we become adults. Instead of speaking our minds, we become conditioned to sit on them. After a while, we stop trying because whatever it is we're trying just seems TOO DARNED HARD.

> *Unless you try to do something beyond what you have already mastered, you will never grow.*
> RALPH WALDO EMERSON

Separate "it" from "you." Recognize that when one of your ideas fail, it's not a reflection on "you." It's a reflection on "it." Failure is part of the process of learning. Your best teachers are your mistakes.

Watch a baby learning to walk. The baby falls, the baby gets up, the baby falls, the baby gets up again. A baby learns without realizing it. And one day, the baby is able to walk because it never occurred to the baby to give up.

Hold your focus on your goal. Think of the bumps in the road—and there are always bumps in the road—as milestones that mean you're getting closer to your goal. Remember Reggie Jackson. He's at the top of the All-Time Whiff List, striking out more often than anyone who ever swung a bat in the majors—2,597 times at all. But he also hit 563 home runs during his twenty-one-year career, which puts him, as of this writing, at No. 6 on the list of All-Time Home Run Hitters.

> *Finding the courage means you believe in what you're doing and that you are secure in your ability to go do something else, that you're not afraid to take it to the monster. Finding the courage means you're not afraid of getting kicked out, knowing you'd land on your feet if you did.*
> DAVE HOWE,
> Richard Saunders Technologies

4. FEAR of the Unknown

Many of us lack initial courage because we think we need to have every step choreographed before we embark on the adventure.

We want a detailed road map with a clearly focused beginning, middle, and final destination, along with a synopsis of all the roadside rests and comfort stations.

Sorry. It doesn't work that way. Consider America's westward migration. The trail to California wasn't paved. There were no  HoJos with HBO and heated pools. The pioneers in their covered wagons had to learn to deal with contingencies—rattle-snakes, wolves, bears, the Rocky Mountains, flaming arrows fired from the bows of war-painted locals atop galloping Appaloosas. And you think you have problems.

It takes ignorance to do new-to-the-world ideas. Ignorance is as big a factor as courage—ignorance of how difficult whatever it is you're trying to do is to do. If someone had sat me down and said, "Guy, let me tell you how hard it is to evangelize a new computer. Everybody's going to tell you they don't want to risk it. It's never been done in the history of man. And, Guy, it took Apple II six years to get software..." I never would have done it.

GUY KAWASAKI,
Macintosh software evangelist

When I first tried to sell ONCE, my storytelling board game, ignorance was in my corner. I didn't know you weren't supposed to sell games to big companies.

So I flew to New York for the International Toy Fair, an annual event at which the toy industry showcases its wares to retailers, and checked into a hotel that might best be described as a bag of fleas.

I was turned down more times than a wino at a debutante ball. I felt like an onion bagel in a doughnut factory. In the end, all I needed was one person in a position of power to say yes. Or at least say something nice. I just had to keep looking until I found that person.

That person's name was Bill Hill, at the time vice president of product development for Selchow & Righter. Bill made his mark in the business as the man who purchased Trivial Pursuit while all the other big game companies were passing on it. Bill took a liking to me and a look at my game. He didn't buy my game, but his insights and encouragement gave me the courage to carry on and, as it happened, ultimately sell the game to Western Publishing.

> *Doug's game had the same magical ingredient as Trivial Pursuit; it started conversations. Doug thought logically and sometimes illogically, but he thought. He didn't copy. Most inventors take something that exists and give it a twist. All Doug's stuff was original. And he believed in it.*
>
> BILL HILL

If you want to be great, you must learn to live with uncertainty. You have to have faith in your ability to adapt and react. Ignorance of the future is not a sign of stupidity—it's part of the human condition.

5. FEAR of Exposure

It's one of the more crippling forms of dread, the fear that a deep-seated insecurity will be dragged out into the light of day. We accumulate variations on this fear all our lives—as in, "I'm not *(smart, creative, tall, good-looking, fill in the blank)* enough."

These fears run deep. They comprise your most formidable barriers to success. They collect, like soap scum in a shower. You need to scour them away. You do this by facing them head on, by ignoring the warnings and moving forward.

Granted, some warnings are for our own good. Like, "Don't touch that hot stove. You'll get burned." The warnings you have to watch out for are the ones designed to inhibit you for no good reason. Like, "Go ahead if you want everyone to see what an idiot you are." You have to ignore this second kind of warning, no matter how authoritative the source.

Think back. What tasks or activities have you always believed you could never perform? In what ways have you allowed yourself to be limited or stereotyped?

Stop and think of five stereotypes you've been saddled with at various times in your life. Which made sense? Which heightened your fears? Which caused you to change plans?

If you're having trouble here, close your eyes. Review your life in *Reader's Digest* terms. Recollect your years in elementary school, junior high, high school, and college; your first girl- or boyfriends; your first jobs and first bosses.

How did these settings and personalities dictate your expectations? How did they whittle down your perspective and carve into your brain ways of seeing things that shackled your thoughts?

Identifying your fears is the first step to freeing yourself from them. Once you've hung signs around their scrawny necks, you can turn your mind up to full power.

HIGH 5 OF COURAGE

Now that we've identified the five fears, let's kick their butts.

First, you must absolutely, positively, unqualifiedly be committed to your idea—and to the notion that you can make your idea happen. You have to commit yourself with abandon.

> *If you don't believe, you won't achieve.*
> RICHARD SAUNDERS

To help you along those lines, I've developed a list of the high 5 sources of courage. I dip into each of these wells to generate, nurture, and maintain courage in my own life.

1. Look to Teammates
Pioneers need partners. Great adventures are team efforts, and big ideas need courageous teams to make them a reality.

The band of people you assemble is your greatest source of courage. They understand the mission. When the forces of the real world are pressing down, you can find support and strength from your teammates.

Teammates might be folks you work with at Giant American Conglomerates Unlimited. Or they might be your fellow members of the cast of the junior class play. Or the architect who is designing your home and the contractor who is building it.

Or you might have just one teammate. Like, say, your spouse—your dearly beloved, the one who promised to love and obey you until death do you part. In my case, her name is Debbie, and I'd never launch a venture without her total support.

If you don't have a mutually supportive relationship, get the relationship fixed. Never, ever set sail on a grand adventure without the support of your spouse. This person must be a portrait of faith and support. If you have that, you're blessed indeed. Anything short of it will deflate your oomph, drain your energy, and puncture your balloon.

> *A good wife and health, is a man's best wealth.*
> BEN FRANKLIN

> *That goes for good husbands and health, too.*
> RICHARD SAUNDERS

When I launched Richard Saunders International, my financing took the form of a most excellent MasterCard. It was expensive, but it worked. In this regard, as in so many others, Debbie was the Queen of Supportiveness.

> *Starting the business meant working extra hours. Whenever we got our MasterCard bill, I'd sign up for extra shifts at the hospital. I was working nights at the time. At one point, I worked eighteen nights in a row at two different hospitals.*
> DEBBIE HALL, R.N.,
> my wife

Children are powerful little courage generators. They have the ability to put your life into perspective, a gift for stripping away the peripherals and finding the essence of a situation.

If you're really scared, try talking to a child about fear. Ask what scares them and how they deal with their fears. In just such a conversation the other day, my five-year-old daughter shared a revelation with me, a revelation that put into perspective how large children's fears must seem relative to adult fears:

Dragons and monsters are what scare me most. When I get really scared, I count to ten and that takes my mind off it.

KRISTYN HALL

Wow! I may have fears in my day-to-day business life. But I never have to come face to face with dragons and monsters.

Talking with a child has a way of making your fears seem not so big. Most adult fears melt away under the scrutiny of a five-year-old. One of the wonderful things about kids is that no matter how great your success or dismal your failure, they'll love you just the same. Your children have total faith in you. Believe in that. Use it to believe in yourself.

Over breakfast, a friend of mine passed this same bit of advice to a major-league baseball pitcher who was going through a slump, a guy who was growing numb to the sound of tens of thousands of people booing. The pitcher's confidence was shot. But when he considered that no matter what happened at the ball park, his three-year-old wouldn't care, he began regaining his faith in his abilities. Once he turned that corner in his mind, he beat the slump.

2. Taking Action

Think of yourself as a deer on a highway. If you freeze in the headlights of an oncoming 18-wheeler, you're roadkill. When fear hits you, it's time to move your hooves. Move your feet, and your body and mind will follow. You may fall on your face, but at least you'll be moving forward.

Fear is often a mirage arising from your own uncertainties. Take action. Any action is better than standing still. In most cases, if you challenge your fear

through action, you'll find it's not nearly as formidable as you thought.

> *I am in the midst of learning to face my fears. It seems that fears are all based on these things: illusion and future thinking, with a side order of "what if."*
> SARK,
> *Inspiration Sandwich*

Think of a group of explorers at the base of a mountain range. They can sit and ponder the fearful vagaries of fate or they can start climbing. As they make their way up the slope and toward the peak, they'll find many opportunities and alternative routes they never could have seen from the base of the mountain.

You can't think and hit at the same time. To really hit, you have to just get out there.

YOGI BERRA

It's difficult to identify new opportunities if you stay put. If you get moving, new opportunities will expose themselves. Besides, once you're moving, you're building momentum. To paraphrase Ben, an ounce of momentum is worth a pound of courage.

Another way to build momentum is to break your fear into pieces. Then act on each piece, one at a time. Celebrate small victories. Realize that each small victory represents another step up the mountain. Manhattan wasn't built in a minute. Small successes add up to increased confidence and positive momentum.

I once led a creativity seminar for 100 executives at a leading corporation. At the end of the session, I gave each executive a paper airplane and asked that they write any suggestions for improving the seminar on the wings. The idea was for them to scribble a comment and let their plane fly, then grab any planes that came their way and expand on the thoughts that were already there.

I got a lot of good suggestions from them. But one plane in particular gave me an insight into the different perspectives on my message. I think Person #3 got the picture.

Person #1: You're not in touch with the real world.
Person #2: Can you help us translate learning to the
real world?
Person #3: JUST DO IT!

3. Covering Your Bets

Contrary to popular belief, most entrepreneurs—and certainly 99 percent of all successful veteran entrepreneurs I've ever come across—are extremely conservative. Entrepreneurs are not daredevils. They don't take long shots.

Rather, they reduce fear by covering their bets. They use a number of tricks to minimize risk and increase their courage, including:

- *Underestimating expectations.* A classic rule of thumb is to round all costs upward and all revenue estimates downward. Then cut all sales assumptions by 50 percent. If you find your plan will work even when it's cut to a fraction of its regular size, your courage will grow.
- *Building back doors.* Figure out fallback positions in the event your initial plan falls flat. The more options you have now, the more courage you'll have tomorrow.
- *Be the best.* When you take the high ground and create something of genuine value, you'll be strengthened. If an idea is true, if it's not of dubious value, you'll be more apt to have the courage to see it through. The best ideas are those that bring out the idealist in you.

When you do the right thing, you can never be wrong.
MARC MARSAN, General Manager,
Richard Saunders International

- *Nonnegotiable ethics and low overhead.* The following story regarding Ben Franklin tells it well:

Soon after the establishment of his paper, a person brought him a piece, which he requested him to publish in the Pennsylvania Gazette. *Franklin desired that the piece might be left for his consideration until next day, when he would give an answer. The person returned at the time appointed, and received from Franklin his com-*

munication, "I have perused your piece, and find it to be scurrilous and defamatory—to determine whether I should publish it or not, I went home in the evening, purchased a twopenny loaf at the baker's, and, with water from the pump made my supper;—I then wrapped myself up in my great coat, and laid down on the floor and slept till morning, when on another loaf and a mug of water, I made my breakfast. From this regimen I feel no inconvenience whatever. Finding I can live in this manner, I have formed a determination never to prostitute my press to the purposes of corruption, and abuse of this kind, for the sake of gaining a more comfortable subsistence."

ISAIAH THOMAS,
History of Printing in America

4. Replaying Success
Another way to heighten your G.Q. (Guts Quotient) is to visualize success.

- **Visualize Previous Wins:** Think back to a moment when, by some sudden, unexplainable serendipity, you created a solution, invented a shortcut, or concocted a new way to reach a goal. Recall a moment of revelation in which the curtain pulled back and you were given an answer from somewhere outside yourself. Hey, you did it once. You can do it again.
- **Recall the Great Ones:** What would your hero do in this situation? If you don't have a hero now, who were your heroes when you were small? How would John Wayne, Amelia Earhart, Zorro, Betty Crocker, Sam Snead, Eleanor Roosevelt, Conan the Barbarian, or Ben Franklin proceed under these circumstances? One of the reasons fear paralyzes is that it befuddles. Often a fearful person's biggest problem is simply in knowing which way to turn. By stepping out of yourself and letting a hero be your guide, you can find that direction.

5. Bursting the Worst

What is the worst that can happen? Think about it, write it down, articulate it. How bad could it get? Then deal with it.

Is the worst case really all that bad? The specifics of the worst case are often much less than your vague imaginings of it.

Then consider that it's not likely you'll allow things to get to a worst-case scenario. And take heart in that.

> *When I'm not feeling creative, I just turn off the word processor, sit back, take a sip of coffee, and say to myself, "Hey, I can ALWAYS get another job, such as coal miner." And then I turn the old word processor right back on and become AMAZINGLY creative.*
>
> DAVE BARRY,
> humor columnist, author

Remember the story about the Spic & Span diamonds promotion from the previous chapter? There's more to it.

The idea was not without its risks. Considering the scope of the Spic & Span line, it was decided we would have to corner the world market on cubic zirconiums for four months. Additionally, there were concerns about how to get the stones in the boxes and what to do to keep unscrupulous individuals from opening the boxes in the store to get at the rocks.

Procter & Gamble's legal, manufacturing, and public relations departments strongly recommended against the promotion—at least until it could be tested.

The manager of P&G's advertising department asked if I had another option. I told him our traditional plan had been to offer a 25¢ coupon and a 35¢-off price pack, which is P&Gese for a discount that's printed on the package itself. The results were predictable enough, seeing as how sales had declined versus the previous year over the past five years we'd taken this route. How much did it cost to stage this traditional marketing event? About $2 million per year.

I told him the diamond promotion would come in at $1.3 million.

The advertising manager knew there was some uncertainty with my diamond campaign inasmuch as it hadn't been tested. He also understood there was very little uncertainty about the coupon promotion; it was guaranteed to be a waste of $2 million.

"Let's do the diamonds," he said. As I pointed out in the previous chapter, the results were glittering.

> *Corporate Americans have a fear of doing anything new. They're comfortable doing the same thing over and over again. You know, "We ran that promotion last year. Let's run it again this year!"*
>
> ERIC SCHULZ,
> Walt Disney Company

We've established that you're not a machine. You're a human being. Otherwise, fear wouldn't be a factor. You'll need courage to get started, and you'll need grit-your-teeth, clench-your-fist perseverance to keep going when war-painted locals atop galloping Appaloosas start firing flaming arrows at you.

But don't fear fear. Make it your friend. Use it to fuel your energy. It prevents complacency. It will make you reach inside yourself and stretch your potential.

> *Years ago, when Ken Stabler was a quarterback for the Raiders, a newspaperman said, "Ken, I want to read you something Jack London wrote: 'I would rather be ashes than dust. I would rather that my spark burn out in a brilliant blaze than be stifled by dry rot. I would rather be a superb meteor, every atom of me a magnificent glow, than a sleepy, crumbling planet. For the proper function of man is to live, not exist. I shall not waste my days in trying to prolong them. I shall use my time.'" And the reporter then asked Stabler: "What does that mean to you, Kenny?" Without hesitating, Stabler said: "Throw deep!"*
>
> MICHAEL WAGMAN,
> *Advertising Age,*
> January 30, 1986

One of the reasons I left P&G was that I no longer had any fear. My work there was no longer new. The edge was gone. It seemed too easy. The opportunities to throw deep were gone.

For all its allure, stability can be too comfortable. Stability taken too far leads to stagnancy. Stability is the absence of change. Dead people are stable.

You'll get your chance to be brave. Remember what the Wizard told the Lion:

> *As for you, my fine friend, you're a victim of disorganized thinking. You are under the unfortunate delusion that simply because you run away from danger, you have no courage. You're confusing courage with wisdom. Back where I come from, we have men who are called heroes. Once a year, they take their fortitude out of mothballs and parade it down the main street of the city. And they have no more courage than you. But they have one thing that you haven't got—a medal.*
>
> *The Wizard of Oz*

It was true then, and it's true now. In keeping with this sentiment, I hereby present you this medal of courage.

The hardest part is taking the first step. Once you get your feet moving, opportunities will present themselves. Here are a few footprints, courtesy of my one-year-old son, Brad. Cut them out, put them on the floor, point them toward the door, and follow them.

ACT II

Eureka! Stimulus Response Explosion

Working with Doug Hall and his lunatic friends has been the most uncivilized experience of my life...if there is a better way to create new ideas, I haven't found it...by the way, Doug is not nearly as tall as he appears in the book.

MARK MICHAUD
Coors Brewing Company

We've found Richard Saunders Invention methods to be different than most. They work.

MICHELE WOJTYNA

The Eureka! experience is the freshest breath of air I've had in a very long time. The fact that something so much fun could be both productive and add value gives me hope for the broader corporate environment of the future.

SHARON HALL
General Manager, Avon Products

Doug brings out (or back) the kid in all of us...to find solutions that are intuitively obvious to an eight-year-old but not to a forty-year-old.

CHUCK HONG
Director of R&D, Proctor & Gamble

Eureka! Stimulus Response Explosion

Act II is a toolbox. It's filled with techniques and examples for making Eureka! Stimulus Response work for you. You'll find contained herein my secrets to making your brain more powerful.

Included are detailed discussions on stimuli—where to find them, how to get them, and what to do with them—along with a range of exercises or Eureka! Stimulus Response Brain Programs for making your Brain Operating System run

more smoothly, quickly, and creatively. These Brain Programs have been proven in the line of fire to increase and enhance the ability of ordinary and not-so-ordinary Americans to think quicker, better, faster. They're the same programs I've used with executives at Pepsi-Cola, AT&T, Procter & Gamble, Walt Disney Consumer Products, Nabisco Brands, Quaker Oats, Nike, Ralston Purina, Eveready Battery Company, Frito-Lay, Folgers Coffee, and many other top corporations.

There's a right way and a wrong way to invent ideas. The Eureka! Stimulus Response method is the right way because it allows you to use your brain as a computer, a processing tool.

The old way is the wrong way. That would be the traditional

approach, that of Braindraining brainstorming, because it attempts to SUCK ideas from your head. It forces you to use your brain as the primary source of ideas, as if it were a library.

Some of the Brain Programs included in Act II are designed to unfetter your mind. Others are aimed at reshaping established perceptions. Still others will help you tap into the unexplored corners of your imagination. You'll find fast-paced Brain Programs for breaking through mental blocks, mining the gold from gut instincts, programming your subconscious, and making chaos work for you. You'll learn how to use your five senses to invent and how to break rules for fun and profit.

You can improve your brainpower with any of the programs described in Act II. In fact, the more different Brain Programs you use, the more fluid and dynamic your thoughts will become.

Sound like fun? You bet. Done properly, Eureka! Stimulus Response is the most fun you and your brain can have, when it's just the two of you. As you move through the book, please don't forget you're supposed to be having fun here. Fun equals creativity; more fun equals more creativity. Remember:

$$\mathcal{E} = (S + B.O.S.)^F$$

Certain brain styles naturally gravitate to certain Brain Programs. In most cases, it's a matter of what you're comfortable with.

Realists prefer the kinds of Brain Programs that are structured, that lead them step by step to a goal, and that use stimuli directly related to the problem at hand. Realists like to ground their thinking on that which exists. They're at their creative best working with tools and in arenas they can relate to on practical terms.

Dreamers prefer the freedom of more open-ended Brain Programs. They're more at home defining their own dimensions in an atmosphere of wide open space. Dreamers are drawn to new horizons.

For their part, Builders find something of value in all the Brain Programs. The issue with Builders is not so much which Brain

Program to use, but how many. Builders are equally at ease with structure and randomness.

To give you an idea which Brain Programs are likely to be most effective for you, I've provided a checklist of which way the winds of preferences blow. All this notwithstanding, the more different types of Brain Programs you bring to a task, the more your brain cells will be pulled, pushed, and stretched. And the more you will jump-start your brain.

Eureka! Stimulus Response Brain Program Preferences

Chapter Area	PREFERRED BY		
	Realists	Builders	Dreamers
201 Prison Break			
1. Mind Dumpster	✔	✔	✔
2. Hitchhiking	✔	✔	✔
202 Stimuli: Where to Find Them, How to Use Them			
3. Stimuli One Step	✔	✔	✔
4. Stimuli Two Step	✔	✔	✔
• Stimuli Prospecting			
5. To Market, To Market		✔	✔
6. Newsstand		✔	✔
7. Hello, Mr. Webster	✔	✔	
203 Common Senses			
8. Candid Comments		✔	✔
9. Magic Moments	✔	✔	
10. Kitchen Chemistry	✔	✔	
204 Flapdoodling			
11. Flapdoodling	✔	✔	✔
205 Jumping the Tracks			
12. 666	✔	✔	
13. Don't Sell Me		✔	✔
14. Musical Chairs	✔	✔	
15. Sears & Roebuck		✔	✔
206 Vandalism			
16. Law Breaker	✔	✔	
17. Eureka! Physics	✔	✔	
18. Tabloid Tales		✔	✔
19. Edison		✔	

Chapter / Area	PREFERRED BY		
	Realists	Builders	Dreamers
207 Franklin Funnel			
20. Do One Thing Great	✔	✔	
21. Be #1	✔	✔	
22. Pin Pricks	✔	✔	
23. Skybridging		✔	✔
208 Dr. Disecto			
24. Dr. Disecto	✔	✔	✔
25. Dr. Disecto Mutant Surgery	✔	✔	
26. Dr. VanGundy's P.I.C.L. List	✔	✔	
209 Borrowing Brilliance			
27. Winning Ways			
• Best of . . .	✔	✔	
• Classic Themes for the Ages	✔	✔	
• David and Goliath	✔	✔	
• Superstars	✔	✔	
• Street Sense	✔	✔	
• The Sure Six	✔	✔	
210 Party Time			
28. Dear Mr. President	✔	✔	✔
29. Pass the Buck		✔	✔
30. Center Stage	✔	✔	
31. Pass the Hat	✔	✔	✔
32. Out-of-the-Blue Lightning Bolt Cloud Buster	✔	✔	✔
33. Battle of the Sexes		✔	✔
34. Roll Call		✔	✔
35. Spin the Bottle	✔	✔	
211 Extra Brainpower			
36. Stimulating the Subconscious	✔	✔	✔
37. Junto		✔	✔

CHAPTER 201

Prison Break

One of the great barriers to original thought is the thought you're already carrying around in your head. When your mind is filled with solutions, it's nigh impossible to conceive a newborn thought.

> *For a tree to bear fruit, dead limbs must be pruned.*
> RICHARD SAUNDERS

As we grow into adulthood, we become mental pack rats. Our minds become cluttered with S.O.S.—the Same Old Stuff. It's like putting up a cement block wall. S.O.S. shuts down idea production. It puts a clamp on our ability to see new thoughts.

Management types can be severely afflicted with this. It can stop up their ears, rendering them incapable of listening, eventually leading to a condition known as:

Mental constipation occurs when you have old ideas knocking around in your head that prevent you from having new ideas and entertaining alternative points of view. The thing to do is flush out the old ideas.

Once upon a time, when I was hired to work on a juice project with a major American food producer, a senior god in a position far superior to my own fell in love with an idea for a new juice using the Huggies diaper trademark. His plan was to license the Huggies name and deliver a juice that would provide nursing mothers with special nutrients so that their babies might grow up to be able to leap tall buildings in a single bound.

At first gasp, the premise was, well, breathtaking. It was also exciting, bold, and fairly far removed from any existing consumer beverage in the Civilized World. I mean, talk about contradicting history. If our team could secure the Huggies name, we believed we'd change the course of world history.

Our hearts pounding, we plunged ahead, writing copy and designing packaging. Then we hit an abrupt snag. Someone raised the obvious question. What color should the product be?

Dark colors raised definite issues. Lemon yellow was not particularly tantalizing either. Once we began associating a real product with the concept, we kept coming up with negatives.

We reported our concerns to the Great One. Huggies Juice was having problems, we told him. But there was good news, too. Our research had turned up five wicked good juice ideas other than Huggies. Unfortunately, he was in no mood to hear about them.

"No, no, no!" the mentally constipated god said. "You're not trying hard enough. Huggies Juice is big, I tell you. You're not listening."

At this point, inadvertently or not, he let slip the reason for his stubborn support of Huggies Juice. The problems we'd encountered were superficial, he told us. New mothers won't see it that way, he said. The emotion they feel for their babies will overcome your petty concerns, he added.

Our suspicions were soon confirmed. The Great One was, in fact, about to become a father for the first time. His wife was full with child. He was, perhaps for the first time in his life, feeling something akin to an honest emotion. He was mentally constipated with it.

We pleaded with him to deep six Huggies Juice. But out of reverence for his position, I led the team back into the consumer

wilderness four times to run the concept past everyday consumers. Each time, the everyday consumers turned up their noses.
And each time, the god told us to try again. The team's enthusiasm waned. At the same time, we continued to work on the five
decent ideas that had come out of the earlier research effort, only
to squeeze the life from them and cause our enthusiasm to wither
even further.

In the end, Huggies Juice died a horrible death. The five decent
ideas and the spirit of the team went with it. All because of mental constipation.

A few months later, I was again called on to develop new products for the same god. Once again, he'd had a vision—this time,
it was at the other end of the age demographic. (I later learned
he'd been spending a good deal of time with his elderly mother.)

I greeted his proposal for Ex-Lax Juice, the high-fiber juice,
with all the excitement I could muster. I returned the next day
with what I hoped would be a potent laxative for his brain blockage: ten package designs and a portfolio filled with advertising
copy. The god spent the afternoon pruning the concept until it
was just to his liking.

Then it was time to test the concept—this time not with mere
qualitative consumer discussions, but with a full-scale national
test sample costing $10,000.

Judgment day finally arrived. The god was pumped, big time.
But his excitement was short-lived, seeing as how Ex-Lax Juice,
the high-fiber juice, had achieved new records for poor taste and
total lack of consumer interest. The god was shocked and dis-
mayed, but he couldn't argue with the findings. A jury of real
people—real elderly people—had spoken.

I took advantage of the god's moment of vulnerability to offer
a vision of new areas for development. It worked. The god heard
me. He authorized a new project based on real needs and actual
consumer interests. Nine months later, a product you've heard of,
one which I unfortunately am not at liberty to mention by name,
was launched in test market with great success.

The point is, mental constipation is a bad thing. It smothers
new ideas. Avoid people who are suffering from it whenever possible. The following is a list to help you identify the symptoms.

You know you are mentally constipated if:

1. Your brain is doubled over with cramps.
2. You are pretty sure you're engaged in a conversation because you see the other person's lips moving, but you don't hear any words.
3. You have an uncontrollable urge to run an enema nozzle up your nostril.
4. Your tongue is parched and swollen from incessant talking.
5. You are seized with embarrassing bouts of verbal flatulence.

Mental blockage is by no means exclusive to the ranks of corporate management. It also happens to everyday people on an everyday basis. You know how sometimes you get a song in your head and can't get it out? Like, say, if you go to Disney World and take the *It's a Small World After All* boat ride? And hours later, the song is still playing over and over in your brain until you can't think of anything else and you're afraid you're about to go absolutely berserk help oh pleasesomebodyhelp-me?!?!?!?!

It's the same deal with ideas.

> *When the ideas aren't flowing, I take a mental laxative by putting some distance between the "problem" and myself. That can mean starting a new project, taking a break, going for a run, playing with the kids, taking a nap.... After my subconscious thrashes things around for a few minutes or a few days, everything falls into place and—Eureka!—problem solved.*
> KEVIN KNIGHT,
> President, Knight Marketing Communications

You can fall in love with an idea. You can be so deeply attached to an idea that you think of nothing else. A better idea may try to woo you away, but you don't know it because you can't take your eyes off the object of your affection. And until you have fully considered your idea, until you have brought it out into the light of day where you can see its warts and jug ears and flabby thighs, you are its slave.

These are the kinds of ideas you bring to the problem-solving process. The ideas aren't necessarily as all-consuming as I've portrayed here. They come in varying degrees of intensity. But it's only natural that you would have them. It's normal for the human brain to anticipate and bring at least a few prefab ideas to the table.

Sometimes these ideas are wicked good and worthy of immediate copyrighting. More often they aren't. But they have to be gotten at before any others can be had. The slate has to be wiped clean.

> *Purging is like hog washing. Management people often have hogs of ideas that need cleaning, remodeling, updating. These sacred hogs tend to be stale and old. It's critical they be washed out as they sap strength, steal motivation. They're so fat they leave no sustenance for younger, leaner original ideas.*
>
> MIKE KATZ,
> Entrepreneur, Trained Brain

The following Brain Programs are good mind erasers, so to speak. The techniques are also good for giving you extra traction when you're stuck in the mud ideawise.

BRAIN PROGRAM #1: MIND DUMPSTER

Mind Dumpster is the ultimate brain purge program. It can sweep old ideas from your mind in less than three minutes. It's also the first step in every creative effort I undertake. A good Mind Dumpster is like a good stretch before a long run.

Objective

To quickly empty cluttered minds of preconceptions, prefab ideas, and blockages so that original work can be undertaken. Mind Dumpster is also a fast way to read the landscape of what's running through your mind and, if you're working in a group, the minds of others.

How to Do It

Get a stack of Flush Cards—3 × 5 index cards, preferably of varying colors—and a fat, juicy pen so that you can write in a bold, assertive hand. Scribble one thought per card. Unburden yourself of any miscellaneous mental luggage associated with the task that you brought to the creative effort.

Just move your pen—the words will follow. Let thoughts flow from the tip of the pen in a stream. But do it quickly, in three minutes or less. The idea is to let it happen, to flush whatever's inside out. That's why I call them Flush Cards.

Music is helpful. I like to spend a few minutes on Mind Dumpster, which is enough time to play the theme from *Jeopardy*, along with a few snippets from *The Three Stooges* theme, *Merrie Melodies*, and *Looney Tunes* themes. All four cuts are available on one compact disc, TeeVeeTunes' *Television's Greatest Hits, Vol. II.*

Let your mind take off in whatever direction you feel tugged to go. Or delve into your own background for ideas. Sometimes I use the following to prompt the dumpster process:

• Graphic images relating to the area of interest
• Rumors and gut feelings about the problem
• Best and worst memories associated with the problem
• Sensory elements: sights, sounds, tastes, touches
• Emotions, positive and negative
• Pet ideas, peeves and otherwise, that your mind connects with the task

After blowing out the impurities from your mind, collect your cards and shuffle them. Let them ferment for twenty minutes or so. Now it's time to play blackjack; deal the cards into piles— which is perhaps a poor term to use in the context of a discussion about mental constipation. At any rate, arrange the cards in stacks of associated thoughts. Then go over them again, adding bulges as they occur to you. Watch out for flying sparks.

Mind Dumpster in Action

As part of the preparation for Jump Start Your Brain, I convened a dozen Trained Brains to spend a Wednesday in June talking about what ought to go into this book. The day began with Mind Dumpster. I asked the Trained Brains this question: "What comes to mind when you think of creativity, inventing, and imagination?"

Here are a few of the thoughts written on the Flush Cards that came back to me:

Flush Cards from Book Eureka! Session

Dr. Seuss
Out on a limb
Amaze yourself
Get more out of life
Why ask why?
Caffeine
Rev up ... magic mushrooms
Jumper cables
Disneyland of the mind
Make more connections
Fear of blank paper
Question everything ... why ... why ...
Reverse the effects of mind cramps
Break, trash, destroy all rules
From darkness to light
Brain food
Wild imaginings
Alive—alert—awake
Fear of speaking up
Fun (listed ten times!)
Kids
Lots of color
Be open to all kinds
Bare feet
Open up your brain nasal cavities
Moan, groan, push ...
!
The Little Engine That Could

These figments of imagination ended up stimulating many of the thoughts in these pages. Such as:

Caffeine/Brain Food. This got me to thinking about the impact of what you put in your body has on what comes out of your head. My first-level response turned out to be the earlier section on the power of caffeine, caloric reduction, and Maine lobster. On further reflection, I realized Brain Food could also be interpreted to include any external factor that affects the act of thinking, so I expanded the section to include environmental aspects that influence creative motivation.

Fear of Blank Paper, Fear of Speaking Up. This card helped me realize what a barrier fear is to the creative process and, conversely, how important it is to have courage. Hence, the courage chapter.

Dr. Seuss. This card set my antennae to twitching. The doctor has always been one of my favorite authors. The card immediately conjured the Grinch in my mind, who called up Ebenezer Scrooge, who in turn recalled a number of CEOs I've known. I fiddled for a while on a section of Corporate Ghosts of Christmas Past, Present, and Future, then decided that the true magic of Dr. Seuss's works lay in their use of utterly original, utterly outrageous characters to tell simple stories and teach simple lessons. I wanted to do that, too. The result is "Yink's 'It'!"—a children's story for grown-ups. It's at the end of the book. I like to think of it as the dessert after the main course. Don't peek. You might spoil your dinner.

BRAIN PROGRAM #2: HITCHHIKING

You're stuck. You can't break out of your thinking patterns. Time to recapture innocent, uneducated, raw thinking. But how? The answer is simple. Move your feet and your imagination will follow.

You might try hitchhiking. Hitchhiking is a time-honored art at the Eureka! Mansion. In

other circles, it's called "adding to," "building on an idea," "providing additional perspective," "adding your two cents' worth," "giving so-and-so a piece of your mind," or "bulging" on another's idea. It's a process of hopscotching from one idea to another.

Hitchiking can be a spontaneous occurrence involving walking and talking to others. Or it can be encouraged, as in a group Eureka! Stimulus Response session. Usually, in a free, open environment, it just sort of happens without much prodding.

Objective

To unchain your brain. To grease the skids inside your head and build mental momentum. To let your imagination play leapfrog with other Brain Operating Systems.

How to Do It

Push yourself away from your desk, stand up, head on out the door, and hitchhike on other imaginations. Take a walk. Through your office, down the hall, out to lunch. Talk to the waitress, the janitor, the cabdriver. Consult the butcher, baker, and candlestick maker. Seek out commonsense people who are blissfully ignorant of the preconceptions, myths, laws, and facts surrounding your task.

Tell them your problem.

> *The best ideas occur to me while I talk to someone else about the problem. If I can get someone else interested, then the process of explaining and defending my old moss-covered ideas causes new shiny ones to occur to me. Sometimes the old ones just get cleaned up, but they look new anyway.*
> DR. PAUL W. FARRIS,
> Professor, Darden School of Business

Ask for a top-of-the-head, off-the-cuff, spur-of-the-moment, commonsense answer.

Most of the time, they'll be happy to help—especially if you're a high-profile corporate executive because then they can go home and tell their families about the poor schmo they ran into that day who couldn't find his or her brain with both hands.

Lay out your situation. Let them in on what you're dealing with and what you're not dealing with so well. Then—and this is the tough part—listen closely. Allow your mind to drink in their fresh, naive thoughts and perceptions.

Listen in particular for pure gut reactions. Look for quick instinctive snapshots of innocent thought. First perceptions often lead to the best solutions. You can mine gold from these virgin thoughts. That's because these people haven't been doing what you've been doing—overthinking and overworking your task until your supply of common sense has depleted itself.

The same principle can come into play when you start a new job. More often than not, you experience a rush of ideas in your first week. As time passes, you become educated as to what you can and cannot say/do/be. You begin to overthink. You lose the ability to leap before you look.

As you listen to your innocent outsiders, pull back and ask yourself, "What's the obvious solution?" Get simple.

The key is to listen. Forget your education, knowledge, credentials, native intelligence, and the conformity facts of life. Seek ways to make innocent, virgin thoughts feasible.

> *TO JUMP START MY BRAIN I talk to people. I think better if I talk things out, so I usually call someone or grab the first person who walks by and engage them in helping to find a solution. If I still can't find a solution, I put it aside for a while and try to look at it later, with a fresh brain.*
>
> BARB KORN,
> Group Director, Ralston Purina

TO JUMP START MY BRAIN I drink coffee—lots of it. Or I talk to someone who has no knowledge of my problem or situation. This translates into fresh, honest stimuli. And I sometimes wander through a grocery store and steal inspiration from other categories— search and reapply or take various ideas and put them together to form a new idea.

BRUCE HALL,
Procter & Gamble Brand Manager

The world is full of fresh perspectives just waiting to be consulted on any subject. And the naive, first-blush response is often the obvious solution—the one you'd missed because it was hiding in a secret place under your nose.

Common sense is not so common.
RICHARD SAUNDERS

Hitchhiking in Action

While dreaming up the packaging and positioning for a new candy for Van Melle called Great Unbelievable Tasting Sweets, I became what is known in the business as "stumped." Great Unbelievable Tasting Sweets—G.U.T.S., for short—is the Russian roulette of the confection world. G.U.T.S. are red balls of hard candy, filled with either a concentrated cherry punch powder or concentrated red-hot cinnamon powder. The deal is, you don't know what you have until it's too late.

My problem was coming up with a way to define the difference between the hot candies and the cherry candies. All my ideas were lame. I'd tried Fire 'n' Ice, Hot Stuff 'n' Cool Stuff, Flamers 'n' Ice Cubes, Sugar 'n' Spice, to name a few. I was stuck in an 'n' rut.

So I started wandering through the offices at the Eureka! Mansion. My first stop was Sandie Glass's office. I spilled my G.U.T.S. on Sandie's desk. She was reminded of little cherries. I explained that the taste was actually a red berry. To which she replied, "Cherry Berries."

Not bad, I thought. It was a fun name to say, and it fit the product's sensory aspects.

Two flights of stairs led me to Randy Mazzola's office. We Ping-Ponged ideas back and forth, and Randy hit on a name for the hot candies—Cherry Bombs.

Cherry Bombs and Cherry Berries. Wow! Another nice fit.

Now I had to concoct a half-baked G.U.T.S. story to explain how Cherry Berries and Cherry Bombs came to be mixed up in the same box. I headed back downstairs to Sandie's office. I asked her, What do cherry bombs do?

They go boom, she said.

Boom became Dr. Boom Boom. Once we had the doctor, the story wrote itself. Here's what it says on the back of the G.U.T.S. package:

Hey Dudes and Dudettes!
The wild and wacky Dr. Boom Boom has invaded the
Van Melle candy factory.

Inside harmless looking, awesome tasting
Cherry Berry hard candies,
he's placed two different surprises.

In the center of most of the candies
you'll find gazillions of CHERRY BERRIES
that rock your mouth with awesome flavor!

BUT BEWARE!
In 2 to 4 of the candies in each bag, he's placed
HOT, HOT, HOT CHERRY BOMBS!!!!

The taste of Great Unbelievable
Tasting Sweets is incredible.
But only try them if you've got the GUTS!

Once again, I'd hitchhiked my way out of the abyss. The solutions to my problem were simple, as most great ideas are. But I was too deeply ensconced in my rut to find them on my own.

> *Sometimes the best solutions come from those not as closely associated with the situation or those who are unfamiliar with everyday business practices.*
> SCOTT BECKER,
> Brand Development Manager,
> Thomas J. Lipton Co.

Hitchhiking works with strangers. But spouses, friends, and family members often make the best sounding boards. I'm blessed with a fountain of insight, common sense, and originality in my own home—my wife, Debbie. On those occasions when I find myself tangled up in knotted notions, tangents, and peripherals, she cuts the cord for me.

Once, when I was working on ready-to-drink Lipton Iced Tea, Debbie mentioned something that made a difference in that project and many others since. I asked her what should be done with ready-to-drink iced tea.

"Make something I can't make myself," she said.

It sounds simple on the surface. But it was strong medicine for me. The simple premise of providing customers with something they can't make themselves has helped me create winning concepts for Green Giant, Planters Peanuts, Lipton Tea, and Folgers Coffee, among many others.

Stimuli: Where to Find Them, How to Use Them

The biggest bonfire starts from the smallest spark.
RICHARD SAUNDERS

Stimu-lee, stimu-la, stimu-lye. However you say it, nothing makes a brain more productive or creative.

Once again, you can choose to brainstorm and simply SUCK ideas from your head or you can use your brain as a computer and process stimuli into ideas.

This chapter details some of the simplest, most common, and most potent sources of stimuli. First, here are a few suggestions:

1. *Stimuli need not be fancy, exotic, expensive, or complex.* A large advertising firm once came to me for advice on building a Eureka!-like facility and stimuli library. I listened as they outlined wondrous plans for a slick work of architecture packed with custom digital CD-ROMS that could be searched with lightning speed and interactive video walls with laser discs.

211

On hearing about all these ultra-high-tech systems and the special operators and time it would take to execute this stuff, I grew more and more fatigued. What about the dictionaries, the magazine rack, the Play-Doh?

The designer explained that the firm's facility was to be state of the art, with none of that old-fashioned crap. I got the distinct sense that the designer was mainly interested in winning design awards. She didn't want to hear about the power of such simple items as Nerf Master Blasters, paper airplanes, and Sears catalogs.

"Clutter, mess, trash," she said. Or words to that effect.

I couldn't be of any help. So I gently excused myself and bid her a warm farewell. I never did hear back as to how those interactive video walls worked out with those laser discs.

Beware of those with more money than sense.
RICHARD SAUNDERS

A stimulus is a fuse for lighting off ideas. It can be anything you think you can use to prod and poke your mind, to make your mind react. Stimuli should include stuff that is related and/or unrelated to your task. A stimulus can be as simple an item as today's newspaper, a rubber ball, a couple dozen cable TV stations, chocolate pudding, a paint chip, a song, or a banana peel. It can be anything that makes you think of something else. More on this subject later in the chapter.

2. *Multisensory stimuli stimulate more ideas.* When I'm trying to solve a problem, I like to smell it, taste it, touch it, hear it, see it. The more different senses I can stimulate, the more my brain responds. At the Eureka! Mansion we have a vast collection of aroma strips to put our minds in different settings, from a carnival (cotton candy) to a country road stand (green apple). We have travel posters to put our brains in Africa, Antarctica, and Argentina without ever leaving the room. We have a music library to put our brains in any culture, rhythm, or mood we want. See (hear, feel, smell, taste) what I mean?

Play-Doh is an item that touches several sensory bases. I don't know why, but the mere act of opening a can of Play-Doh puts me in a fun condition. Part of it is the smell, which sends me back to my childhood. Part of it is the way it feels—so submissive, squishy, and warm. Part of it is the way it looks—a big, bright, happy lump. It makes me want to do something with it. It gives me ideas.

STOP

Experience it yourself. Put this book down and go to the nearest toy store. Buy a sixpack of Play-Doh. Smell it, feel it, fiddle with it. Doesn't it make you feel, well, playful? Doesn't it tempt your imagination?

3. *Related versus unrelated stimuli.* I've found that the more the stimuli are related to the creative challenge, the greater the quantity of ideas are produced. As stimuli become more unrelated, abstract, or obscure, the number of ideas drop, but the insights that result are more original. In my creative efforts, I try to use a blend of the related and the unrelated.

   For example, if I'm looking for ideas for new soft drinks, I might use bar drink guides, fruit catalogs, and cookbooks as related stimuli. I might also tune into MTV, take a walk through Toys "R" Us, and leaf through *Rolling Stone* magazine for unrelated stimulus.

4. *Beware of stimuli overload.* It's possible to get too much of a good thing. Just as a baby closes its eyes, clams up, and shuts down when its mind is filled with too much stimulus, so, too, will your mind. Symptoms of stimuli overload include a blank stare and a diminished attention span. When this happens to you, cover the stimuli with a cloth or put them in a brown paper bag. Slow down and spoon-feed your brain by randomly pulling out items one at a time.

BRAIN PROGRAM #3: STIMULI ONE STEP

There are two basic ways to process stimuli into ideas—the One Step and the Two Step. With the first, you make a direct connection from stimuli to idea in a single leap of imagination. With the second, you identify the attributes of various stimuli, then apply those traits to your task.

Objective

To transform physical stimuli directly into ideas. To translate objects straight into thoughts and ideas. Alexander Graham Bell was having difficulty designing a receiver for his telephone. He used a Stimuli One Step of a most direct manner to find a simple solution; he asked a doctor friend of his for a human ear taken from a cadaver. Bell then designed an earpiece to match.

How to Do It

Look, smell, feel, touch, listen to as much stimuli, and as many different kinds of it, as possible. Move quickly. Tear through stimuli like a lawyer lunging for loopholes. With the One Step, you're looking for first-glance ideas. You look and a thought occurs.

As you riffle through the stimuli, keep sight of your task. Otherwise your mind may wander off into the stimuli itself and you'll lose sight of the problem.

I find it helpful to have a stack of index cards on hand while going over stimuli. Any time I see a piece of an idea that might later prove helpful, I scribble it on a card. This keeps me moving, so that I don't get hung up on any single piece of stimuli.

One Step in Action

Before Debbie and I moved into our new home, we wanted to finish the basement and turn it into an office for my creative and development efforts. It was also to become the first Eureka! Stimulus Response room.

The ceiling was a problem. I've always hated drop ceilings because they make me feel claustrophobic. Drywalling was out because I would need access to the wiring and plumbing.

I reached for some stimuli. Thumbing through a sequence of home design books and magazines didn't prompt anything. My favorite source of ideas, the Sears catalog, turned up nothing.

Finally, having despaired of finding a solution in a dozen volumes on home improvement, I found balm for my basement woes in *Vogue* magazine. I picked up a copy and latched onto a photograph of a clothing store with exposed rafters and track lighting, all painted the same color.

The answer was simple—spray paint the entire basement white from top to bottom, then hang halogen track lights from the rafters. The best way to address the ceiling issue was to not put in any ceiling.

The results were spectacular. Many people have commented on how spacious the basement feels. Despite the exposed rafters, the consensus is that it doesn't look like a basement.

The idea for the no-ceiling basement ceiling wouldn't have

come to me had I simply sat and engaged in Braindraining. It took a spark to light the fuse.

One note on the Stimuli One Step: It may not seem, on the surface, especially sophisticated or complicated. It may appear too ridiculously simple to yield worthwhile results. You'll change your mind once you try it. It's not necessary to go through a series of complex machinations to find the best ideas. Often the simplest, straightest paths are the most effective.

BRAIN PROGRAM #4: STIMULI TWO STEP

This one's slower and more deliberate. It creates ideas through analogy. Instead of the direct literal associations you made with One Step, here you break the stimuli into their elements, then apply those traits to solving your task.

Objective

To identify the characteristics of stimuli and then meld them to your task. To concentrate not on the stimuli, but on the elements that make it what it is.

How to Do It

Using either a related or unrelated stimulus, list all the features, traits, and elements you can find in it. Look at it up close, from afar, and from different angles. List emotional, physical, or interactive elements. What features, elements, or mechanisms make your stimulus move, act, or deliver excitement?

Consider how these elements could be applied to your task.

Locating abstract elements in stimuli and reassembling them in different configurations can be akin to strapping jet engines to your thinking machine.

You can do the Two Step with virtually any stimuli. But when you're first getting started, you'll probably find it's best to use stimuli that are in some way similar or related to your challenge.

For example, you might find a book about animal habitats helpful in prompting ideas for new construction methods. A study of the hundreds of ways different species of birds build their nests, for instance, is likely to suggest to you new ways to assemble your factory, clubhouse, or backyard deck.

Let's take another tack. Let's say your challenge is to come up with ideas to amuse your five-year-old nephew, Bernie, on a rainy Sunday afternoon. All you have is the Toys "R" Us advertising supplement from the newspaper.

You don't need the actual toys that the supplement advertises. What you need are their operational elements. Look at the toys. What do they do? How are they used? What makes them fun?

Once you have the answers, you can make it happen for Bernie with everyday stuff.

The supplement is advertising a sale on Nerf products. What is Nerf? Well, it's soft stuff you can toss around, fling, and shoot indoors. So how might you duplicate the Nerf experience without the actual Nerf stuff?

How about using rolled-up socks as shot puts? Or couch pillows for Frisbees? Or a rubber band and tongs as a slingshot, using paper wad ammo?

Involve Bernie. He doesn't need the toys, he needs the analogies. A squeeze bottle makes a perfectly good squirtgun. Pots and pans make for a perfectly good drum set. And when Bernie's sister, Iodine, comes over, you can cut out people and things from magazines, glue them onto cardboard and make your own stick puppets.

Two Step in Action

Once, when I was with a team assigned to develop new recipes for a cookbook, we decided to use the beverage Clearly Canadian as a stimulus. We listed its basic elements: It's clear, it comes in a glass bottle with its name painted on the surface, it feels healthy, and it's expensive.

Then one of the team members mentioned something else. It was a surprise to her, she said, that it had such a full taste.

Building her thought into a launching pad, the team quickly developed dozens of new bakery products around the theme of surprise. We did muffins and cookies crammed with jelly and chocolate-chip surprises on the inside. We did inside-out cakes with the frosting in the center and the cake outside. We did peanut butter eclairs, with chunky peanut butter.

The simplest impression opened a rich vein of ideas—rich in more ways than one. But the links we made were courtesy of a single characteristic of the stimulus, a single analogy.

All kinds of ignition systems are readily available for sparking original thoughts for icons, images, and names. Here's a list of idea grenades you can use to bombard your Brain Operating System:

Stimuli Prospecting

- *Chip City:* If the task requires an extraordinary hue, raid the paint chip display at your neighborhood paint store, where you'll find an array of carefully considered names for every tint and shade on the color wheel.

  Paint chips can be an almost bottomless source of stimuli for names, icons, and images. There's a whole world beyond red, white, and blue. Somehow, colors like Glidden's chocolate kiss, forget-me-not, gold coast, eggplant, flamenco, scrimshaw, orchid puff, smoked pearl, and fjord seem a bit more vivid. They conjure images, moods, and emotions.

- *Greeting Cards:* Speaking of images, moods, and emotions, a good place to go prospecting is your local card shop. The Valentine's Day section, for instance, can be helpful if you're looking for ways to put love into words, even if you don't care enough to send the very best.

- *Video Rental Stores:* When Ben Franklin founded the new America's first public library, I doubt whether he realized the culture's most popular libraries would one day be oriented more toward flickering images than words. Aside from providing escapes from reality, movies are a great way to teleport yourself to any locale in the galaxy—from travel videos to *Jurassic Park* to *2001: A Space Odyssey.*
  Rocky gave me the inspiration for a new make-it-at-home beverage combination. Remember the scene where Rocky gets out of bed, opens the fridge, cracks a half-dozen raw eggs into a glass, and chugs it down? I later developed a number of new beverages where the client's product is mixed with everyday fruits and juices. And it goes down a lot easier than raw eggs.

- *Specialty Catalogs:* There's a catalog for everything. Catalogs are a rich, often untapped source of stimuli for ideas. I especially appreciate the way the copy and visuals in catalogs are so tightly focused. In the mail-order business, either you get the idea in a hurry or they don't get the sale.

- *Wallpaper Catalogs:* This is a resource most creative teams never think of using. A good wallpaper catalog can be a rich source of styles, moods, textures, images, and icons.

- *Coffee Table Books:* You know the type—big, fat, awkward, won't fit in your bookshelves. Name a subject, and you can find a book of pictures it inspired. Such books are abundant sources of material for idea stimuli. Best of all, they're often marked down.

- *Play-Doh:* The smell alone can sweep you back to childhood. Squash it, roll it, mold it, conform it to your will. Turn it into a 3-D likeness of the image inside your brain. Take a few cans to a staff meeting and pass them around. Stash a can of Doh in your attaché. Accentuate your Play-Doh sculptures with Popsicle sticks, pipe cleaners, and the plastic facial features that come with every Mr. Potato Head.

  If you can't spring for a carton of Play-Doh or if your sculptures call for massive amounts of it, here's the Eureka! recipe for a wicked good homemade version, courtesy of Loretta Gordon.

STIR TOGETHER IN SAUCEPAN:

1 cup flour
1/2 cup salt
2 teaspoons cream of tartar
2 tablespoons vegetable oil
1 cup colored water

  Heat mixture on stovetop burner over medium heat, stirring constantly. Mixture will thicken quickly. When mixture forms a ball, remove from heat. Be careful not to get burned! Knead dough thoroughly. As it cools, it will become pliable and ready to play with in minutes. Mix in a little vanilla if you want the aroma to match the stuff from the toy store.

- *Music:* Fast music, slow music, up music, down music, loud music, and soft music—it all has tremendous thought provoker value. Whatever mood you want to be in, whatever attitude you're trying to develop, there's a piece of music that can take you there.

- *Cookbooks:* Tomes de cuisine can be a handy resource if your task has any connection with food. Here you can find names and combinations of ingredients to provide insights into anything of an edible persuasion. Of particular value are cookbooks with personality that offer variations on common themes.

- *Cable TV:* Take the classic man-of-the-house approach with the remote control. Flip through the channels at a minimal rate of one per second. No slower. Bombard your brain with images, scanning up and down through the channels like a person possessed. Don't just stare at the screen—absorb the images. Let them light fuses in your brain.

- *Dr. Seuss Library:* At the Mansion, we're the proud owners of a complete Dr. Seuss collection. When a team is mired in reality, I pass out Dr. Seuss books to all concerned and invite them to invent à la Seuss. The beauty of Dr. Seuss's work is that very little is tied to the real world. Instead of People, Places, and Things, he writes of Wockets, Solla Ollew, Thidwick, and the River Wah-Hoo. When I'm working on children's products, the doctor is a sure cure for Real World Adultitis.

- *Puppets:* It's often easier to get people to verbalize their thoughts if they're not the ones doing the talking. A collection of puppets can be useful in articulating ideas and developing unusual personalities or proprietary characters for new products. When working with  children, I ask them to make puppets from brown paper sacks. It helps kids give form to their imaginations and develop greater depth and personality to their ideas. It can do the same thing for grown-ups, too.

- *Grab Bags:* This exercise blows the process of forced association into three dimensions. Fill a grocery bag or similar conveyance with dime-store toys—little cars, funny glasses, squirt guns, cartoon figurines, balloons, buttons, et cetera and so on.

BRAIN PROGRAM #5: TO MARKET, TO MARKET

The world is filled with thoughts. Ideas fill the air we breathe. The idea of To Market, To Market is to take advantage of the environment around us, wherever we happen to be at any given moment.

Take a walk and look at the world around you. It doesn't matter if you are in a large city or the country. Look at nature, what is it doing? How is it responding to the wind, animals, cars, etc.? Again, observation to gain new stimuli is the key. One of my most remarkable discoveries this year came from watching how leaves dried and curled, and its relationship to a similar problem I was having in obtaining curvature in a snack product. All of the answers to our problems probably are as close as outside our windows. And if all you see is a neon sign and a brick wall ... you're trying too hard. Laugh at yourself and try again. It works.

JEFFREY A. STAMP, PH.D.,
Principal Scientist,
Frito-Lay, Inc.

Objective

To translate the stimuli of flea markets, stores, national parks, museums, and/or construction sites into ideas. To go someplace and mine it for visual stimuli.

How to Do It

Head on out. Just get in your car and drive to Main Street, the park, or a part of town where you don't normally go. Or take a walk through a shopping mall. These monuments to conspicuous consumption are terrific places to watch people and fill the mind with multihued thought bubbles. As you wander, make a mental note of anything that strikes your fancy. You probably do this all the time anyway, don't you?

If you're brave, take an instant camera to capture ideas. Beware: The natives at stores sometimes take offense at strangers with cameras. I advise either getting permission or making a rapid preemptive strike.

Stay focused on your object of inquiry. Keep repeating your challenge. Force-associate that which you see with that which you need to solve.

Don't limit your market walking to the upscale. Seek out the lowscale, too. Be an equal opportunity idea hunter. Check out the ghetto, the flea markets, the local St. Vincent De Paul store. One man's trash is another's treasure, don't you know.

To Market, To Market in Action

My clients have used To Market, To Market in expeditions for all manner of ideas. Once, when searching for ideas for new types of merchandising displays for grocery stores, we sent teams to department stores with Polaroid cameras. The teams stalked aisles of perfume counters, sporting goods displays, bookstores, and, yes, even the lingerie cases at Victoria's Secret. They returned with a stash of photos that stimulated fresh, original thoughts—at least in the context of your typical grocery store.

I used the formula of To Market, To Market back when I was embarking on a career as Merwyn the Magician in junior high school. In those days, I didn't have any money for fancy equipment. On the weekends, I'd head to the local Goodwill store and the flea market to go shopping for new props and ideas I could add to the act.

One weekend, I picked up a matched set of plumber's helpers that were just right for juggling. Another weekend, I bought a twenty-five-cent toilet seat. It was an impulse purchase, one that felt right, but for no apparent reason. But my brother, Bruce, turned it into one of the funniest elements of the show.

The idea was a twist on the old Rocky and Bullwinkle gag, where Bullwinkle kept trying to pull a rabbit out of his hat and kept failing.

Dressed as Boo Boo the Clown, Bruce would appear onstage with the magician—yours truly—and say, "Hey, Merwyn! Watch me pull a rabbit out of my ... toilet seat." Then he'd hand me the seat, lift the lid, reach through the hole into his jacket—in full view of the kids—and pull out a rubber snake. Or a roll of toilet paper. Or a bowling pin. After two or three of Boo Boo's failures, I'd pull a rabbit from a hat.

The gag was a staple of the act. The prop cost a quarter.

If your mission is to dig up an idea for a school project, a plan for redecorating your family room, or a costume for Halloween, take your pick and shovel to your local markets.

BRAIN PROGRAM #6: NEWSSTAND

Newspapers, magazines, and radio and TV news outlets are largely dedicated to reporting trends. These same information-mongers are also slaves to public interest.

To varying degrees, the news media conduct research to identify subjects of interest to the public. And if you want to sort of learn about what tickles America's fancy, stop by a news-stand. I say "sort of" because the media occasionally attempts to predict trends rather than simply report them.

Hardly a subject exists that hasn't inspired a magazine, from *Soldier of Fortune* to *Self* to *Boy's Life* to *Plywood Today*. Collect them, trade them with your friends, use them as stairways to idea heaven. Need ideas for fund-raising? Look to women's magazines for crafts you can make and sell. Need a theme for your party this weekend? Peruse the headlines for the controversy *du jour*.

Objective

To open your mind through current events and trends, as measured by the media. To leverage the hours of research bought and paid for by news outlets to your own advantage. You never know when an idea will pop out at you from the cover of a magazine or a front-page photograph.

How to Do It

Let your fingers stroll through a pile of magazines and newspapers. The randomness of this process is in and of itself a cattle prod to new thoughts. As your mind fills with images and statements from the publications, they become jumbled and connected in new ways in your mind.

A number of Brain Programs can be executed with news media images and icons, among them:

Captions: You'll need magazines with lots of photos. Use magazines or photos that have at least a tenuous tie to the task. If you're working on ideas for children, get magazines that feature lots of kids in the pictures. If you're trying to launch an aerobics class, use a fitness magazine.

Write captions, titles, names, and/or brief descriptions that relate your task with your selection of photos on Post-it Notes and plaster them on the various images. If you are working on a new sports beverage, for example, you might mix images of waterfalls, rainstorms, and seascapes with photographs of athletes, cowboys, ballerinas, middle-aged men mowing the lawn, or anyone else who is in any way exerting him or herself.

Work as quickly and as instinctively as you can, with no regard to the practical and feasible. Let the images provoke new and original thought patterns. After having covered the pages with yellow flaps, spread the images across the floor and begin to develop full-blown solutions—borrowing and swapping ideas from the images and your own handwritten thoughts.

I believe so devoutly in this exercise that I've amassed a humongous library of photographs, picture postcards, and illustrations clipped from hundreds of books and magazines over the years. They're filed under such linear headings as KIDS, COUPLES, SPORTS, WET, and MORNING, along with such abstract headings as SPEEDY, POWERFUL, WARM, and WOW.

Trend Scan: This approach is for those who just can't live without numbers. At the Eureka! Mansion, we subscribe to slews of magazines in a flood of categories. The covers and tables of contents are copied and filed in a reference library under the heading THOUGHT STIMULATORS.

To get a fix on trends, we sometimes track and tabulate magazine articles into what we call the Eureka! Stimulus Response Index. It's not as well known as the Dow Jones Index, but it's more valuable in terms of inventing ideas. If you want to know what's hot and what's not, simply look at the covers. AcuPOLL Research conducts testing for magazines looking to capitalize on subjects and celebrities that have the greatest potential to generate newsstand sales. So what you see is what consumers say they want.

All publications have something to offer when you're looking for ideas. But I have a few favorites:

- *Tabloids:* These oft-shunned pieces of journalism represent America better than any glossy, big money periodical packed with Ralph Lauren ads. I find them a valuable source of creative inspiration, especially *Weekly World News*, which in late 1992 broke the story that five U.S. senators were actually aliens from outer space. While other members of the media report facts no matter how boring, the tabloids always deliver excitement—IN SCREAMING HEADLINES WITH PLENTY OF EXCLAMATION POINTS!!!!!!!!!!!!!!!!!!!!!!!!!!!!

- *The Smithsonian* and *National Geographic:* Either publication is just the ticket if you're looking for inspiration to create an exotic or historical context. Nowhere else can you learn so much about the Arctic circle, the stone crab and the mudmen of Lower Umbroglio. I once bought a steamer trunk filled with *National Geographics* at a library book sale for a nickel apiece. That afternoon, I mined them for dozens of wicked good ideas. The result was three winning concepts for new soft drinks.

- *USA Today:* It's the trendiest of the trendy. While roundly criticized in Big J Journalism circles as the publication for those who don't have time for TV's fuller coverage, *USA Today* delivers facts, figures, surveys, and information in snapshot form. *USA Today* is fertile turf for material to stimulate ideas.

Newsstand in Action

At one point while developing a new bottled water, I gathered every picture of natural water I could find. These included photos of oceans, waterfalls, rivers, lakes, glasses, open sewers, and so on. I laid out the images, stepped back, and drank in the view.

I assembled the images into three sets—depending on whether they made me believe the water would taste terrific, merely OK, or horrible. As my mind processed the images, I saw patterns in the terrific images that were missing from the horrible images. Such factors as movement, coldness, clearness, and lack of a human presence were far more common in the terrific images.

From this, I whipped up a list of package design traits. Later testing showed that applying these factors to the package design made a major difference in the way consumers reacted to the product. The actual traits and principles are, regrettably, a zealously protected client secret.

BRAIN PROGRAM #7: HELLO, MR. WEBSTER

Name a thing and you make it real.

Whether it's the name of a product or a process or a color or a type or a formula or a three-legged dog, people will not take it seriously until they have something to call it. Like a name.

Would a rose by any other name smell so sweet? Maybe so. But how would you know what to ask for at the flower shop?

Names have a broader application than products and services. Names can also be applied to promotions, parties, teams, and events, among other nameables. A good name tells the world what you stand for and whether you're worth heeding. If you don't name it, the masses will. Worse yet, they'll brand your product GENERIC. And generic products always sell for less.

When you have a wicked good name for an idea, even the dullest idea comes alive. When a name isn't there, the idea can easily be lost in the explanation.

Focusing on the name of your object of inquiry has advantages beyond the acquisition of a trademark. Focusing on developing a name forces you to articulate your thinking with a brevity and simplicity that delivers success.

During the summer of 1902, Willis Haviland Carrier was working for a publishing company in New York that was having problems with its printing inks. Day-to-day fluctuations in humidity changed the way the ink looked on the paper.

Carrier realized he could stabilize the moisture if he chilled the air. So he designed a system for blowing air over cooled pipes. It worked. Eureka! He called it Apparatus for Treating Air.

About the same time, a textile engineer named Stuart Cramer had an opposite problem. He needed to add humidity to his factory to condition yarn. He called his system Air Conditioning. The term caught on. Carrier liked it so much that he adopted it for his equipment and dumped Apparatus for Treating Air altogether. The air conditioner may well have become a success had it been marketed as Apparatus for Treating Air. But somehow, I don't think it would have caught on quite as quickly.

Objective

To identify and create names for ideas. Giving an idea a name, a handle, a point of proper noun reference makes it easier to describe, tout, and ballyhoo.

How to Do It

In my search for names, I've discovered a remarkable fact—most dictionaries are packed with words from beginning to end, many of which are perfectly suitable to use as names.

Tom Attea, a wizard of a copywriter, taught me how to find a name in a dictionary. The process is simple. Read the dictionary. Write down every name, word, or word bit that relates to your task. In a day or so, you'll have amassed an amazing list of words and dramatically enhanced your vocabulary. Now mix and match the words on your list until the right name jumps off the page, grabs you by the throat, and hollers, "WHERE YA BEEN ALL MY LIFE?"

A less extreme approach is to review thesauruses, as well as copies of the *New Comprehensive American Rhyming Dictionary* and Richard Bayan's *Words that Sell*. The world atlas is also helpful if you're trying to establish a connection with a far-flung locale—as in, say, the halls of Montezuma or the shores of Tripoli.

Hello, Mr. Webster in Action

My good friend Doug Evans owns one of the largest landscaping supply companies in Greater Cincinnati. One of his products is an ultrarich soil, made from recycled human fecal matter, et al., processed at a wastewater treatment plant in Hamilton! Ohio. In a sense, the entire population of Hamilton! is working for Doug on a daily basis.

It's a fine product. Tests conducted by soil scientists show that it's remarkably rich in key nutrients needed to sustain just about any form of plant life. The challenge for Doug is what to call it. Potting soil just didn't cut it.

While consumers are in love with the ideas of recycling and rich soil, the notion of recycled poop is a little hard for most people to swallow, pardon me very much. Still, Doug needed a name. This was clearly a job for Mr. Webster.

One sunny afternoon, I retreated to the bathroom with a copy of *Webster's New World Dictionary* to ruminate over Doug's problem.

Ideas were developed and tested with consumers. I was disappointed to learn that some of my favorites—Caca Doodle Doo Doo, Perfect Poop, Waste Power, Nutra-Doo, and Farm Feast— scored poorly. But consumers did take to Fertilasoil, Magic Manure, Genesis, Fertonix, EcoScape, OrGanix, and GRRROW. Notice the wide variety of names. Notice how each has its own feel, its own identity. In my experience, you only get this range of ideas by reading the dictionary, by shaking hands with Mr. Webster.

CHAPTER 203

Common Senses

The five senses are extraordinary collectors of information. Most of us trust them, but we barely use them.

An idea that backs up a claim of greatness with sensory support makes it easier for people to believe that claim and, as a result, makes it more likely that they'll give it a try. Three shining examples are Glad Bag's blue-and-yellow-make-green seal, Pepto-Bismol's pleasingly pacifying pink, and the Oral-B Indicator toothbrush, with bristles that change color when it's time to replace your brush.

Color kicks up a lot of interest in new products. The wide range of clear products that have been introduced express a halo of purity and cleanliness. Blue beverages from Hawaiian Punch, Kool-Aid, and Jell-O appeal in a big way to kids due, I think, to the fact that blue potables are revolting to parents.

Likewise, natural foods draw more consumer interest when they look natural; an ugly food with odd-size chunks and imperfect lumps is more convincing than homogenized pellets of perfection. The label on Paul Newman's salad dressing, for instance, advises that the bottle be shaken to mix natural ingredients before opening. The message is that natural stuff separates, artificial stuff doesn't.

BRAIN PROGRAM #8: CANDID COMMENTS

When you're exploring new territory, it helps to get the lay of the land. Before a wagon train headed across the prairie in the westward expansion, a scout would be sent ahead to learn what dangers and opportunities lay ahead. That's the idea of Candid Comments.

This exercise is also handy if rigor mortis is beginning to set in where your task is concerned. It can help you see your task through new eyes.

Objective

To hit the streets like a news reporter and dig up information and insights to solve your task. To be your own Gallup pollster, gathering information, opinions, and insights you can use to build ideas.

How to Do It

Take a walk. If you don't have a video camera, take a tape recorder or a notebook with you. Go to the scene of the challenge, where people are involved with your area of inquiry.

Go to the recess at your PTA school you need to raise money for. Go to where people are using your product or the competition's product. Start asking questions. Spend the day interviewing as many people as you can.

Catch people on location, while they're involved with your area of inquiry. How do they feel? What are their moods? What kind of day are they having? What's good, what's bad? What advice do they have? What would make it better? Less of a pain in the neck? More memorable? More fun? More of an experience?

With every answer you get, follow up with my three-year-old's favorite series of questions—Why? Why? Why? Why?

Who, what, where, when, and how are good ones, too.

Lap up everything surrounding your situation. See it, feel it, touch it.

> *Believe none of what you hear and half of what you see.*
> BEN FRANKLIN

Sharpen your sense of the attitudes, emotions, and motivations swirling around your task. Candid Comments can help you understand what people are really feeling and thinking, as opposed to what they say they are.

> *Candid Comments is one of my faves. I'm a very visual person, and this exercise helps me see things, as opposed to just looking at them. It's the voyeur in me. I've always liked watching people, studying people. When I worked at Drackett, I took a video camera into people's homes and watched them clean house. They'll tell you one thing, but they'll do something else. You can get a wealth of ideas by watching people.*
>
> DIANE ISEMAN,
> Trained Brain

Review your tapes or notes, then review them again. If you have it on tape, play the tape over and over and over, as if it were background music. Brainwash yourself. If you have it on videotape, look into the people's eyes and listen to their voices as they answer your questions.

What do their nonverbal responses tell you that their verbal responses don't?

Generally around the tenth viewing, I stop hearing the words. But I start seeing pure reactions and developing a reading of people's real inner feelings.

Granted, Candid Comments is not easy or quick. But it works. There is no finer way for getting a fix on what people want and what they don't want. Often enough, it turns out to be an express lane to the Mother of All Ideas.

Candid Comments in Action

On occasions when I'm hired to work on a new category of products I don't know much about, the first thing I do is hit the streets.

When I was asked to soup up Duncan Hines cake mixes, I went to grocery stores and watched people at the in-store bakery and in the baking supplies aisle. After about an hour, I realized shoppers wanted stuff that was, in baking parlance, "decorated." They were buying frosted and festooned cookies and cakes, turning up their noses at the plain, simple, unadorned cakes and cookies.

This observation led to the invention of Duncan Hines Pantastic Party Cakes, a line of cake mixes that come with their own molded pans and decorations so that people can make bakery-style cakes in their own kitchens that look like Garfield the Cat, Kermit the Frog, Miss Piggy, or a major-league baseball stadium.

My coauthor, David Wecker, swears by Candid Comments. Any decent journalist does. He has used the approach in newspaper stories that tied a Clark County, Ohio, sheriff to a stolen car ring; led to federal fines against the Frigidaire plant in Moraine, Ohio, for ignoring repeated safety warnings about a 10,000-pound punch press on which an underage female employee lost an arm; and beat the police to a city commission candidate in Covington, Kentucky, who was eventually convicted of murder.

Once, he was working a Saturday shift at *The Kentucky Post* when a report came over the police radio that a woman had been found decapitated in her apartment. The competing news media waited for the police report and did the basic who-what-why-where-when crime story, the kind that ends with the phrase "Police have no suspects."

David and another reporter, Gary Webb, went to the scene. They knocked on doors, talked to neighbors, found out who the woman's friends were, and then went and talked to them. Before the morning was out, the two learned that the dead woman had been dating the city commission candidate, that she had become pregnant, and that the candidate had been unable to persuade her to have an abortion.

David and Gary went to the candidate's house and talked to him. Where had he spent the night? When was the last time he had seen the dead woman? Did he kill her? The candidate was flustered, to the point that his denials began to contradict each other. He wove a tangled web, and he didn't notice that the reporters were taping the conversation.

They thanked him for his time and went on their way. As the day wore on, they called the candidate two more times, asking his help in clearing up certain confusing issues and taping his responses.

The more the candidate talked, the more his story unraveled. Along the way, David and Gary found two people who had seen the candidate climbing the stairs to the dead woman's apartment late the previous night.

The next edition of *The Kentucky Post* carried a banner story establishing that the candidate was one of the last people to see the woman alive and that he was unable to account for his whereabouts on the night she was murdered. When police caught up with the candidate, he denied ever talking to Gary and David, unaware that they had his voice on tape. Their subsequent stories implicated him even deeper.

The candidate didn't get elected. He got convicted and sentenced. As of this writing, he's still in prison. David doesn't regard the case as an example of great investigative journalism. It wasn't a difficult story, he says. It was a simple matter of hitting the streets, asking lots of questions, and listening.

BRAIN PROGRAM #9: MAGIC MOMENTS

"First words"

We measure our lives in moments of experience. Our first step, our first kiss, the first time we got behind the wheel of the family car and backed it out the driveway—these are the kinds of moments we enshrine in our own personal halls of fame.

They're Magic Moments. We spend our lives in search of them. The more we collect, the better we feel about ourselves.

Magic Moments reach into the far corners of our lives. They can play a key role in determining what choices we make, how we cast our votes, what products we'll buy. Consider the following:

Pretend the boy on the box is your son. Why would you buy this item? Would you be buying a rocket? Or would you be buying the look on your little boy's face at the moment the rocket takes off, trailing a plume of smoke as it disappears into the clouds? Would you be buying a thing or would you be buying an experience?

If you're like me and 99 percent of the rest of America, you pay for the rocket. But you buy the moment. Such shimmering spaces in time have an immensely powerful allure for people. If you can isolate the Magic Moments associated with a task, if you can use them to create scenarios where people can project themselves into the picture, where they can see or feel or touch or anticipate the moment, you'll be able to squeeze off all sorts of wicked good ideas.

Objective

To cut to the essence, the core of your creative challenge. To identify areas of opportunity for creative exploration. To find the critical moments that motivate, excite, and thrill.

How to Do It

Gather any props you'll need to role-play the experience.

If, for example, you're working on a new bread product, you should have a toaster, butter, jam, a knife, a plate, a loaf of something—the works.

Or if you're trying to land a job, you should have an interviewer, a résumé, and the clothes you would wear to an interview.

Let's say your task is to build a better cat food. In this case, you'll need a bowl, a supply of cat food, and something approximating a cat. I lean toward the stuffed variety because they're less finicky and won't wet on you.

You can use lots of ways to capture your Magic Moments—a simple notepad, a video camera or, my favorite, a Polaroid instant camera.

The object is to role-play the challenge before you. Play each role that comes into play. If you're inventing a better mouse-trap, consider the challenge from the points of view of the mouse, the harried homemaker, the man of the house, the bait. What happens when the trap is baited? When it snaps shut? When it's time

to get rid of the body? Take notes or photographs of each step as you go, as if you were creating a storyboard for a TV commercial.

Or, to use cat food as an example, your first Magic Moments might occur when your cat wakes you in the morning as a prelude to the daily feeding ritual. Set the scene and photograph it. Play with it. Have fun.

Your second Magic Moment might occur when you reach for the cat's food in the cupboard; you shake the box, the cat comes running. Maybe your third Magic Moment happens when the cat chows down and you stand back to bask in the warm glow of pet owner accomplishment.

Take it back further if you like, all the way to the store shelf. Stretch it into the future. Think of each Magic Moment as an opportunity. Find and photograph as many as you can.

After you've gathered your pictures, ask some questions.

- Which moments can be made more satisfying? How?
- Which moments haven't been fully tapped?
- What are the best, most exciting, most intriguing moments?
- What are the worst, most annoying, most aggravating moments?
- Which moment should be your focus?
- What are your feelings during the various moments?
- Where is the most magic?
- What is the defining moment?

Having defined the Magic Moments and the elements of each moment, take another look. Think of each moment as an area of opportunity. Look at each moment as a stepping-stone to a great new idea.

As you search for Magic Moments, think about how each of the senses is awakened during them. Regard the task in terms of the way it feels, smells, sounds, tastes, and looks.

Isolate the Pavlovian responses—the *psssst* when you open a cold can of Pepsi; the rich, dark aroma of fresh-brewed Folgers the first thing in the morning; the squeezable softness of Charmin; the snap, crackle, pop of Rice Krispies; the whiter whites of Tide.

Think about the feelings those responses elicit. Do they make you feel cooler? Ready to start the day? Pampered? Hungry? Clean? None of the above?

Great ideas have been built with sensory Magic Moments. Seeing is only part believing. There's also touching, smelling, tasting, and hearing.

Magic Moments in Action

One of the magic moments in my life was when I proposed to Debbie. Like any other guy who has ever proposed marriage, I was looking for an idea to make the moment ultramemorable. I thought about hiring a skywriter, mailing myself to her, plastering my proposal across a billboard on an interstate highway. But those ideas didn't feel sufficiently romantic.

I began thinking of the act of proposing in terms of a Magic Moment, specifically, the moment when the diamond would for the first time be reflected in Debbie's eyes. I could produce the ring through sleight of hand, but that's the kind of thing she'd expect of me.

I zeroed in on the diamond, on how light glinted from it. Diamonds have facets, facets create sparkle, sparkle is magic. What else sparkles? Diamond, glass, crystal. Voilà! I had my idea.

I asked Debbie to a play at a summer theater. On the way to the theater, I stopped at Greeley Park, explaining that it might be nice to have a picnic under our favorite tree before going on to the show. I spread a blanket out on the ground, uncorked a bottle of champagne, and poured some into a pair of long-stemmed Waterford crystal glasses. I turned my back briefly and dropped the engagement ring into one of the glasses. Then I handed Debbie the spiked drink.

She was impressed at the service. Then she looked into her glass. At first, she thought it was scratched. She swirled her glass, then she saw the ring. I blurted out my proposal. She accepted, pulled out the ring, dropped the crystal glass, and started crying. For an awkward moment, I confused her tears for despair. She quickly assured me I was wrong.

I took a picture of Debbie with her ring and the champagne glass under that big old tree. Of all the photographs in all our photo albums, it's the most magical.

Here's another example of Magic Moments in action. The school my elder daughter attends was looking for room mothers to help out in classrooms. The leaflet the school sent home was a masterful piece of Magic Moment leveraging. It included clip-art illustrations to not-so-subtly remind moms of the big three school events they would be involved in should they choose to be room mothers. Placed strategically in the copy were images of a Halloween witch, a Christmas tree, and a Valentine.

ROOM PARENT SEARCH

If you have an interest in being a room parent for the 1993-94 school year, please sign up NOW!!!

Name: _____

Child's Name: _____

Grade: _____

Please return to school as soon as possible Thank you.

Talk about your gut punches. The message was this: If you want to attend the three best parties of the year, you'd better sign up to be a room mother. The school quickly filled its vacancies.

BRAIN PROGRAM #10: KITCHEN CHEMISTRY

Play with your problem. Spill it out on the table and put your fingers in it. Bake it, shape it, bend it, spin it over your head like a lariat. Do it once following the directions, then do it again without them. Add ingredients. Take away ingredients. Be a mad scientist.

Once you've given your task three dimensions, once you're able to see it from the north, south, east, and west, you'll have a better idea which direction to take it.

Objective

To invent ideas based on interaction with your subject of inquiry. Kitchen Chemistry involves playing, prototyping, and modeling alternative solutions. It's a tinkerer's dream.

How to Do It

When I'm called upon to create new food or beverage products, I routinely knead, scald, freeze, whip, shake, boil, mix, fry, and bake the client's products and competitive products. This is especially valuable if you're not a product development or technical person. If you're working in a corporate setting, ask your product development people to set up a play session for you.

As you approach your task, try building it in miniature. If you're looking for a marketing idea, frame it inside a commercial. If you're working on a Boy Scout fund-raiser, frame it inside a brochure or a poster. Consider what you'd call your idea. What claims will you make? What makes it the best? How would you explain it to make people interested?

When you play with your ideas and visualize your thoughts in three dimensions, you can see what works and what doesn't. You find ways to make it the best it can be.

Kitchen Chemistry in Action

I've always loved playing with my food and my products. When I was on the Safeguard soap detail, I developed a fork demonstration. You probably didn't realize it, but if you stick a fork in a bar of Safeguard, it goes in smoothly. If you stick a fork in a bar of Dial, the bar splinters.

So what? Well, at the time, I was looking for a way to establish Safeguard as a deodorant soap that was also soft on your skin—not harsh like (*ahem!*) Other soaps. My fork demonstration would have been a good way to make that point visually. But

I was naive in the ways of corporate salesmanship and was unable to get management to buy the idea.

Too bad. A few years later, Lever Brothers introduced Lever 2000, a bar soap that featured a similar combination of deodorant and skin conditioner that generated record sales.

On another occasion, Kitchen Chemistry proved that Soft Scrub liquid cleanser, while generally thought to be safer for delicate surfaces than Spic & Span powder, was in fact far from it. This was a major point of distinction. The result was an advertising campaign that showed Soft Scrub leaving gouges on one lens of a pair of plastic sunglasses, while the Spic & Span lens remained as smooth as, well, glass.

My father used a parallel process to create designs for our home. Before he committed hammer to nail, he would build miniature models. He drew the plans to scale and cut tiny furniture templates from graph paper. He spread the whole thing across the dining room table and walked around it, inspecting it from this angle and that. He looked at his model as if he were already living in it.

Once his mind's eye could see it, he could build it. A blueprint wasn't enough. I've taken the same approach in designing modifications to our home and the Eureka! Mansion. The only difference is that I build my home improvement models on a Macintosh computer using Aldus Freehand.

Take the problem and reduce it down to visual analogy.
Go collect how much fat is in a product and see it for
yourself! If you're writing ad copy, get the product and

don't just use it, play with it. This is where you can really let your child come out.

One of my trademarks at Frito-Lay is that everyone can find me playing with ingredients. I've even been accused of using magic foo-foo dust. People will roll their eyes as Jeff is scurrying around finding new ways to play with snack foods.

For example, we determined how to redesign a prototype snack's piece shape to make it stronger by learning how it broke as we played horseshoes with it. As we played, it became apparent that the pieces always landed a certain way under force, and sure enough, the same phenomenon was happening during mechanical transfer at the packaging machine.

JEFFREY A. STAMP, PH.D.,
Principal Scientist,
Frito-Lay, Inc.

CHAPTER 204

Flapdoodling

Great Flapdoodling sheets are like great old Ford pickups. They're not gussied-up fashion statements. They're just plain functional. They do real work.

RICHARD SAUNDERS

To invent a wicked good idea it helps to be able to see it. Or to put it another way, Flapdoodle it.

Flapdoodling is a process for display thinking. It's a way of collecting and structuring ideas so that they can go forth and multiply. It's a method for recording, free-associating, and, most of all, making chaos work for you. Flapdoodling is a simplified variation of a display thinking system called Mind Mapping invented by Tony Buzan.

The traditional approach to note taking and outlining is to start at the top of a sheet of paper, work your way in a linear fashion to the bottom, and continue again at the top of the next sheet. You work in one dimension. Ho-hum.

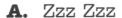

A. Zzz Zzz
  1. Zxy
  2. Zwv

B. Yaz YAZ
  1. Xxy
  2. Xwv

You learned the outline format in the fifth grade. The problem is, it doesn't give your ideas much room to mingle, flirt, or buy each other drinks. As a result, your ability to bulge on your ideas is limited. Opportunities for connecting, cleansing, and enhancing are lost.

Flapdoodling works in two dimensions. It has latitude and longitude. It's messy, free-form, alive, and dynamic. It's the next best thing to producing a printout of your brain.

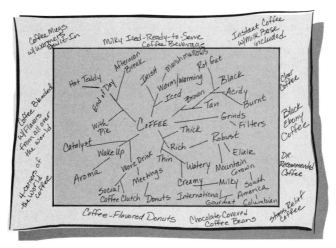

You can Flapdoodle in longhand on paper, with a hammer and chisel on a slab of granite, or, thanks to a program from Inspiration Software, Inc., on your Macintosh. For more information about Inspiration, call 503-245-9011. They're hardly ever out to lunch.

BRAIN PROGRAM #11: FLAPDOODLING

Objective

To allow you to record ideas in such a way that they can bulge, build, and hitchhike on one another. Flapdoodling is a way to invent ideas as well as a means of recording them. The process helps you see a range of alternatives. The discipline of Flapdoodling helps prevent you from simply taking the first path, the first idea that winks at you. The next idea is often a better idea.

How to Do It

Get a nice big sheet of paper—say, twenty inches tall by twenty-six inches wide. I use king-size clipboards to make Flapdoodling more conducive to stretching out on a couch. Or you can lay a chartpad on a table like an extralarge placemat. Or spread a paper tablecloth across a conference room table.

The first step is to define your objective. What is your task, mission, or problem? Maybe it's just a word—a who, a how, a when, or a why. Write it in the center of the page, using a juicy, squeaky colored marker with a nice, fat, assertive stroke. That's your epicenter, your point of departure. Draw a box around the task. Or, if you're feeling particularly mental, try a hexagon or other multisided gon. For each corner, push yourself to come up with one, two, or more different areas of exploration—associations, ideas, or related elements.

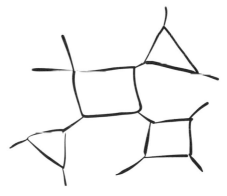

Unleash your imagination. Send it skyward. Begin to free-associate outward in spokes from the epicenter, allowing each spoke to sprout spokes of its own as you work further and further from the center. The further you go, your thoughts will become less grounded in reality and move increasingly in the realm of the new and different.

If necessary, prod your brain at bayonet point. Through the act of forcing a variety of options, your mind will open itself to a wider spectrum of alternatives—as opposed to keeping a narrow perspective and limiting the scenarios you have to consider.

You'll end up with a sheet that, at first glance, will look as if it was used to sop up an ink spill. But as you hopscotch out from the epicenter, your stream of consciousness will begin to flow. Connections will present themselves. Ideas will bubble to the surface, as if with wills of their own. The randomness of it can hardly help but reveal free associations that wouldn't otherwise emerge in a more logical, linear, lunkhead format.

Finally, dress the Flapdoodle for stardom. Draw circles or boxes around wicked good ideas. If you're feeling particularly colorful, use different colored markers to make your thoughts bounce off the page. With Flapdoodling, you'll find ideas come in clusters, like grapes. Circle the ones that strike you as Aha! kinds of ideas. Draw stars and exclamation points around the ones that make your heart flutter.

Flapdoodling in Action

Here's a real-world example of how I used Flapdoodling to come up with an idea for a birthday present for my wife, Debbie.

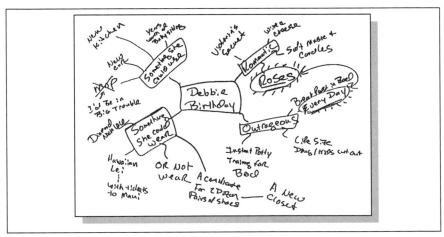

Act II: Eureka! Stimulus Response Explosion

The epicenter of the Flapdoodle sheet was "Debbie Birthday," shorthand for "What to get Debbie for her birthday?"
The first four spokes looked like this:

1. Romantic
2. Outrageous
3. Something She Could Wear
4. Something She Could Use

Each spoke provided a departure point of its own. The next level of the Romantic and Outrageous spokes sprouted these thoughts:

1. Romantic
   a. Roses
   b. Soft music and candles
   c. Wine and cheese
   d. Victoria's Secret
2. Outrageous
   a. A life-size cutout photo of me and the kids
   b. Breakfast in bed every day for a year
   c. Instantaneous potty training for our son Brad

As I scribbled thoughts out from the spokes, my mind started jumping the tracks back and forth from Romantic to Outrageous. "Roses" and "every day" connected themselves. So maybe I should buy her roses every day for a year? Nice idea, but too expensive.

Then again, a bouquet of fresh flowers lasts about a week. What if I had flowers delivered to her once a week for a year? That way, she'd have an unending stream of fresh blooms for the next 365 days. Eureka!

I arranged a frequent buyer delivery program with a local florist, setting up Wednesday as the delivery day to brighten the middle of the week. She loved them. Her weekly bouquet has since become a birthday staple each year. Truth be told, I intend to send her flowers every week for the rest of her life! (Isn't that romantic!) You'd think the thrill would wear off. Never.

One of the fundamental laws of interpersonal physics is that you can never give a woman too many flowers or a child too many stuffed animals.

RICHARD SAUNDERS

Here's another example of a Flapdoodle sheet that led to the creation of a new chewy candy for kids who wanted to see what it's like to be a species other than human. It comes in a package shaped in their choice of bear, lion, pig, or ape snouts.

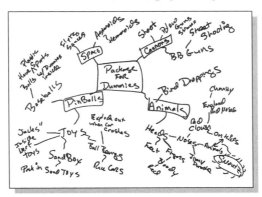

The task was to create a new packaging for a product Van Melle Candy Co. called Dummies, which took the form of small, chewy pellets. In this case, the Eureka! Stimulus Response team had extra motivation. Dummies was a neat product, but sales were lagging. Unless we could come up with a way to salvage it, Van Melle was thinking about selling the equipment used to make the product and closing the line.

At the center of our Flapdoodle board was our target—Package for Dummies. These four spokes radiated from it:

1. Pinballs
2. Space
3. Animals
4. Cannons

These smaller spokes sprouted out from Animals:
3. Animals
   a. Heads
   b. Bird droppings

The Heads spoke prompted still smaller spokes:
   a. Heads
   b. Feet
   c. Fingers
   d. Noses

Noses led us to Jimmy Durante, Clowns, and back again to Animals. The Jimmy Durante tangent was too obscure; at least it would be to anyone under the age of thirty. But Clowns sparked discussion. What are clowns? Well, a clown isn't really a clown— it's a person dressed up in a costume, which usually includes some kind of fake nose. Kids like to dress up. What about clown noses?

But we wanted more variety. Clown noses, for the most part, are uniformly round red beezers. Animals come in a lot of different varieties. And they have noses. Well, not noses exactly. What is that thing animals have instead of noses?

"Snouts!" one of the Trained Brains shouted.

And that's just what we called it. Except we took away the second "s" and added a "z." Snoutz is a soft blob of sweet candy that comes in a cup that's shaped like an animal snout. It comes in Apple-APE, PIGGY-Cherry Berry, Blue Rasp-BEARy, and Lemon-LION. When you've finished the candy, you attach a string to the cup and strap it across your own snout.

Three months after the session, Snoutz was presented at a candy trade show in Washington, D.C.

Later, when you go back over your Flapdoodle sheets, you'll be able to trace the lineage of each idea back to its organic roots. The sheets are like instant replay diagrams; they provide a play-by-play of the thoughts that led you to a certain destination, enabling you to work backward to earlier plays that may have been neglected in the initial blast of creativity but are often worth exploring later.

Part of the beauty of Flapdoodling is that it allows for continued growth. After your initial Eureka! Stimulus Response effort, you can return to your Flapdoodle and push the branches out further. You can continue to add ideas and new connections long after your initial spurt of creativity.

251

Linear lines on paper lead to linear ideas. Wicked good
ideas come from coloring outside and across lines.
RICHARD SAUNDERS

Try this variation on the Flapdoodle theme if you're working in a group. Divide into small groups of three or four people and give each group a Flapdoodle sheet. Let them work a few layers outward, then have them pass their sheets to the next group for continued layering. When your Flapdoodle comes back, you may not recognize it. But your initial ideas will have been enriched, fortified, and polymerized to a high gloss under the buffing brushes of other perspectives.

OK, it's your turn. Time to see it, feel it, touch it. Your mission is to create ideas for a weekend outing—for yourself, your nearest significant other, or your whole family.

I'll get you started with the first spokes of your Flapdoodle. You can take it from there. Get a sheet of paper, oversized if you can, 8 1/2 by 11 if you have to. Copy the Flapdoodle spokes listed below on the sheet.

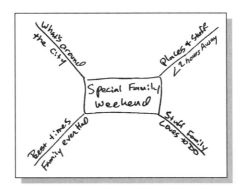

Want to learn more about display thinking? Learn from the display thinking masters. Check out the two best books on the subject:

- *Mindmapping*, by Joyce Wycoff
  Published by Berkley Books, New York, 1991

- *Use Both Sides of Your Brain*, by Tony Buzan
  Published by E. P. Dutton, Inc., New York, 1974

CHAPTER 205

Jumping the Tracks

All your life, you've been told to organize your thoughts. You've been taught to make your thoughts march like prisoners of war in tidy little regiments through your brain.

Maybe it's time to disorganize.

Organized thought leads to formula thinking. Corporations are very big on organized thought. In most large blue-blood corporations, it seems as if everything is based on precedent. All recommendations are couched in terms of how they compare to previous corporate experience.

I have deep respect for tradition when it comes to proms, weddings, and world history. But tradition doesn't count for much when you're searching for wicked good ideas.

Wicked good ideas happen when you break free from established channels of thought. They come from drawing outside the lines and going the wrong way down one-way streets.

The brain naturally tends to operate in neat patterns and tracks. But creativity comes from chaos. Wicked good ideas don't surface through logical conscious process. They emerge through the ragged edge of the subconscious, like thieves in the night.

The Jumping the Tracks programs are designed to force associations between seemingly unrelated aspects of a task. They offer practical steps for shedding the shackles of linear thinking. Some exercises rely on stimuli related to the problem at hand. Others use stimuli with little or no connection.

> *The more a stimulus is related to the problem, the greater the chances of ending up with a great quantity of ideas. When the stimulus is unrelated to the subject matter, the ideas may be fewer but the potential for a major breakthrough is enhanced dramatically.*
>
> RICHARD SAUNDERS

BRAIN PROGRAM #12: 666

This is one of the most provocative, productive Brain Programs in my Eureka! Stimulus Response repertoire.

The name is rooted in the Eureka! Trained Brains' warped senses of humor and disrespect for authority.

Throughout much of the 1980s, Procter & Gamble was besieged with an unfounded and vicious rumor based on a misinterpretation of its man-in-the-moon logo. It was the opinion of the rumormongers that certain elements of the logo were satanic in nature and that, by extension, P&G was a nest of satan worshipers. While I can testify that not all Procthoids are angels, neither have I met any Beelzebubs.

In any case, due to my P&G background, the Trained Brains dubbed this exercise in honor of my former employer, using a number that has biblical references to the Antichrist. *Tsk.*

Despite repeated attempts to rename the exercise, the name stuck. The fact is, the exercise is certainly no crapshoot. It uses three dice, each of which has six sides. It's an unfortunate coincidence. So with apologies to those who find the name offensive, let's press on.

Objective

To force-associate related elements of a problem in random sequence. To bring together the different elements with the roll of the dice and increase the number of mental connections that would not have been forged otherwise. To follow the dice wherever they lead.

How to Do It

Divide your task into as many separate aspects as you can. List all possible areas of exploration, along with characteristics that might be used to define each area.

When our challenge was to invent ideas for new board games, the list of areas of exploration included:

- *Target audience* (boys, teens, seniors)
- *Types of game boards* (cloth, three-dimensional)
- *Theme* (music, sex)
- *Scoring devices* (poker chips, dollar bills)
- *Subject matter* (politics, the future, the past)
- *Materials* (rubber, kites, masking tape)
- *Types of power* (electricity, brainwaves, muscles)

From your list of areas of exploration, select three to pursue in 666. In the case of our search for a board game, I selected *Target audience*, *Themes*, and *Materials*.

Now create six options for each of the areas of opportunity. 666 is at its most effective when the areas of exploration are related to your task. You'll find a stack of starter lists you can borrow from 666's cousin, Dr. Disecto, in Chapter 208.

Arrange your lists in columns, like this:

WHITE DIE	BLUE DIE	RED DIE
THEME	TARGET AUDIENCE	MATERIALS
1. Food, Food, Food	1. Seniors	1. Invisible Ink
2. Sex and Rock & Roll	2. Teens	2. Nylon
3. Laughter	3. College Age	3. Masking Tape
4. Best/Worst	4. Roseanne type	4. Sponge Rubber
5. Gossip	5. Yuppies	5. Kites/Gliders
6. Family Reunion	6. Couples Only	6. Bouncing Balls

You're ready to roll. Use three dice, each of a color to match the columns. Toss the dice and match the numbers on each die to the trait in the appropriate column. See what thoughts the linkages inspire. With each toss of the dice, you'll see a new pool of opportunities. When the well runs dry, roll again. When three consecutive rolls fail to yield any good ideas, move on to a new list of areas of exploration or another Brain Program.

In any case, use the combinations that emerge with each toss of the dice strictly as starting-gate stimuli. They don't have to be taken literally. In fact, it's better if you don't.

At one Eureka! Stimulus Response party, I inadvertently let four RWA clients form a group by themselves, without any Trained Brains to skew the mix. In no time at all, they were utterly discombobulated. They read their first three-item sequence out loud as if it were a sentence and began complaining it made no sense whatsoever.

Of course it didn't. The point of 666 is to trigger ideas outside the normal orbs of thought.

666 in Action

I wanted an idea for a new game. The roll of the dice, using the list shown above was 2, 2, 3. That added up to Sex and Rock & Roll, Teens, and Masking Tape.

What a combination. My thoughts unfurled along these lines:

Rock 'n' roll had been done. That left sex. What do fourteen-year-old kids want? They want to touch members of the opposite sex.

How might they be allowed to climb all over each other without anyone getting too upset and/or pregnant? What if players were to get tangled up in each other in a way that would be more humorous than amorous? What if they were to wrestle with their clothes on?

What if they tied themselves together with masking tape? Or something like masking tape. Something that would come off easily. Like Velcro.

The result was Octopus, a game that has parallels to Twister, but in 3-D. Players attach different colored Velcro bands to their wrists, ankles, and head. With a roll of a big foam die, the players attach and entwine themselves around each other—wrist to ankle, ankle to head, and so on, depending on what colored band is where—until they're physically unable to make the next required connection. Random House liked it well enough to license it.

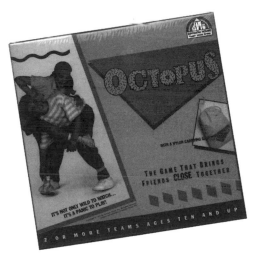

257

I wish I'd had Octopus when I was fourteen. Or I wish I'd had 666 so I could have thought of it.

The advantage to 666 is that it creates a context—albeit a twisted, bizarre context—that's almost always entirely new. So it almost always leads to fresh ways of bulging into the Great Beyond.

BRAIN PROGRAM #13: DON'T SELL ME

Don't Sell Me is based on the premise that people hate to buy things. What they want is to have their basic needs and desires satisfied. As in:

    —Don't sell me clothes ... Sell me attractiveness.
    —Don't sell me shoes ... Sell me feet that feel refreshed.
    —Don't sell me books ... Sell me knowledge.
    —Don't sell me a lobotomy ... Sell me peace of mind.
    —Don't sell me Barry Manilow. Please.

Objective

Don't Sell Me forces you to zero in on intangibles. It asks you to think more about implications, less about the task itself. It moves your perspective away from things and more toward feelings, hopes, emotions, and benefits. Don't Sell Me is the scenic route to new awarenesses of the essence of your task. It takes you right to your mission's core, but from a variety of emotional directions.

How to Do It

Define your mission. What are you trying to accomplish? What are you trying to change? Who do you want to listen?

Now complete the following statement:

Don't Sell Me (Your task in concrete terms)...
Sell me (Your task in abstraction)

Complete the statement as quickly as you can. Fill in the blank a dozen times or more. Let your pen move. You're looking for soft stuff—the feelings, emotions, attitudes, results, consequences, secondary benefits, gut instincts, intuitions, and perceptions that drive your day-to-day existence.

After completing the statement a dozen or so times, set the list aside for ten minutes and do something else.

When you return to your list, focus on each blank one at a time. Concentrate on the pieces, not the aggregate. When you attack a problem in its totality at one time, you can quickly become overwhelmed. Better to be underwhelmed. Or just plain whelmed.

Use each of your statements as a springboard to new ideas. What comes to mind? What new thoughts does each statement prompt? Look at each statement as an opportunity to solve a part of the task. Consider each as an element of the challenge. Or a new direction from which to approach the challenge. Let each represent a separate need, like a moon orbiting the task. Address emotions, feelings, and perceptions. Look for weaknesses to fix and strengths to trumpet.

Don't Sell Me in Action

I love this Brain Program. I had some friends over and we plugged it in to help invent this book. Here are some of the ways we filled in the blank:

Don't sell me CREATIVITY BOOKS ... Sell me *"confidence in my brain."*

Don't sell me CREATIVITY BOOKS ... Sell me *"creative juice."*

Don't sell me CREATIVITY BOOKS ... Sell me *"a renewal of my childhood."*

Don't sell me CREATIVITY BOOKS ... Sell me *"success in the corporate world."*

Don't sell me CREATIVITY BOOKS ... Sell me *"a life I can be excited about."*

Don't sell me CREATIVITY BOOKS ... Sell me *"a blueprint for achieving greatness."*

Don't sell me CREATIVITY BOOKS ... Sell me *"spirit."*

Don't sell me CREATIVITY BOOKS ... Sell me *"enthusiasm and energy that lasts."*

The ideas of *"confidence in my brain,"* *"spirit,"* and *"enthusiasm and energy that lasts"* helped me think about the importance of courage and enthusiasm, along with having the inspiration and wherewithal to challenge conformity. There's a certain element of evangelistic fervor in these pages, in case you hadn't noticed.

The ideas of *"success in the corporate world"* and *"a life I can be excited about"* underlined the importance of examples of creativity techniques in action in both professional and personal environments.

Once during a soft drink project for Pepsi-Cola, I completed the Don't Sell Me phrase with the following results:

Don't sell me SOFT DRINKS ... Sell me *"fun."*
Don't sell me SOFT DRINKS ... Sell me *"good taste/flavor."*
Don't sell me SOFT DRINKS ... Sell me *"outrageousness."*
Don't sell me SOFT DRINKS ... Sell me *"refreshment."*
Don't sell me SOFT DRINKS ... Sell me *"a break in the day."*
Don't sell me SOFT DRINKS ... Sell me *"excitement."*
Don't sell me SOFT DRINKS ... Sell me *"revolution."*
Don't sell me SOFT DRINKS ... Sell me *"perpetual youth."*
Don't sell me SOFT DRINKS ... Sell me *"a piece of America."*
Don't sell me SOFT DRINKS ... Sell me *"thirst elimination."*

I sat and pondered. I bathed my brain in these thoughts. While soft drinks are about flavor, taste, refreshment, and slaking thirst, they're also more than that. They're part of our lives, a reflection of Americana and a symbol of youth. Or youthfulness.

Hmmmm. I was drawn to *"fun,"* *"outrageousness"* and *"perpetual youth."* What could you do with a carbonated soft drink that would be outrageous and fun? What's the funnest, funniest thing a soft drink could do or be?

In a remote crack in my mind, I saw Larry, Curly, and Moe attacking each other with seltzer bottles. Eureka! I whipped out my trusty PowerBook and blew out the copy in ten minutes. The next page details what the concept board and copy looked like:

Stooges ALL-NATURAL Seltzer

Stooges Seltzer... **For Those Who Know How to Laugh**

It's with great pride that Pepsi introduces new Stooges ALL-NATURAL Flavored Seltzer. Named in honor of those classic Kings of American Comedy: Curly, Larry, and Moe. Just shake the product, push down on the special top, and spray into your mouth for an all-natural taste that can't be beat. Flavors include Citrus Curly, Lemon Larry, and Mandarin Orange Moe.

I faxed a copy to Pepsi's world headquarters in White Plains. The client laughed and approved it for testing as part of a collection of thirty other ideas. She told me she felt sure Stooges Seltzer would be either a big winner or a huge bust, so to speak.

I held my breath during AcuPOLL's concept testing. A jury of honest-to-gosh real Americans was assembled to record responses on AcuPOLL computer terminals. In an instant, reactions to various concepts were translated into letter grades—A to F—reflecting how the panelists' responses compared to previous tests of similar new product. An A grade means an idea scored in the top 20 percent of previously tested concepts. An F puts an idea in the bottom 20 percent.

As the votes came over a central computer terminal, the grade flickered from A to F and finally leveled off at C. Rats. I hate average.

At second glance, I found hope in the histogram of how the votes shook out. It showed that the C grade was not reflected in normal parabolic distribution of votes, but by a polarized combination of extremely negative and extremely positive reactions. Stooges Seltzer was clearly a concept that caused controversy. Hope still existed.

I asked Jack Gordon, president of AcuPOLL, to find out what people liked and didn't like about Stooges. The responses led us to what we were to confirm later in statistical analysis. Stooges was a concept with a clear male/female split. Men gave the idea an A+. Women gave it an F.

Later, I asked my wife whether this means that "those who know how to laugh" pretty much just includes men.

"Don't think so," she said. "It means women are the ones who have to clean it up."

When the AcuPOLL report was presented to Pepsi, I tried gallantly to put an emotional spin on the results, pitching Stooges as an idea with magnum drama and excitement. Unfortunately, considering its average overall grade and the fact that another concept had scored an A+, I was not gallant enough.

The A+ idea had set test records. This was a test of an idea for a cola with a new generation of taste, and its score shot off the top of the charts. It was called Crystal Pepsi.

The idea for Crystal Pepsi was cool. But in my heart, Stooges was the hometown favorite.

BRAIN PROGRAM #14: MUSICAL CHAIRS

Step outside yourself. Take a different seat. Forget who you are. Put on a different pair of shoes. Try a different hat. Slip into someone else's point of view.

When an idea has me stuck, I jump into the idea and pretend I'm inside on a micro scale. For example, when I was doing my doctoral research on aspartame (NutraSweet), I wanted to understand how the sweetener might behave in a food system and where it went during processing. So I would often pretend I was a molecule of aspartame, and mentally visualize how I might react under a certain set of experimental variables. It may seem like a corny thing to do, but it works. Many hurdles in my research were cleared once I got "inside" the problem.

JEFFREY A. STAMP, PH.D.,
Principal Scientist,
Frito-Lay, Inc.

Objective

To look at your problem from a different perspective—a different seat in the bleachers, on the bus, in the cockpit. To provide new insights and information from other elements of the task. To kick start your imagination with different points of view.

How to Do It

Look at your task through somebody else's eyes. Sit in that person's chair.

Start with someone who has no understanding of your task. If you were your mom, how would you see it? How would you react at first blush? Where would you look for answers? What would be your concerns?

Get more specific. Look at the whole family. Consider the needs, desires, and spins of the middle teenage son, Aunt Gladys, sister Sue, and the family gerbil.

Do a double-take and look at it from the slant of someone who has been involved in the challenge for years. What mind ruts would you travel? What would you regard as the immutable facts? What would be your beliefs? Which established mind ruts offer an opportunity to contradict history by contradicting them?

Amplify your challenge. Move the chair at the extremes. Exaggerate the issues by taking the most stuck-in-the-mud right-wing conservative view, then the far-leftist bleeding-heart throw-money-at-every-problem liberal view. What are the stereotypes? What seemingly carved-in-stone perspectives are out there?

Put yourself in chairs from other lands. Imagine your challenge in the hands of Lady Di, a Sumo wrestler, an Eskimo, a French chef, a Zulu chieftain, a Ukrainian peasant, a hula dancer, a Rastafarian, a desert sheik, a Norwegian fisherman, the wild man of Borneo. What insights might they have to expand your perspective? What can you borrow from their worlds to make your challenge easier?

Put your chair in a time machine. How would Ben Franklin handle the challenge? George Washington? J. Edgar Hoover? John Wayne? Jed Clampett? Sgt. York? W. C. Fields?

WHEN I NEED TO JUMP START MY BRAIN, I call my mother. She has a knack for simplifying things in my mind and making the solution attainable. Getting back to a childlike mind-set is easier if you are the child. So call your mother; even though you're all grown-up, you're somebody's child.

DEBBIE DELLE CAVE

Musical Chairs in Action

A great time to use Musical Chairs is when you're working on ideas for motivating and involving children.

I was faced with such a challenge when Procter & Gamble acquired Hawaiian Punch, a brand in serious need of jump-starting.

First, I looked at the product from an adult's perspective. The line seemed complete, albeit somewhat complicated. Hawaiian Punch seemed to be available in about a jillion flavors and colors.

Then I looked at the product as if I were a kid. To a child, it was simply Hawaiian Punch, a fruit drink that came in colors.

Seated in the child's chair, I couldn't remember all those flavors and colors. In particular, I was confused by the four red flavors. I could never remember which red I liked.

Looking at the product test data, one flavor stood above the others—Fruit Juicy Red. I had a radical thought. What if all Hawaiian Punch was Fruit Juicy Hawaiian Punch? Instead of changing the flavors from product to product, what if color was the only thing? What if all Hawaiian Punch offered was Fruit Juicy Red, Fruit Juicy Green, Fruit Juicy Yellow? What if we had a Fruit Juicy Blue?

My adult persona liked the simplicity of the idea. At least you'd be selling everybody's favorite taste. And from a kid's perspective, you could just ask for your color. Plus, you'd get a sickly reaction from grown-ups who, for the most part, don't find blue particularly drinkable.

The change rolled national. Since then, Hawaiian Punch sales, as tracked by Information Resources, are up 16 percent. Moreover, the product is purchased by 19 percent more households than before—a figure that translates to an additional 3 million homes. Which means a whole lot more kids are walking around with red mustaches, blue mustaches, and green mustaches.

I often invoke the spirit of Franklin for answers. Not long ago, I was tempted by an opportunity to hire a half-dozen people to run a growing business selling Jump Start Your Advertising training seminars for client and advertising agency teams. At the same time, the thought of having more people on staff, more overhead, and more meetings turned my stomach. I'm an inventor, not a manager.

I wondered how Franklin would deal with it. Franklin kept his personal staff small, yet his business interests and wealth grew significantly. His did it through dozens of partnerships and joint ventures.

I took the same approach. Instead of hiring the people, I proposed a joint effort to their ringleader. She would operate the business; I'd provide insight, investment capital, inspiration, and publicity. She accepted.

Ben would have been proud. The Jump Start Your Brain message is communicated to an important audience. And I stay focused on what I enjoy most—and what I do best.

BRAIN PROGRAM #15: CATALOG CITY

Legend has it that you can find anything you want in the Sears catalog. This exercise proves the legend true. Indeed, it was my understanding as a kid growing up in Maine that Santa's elves worked for Sears in the off-season.

(Note: It was with deep sorrow, while watching CNN in a Los Angeles hotel room, that I learned that Sears was discontinuing its catalog. Writing letters to Santa Claus will never be the same. Although the Sears catalog is gone, I like to keep its memory alive with this Brain Program.)

Objective

To help jump the tracks in minds familiar with the intricacies and implications of the task, jarring them through the use of unrelated stimuli.

How to Do It

Get a Sears catalog. Go for the big Spring & Summer issue. Or the Fall & Winter book. In either case, you want the lexicon with a little of everything.

If you don't have a copy in your closet, attic, or outhouse, try to get one. It doesn't matter how old it is. Some say Sears catalogs improve with age. If, however, you exhaust the possibilities, any other good-size publication with pictures or illustrations will suffice—such as the J. C. Penney catalog, photo encyclopedias, or, in a pinch, the yellow pages.

Having acquired your catalog or functional alternative, randomly select a two-page spread. For those of you who have trouble making decisions, use the following numbers. Start at the first number and proceed in left-to-right, top-to-bottom sequence until your task has a solution.

123	666	384	102	29	
583	723	73	63	723	261
726	99	263	827	364	
276	348	623	45	476	832
112	343	482	763	451	
239	899	400	101	48	70

Having settled on a page in your catalog, let your eyes do the walking. Look at the page as a puzzle to be solved. Use the images on the pages as stimuli.

- What new thoughts do the images provoke?
- If the images shown were a magazine advertisement for your problem, what would the caption be?
- If you were in one of the pictures or illustrations, how would you see your challenge?
- What functions, movement, and/or actions could be effective?
- What in the pictures could you use as a crowbar for opening up solutions?

I find that the Flapdoodling techniques described earlier help push my mind to transform the unrelated images on the page into solutions. The key is to not overthink it. Let your mind hopscotch from one association to another.

When the pace slackens, try another number. And another. And another.

Catalog City in Action

I was redesigning the master bathroom of our newly purchased home. To the right side of the master bedroom was a small bathroom, with a vanity, toilet, shower stall, and no windows. On the left were two clothes closets. A hallway exited from one end of the bathroom.

My challenge was to find a way to fit a tub and picture window in the bathroom. I turned and twisted the design. No matter how I maneuvered it, we ended up with too little space.

I turned to my trusty Sears catalog and opened it to a layout of foam couches and chairs. In one picture, a dog was sleeping beside a chair and couch. One of the couches was shown in an insert photo folding out into a bed.

Was there any way I could fold out the bathroom? Nope. Dead end. The only other photo on the page was of a woman placing a blanket into a storage area behind the couch. The couch had a storage area beneath the pillows. It got me thinking.

Eureka! What if I put a storage area in the bathroom? What if I put the bedroom closets in the bathroom? Could I then use the hallway for the bathroom?

I grabbed a measuring tape and measured the bathroom. It would work. By moving the closet inside the bathroom, we would have ample room for a double sink, toilet, shower stall, whirlpool tub, and bay window.

With a quick parry and thrust at the Sears catalog, our master bathroom was transformed from a torture chamber into an oasis of personal hygiene.

CHAPTER 206

Vandalism

Never underestimate the power of giving overt permission to break rules. Telling someone they can be open and creative on one hand and telling them to break the rules on the other are two different hands.

RICHARD SAUNDERS

We learn early on that rules are to be followed. Some rules—the Golden Rule, for instance—teach us how to behave in a civilized manner. Other rules are Don't Rules, which are rules that, for the most part, have come into being for our own good and are almost always handed down to us by individuals who have more authority than we do. Such as: Don't  Touch That Hot Stove, Don't Run Through the House with My Good Scissors, and Don't Talk Back or You'll Get a Good Spanking! As opposed to a bad spanking.

Patents are issued only to those who contradict experts.

RICHARD SAUNDERS

But there's a disadvantage to following all the rules all the time. We can drift mindlessly on the Sea of Conventional Wisdom, to the point that we fail to notice the wicked good creatures of unconventional wisdom when their dorsal fins break through the surface of our subconscious minds.

Ergo, we sometimes need permission to break the rules in order to see what's behind, beneath, above, and beyond them. Unless you're given the OK to go ahead and vandalize a rule now and then, it can be difficult for you to challenge your thinking, to push your thought envelope outward. Indeed, the more knowledgeable you are about the task at hand, the more difficult it can be.

The exercises in this chapter are here to encourage the anarchist in you. They're here to tell you, hey, it's OK to break the rules.

> *I like to turn the problem inside out by asking myself seemingly irrelevant questions. For example: What if this were a place? What if it happened on the moon? What if they named a street after it? What if it had no top? These "what ifs" get me going. It's sort of like playing your own private party game. If this doesn't work, I eat chocolate. That never fails.*
>
> LIZ NICKLES,
> author and cofounder,
> Direct Dialogue

BRAIN PROGRAM #16: LAW BREAKER

The direct assault is often the most effective. Law Breaker is the most flagrant, brazen challenge to conventional wisdom I know of, short of a Molotov cocktail.

Objective

To consider your task in terms of the regulations, traditions, clichés, and/or popular conceptions attached to it. To examine what happens when you ignore, circumvent, or twist the intent of those laws.

How to Do It

List the laws, truths, perceptions, myths, and absolutes surrounding your task. Search for the most obvious facts, the ones that could never change. Here are a few examples of Great Laws through the Ages to illustrate:

Fruit drinks are colored
The world is flat.
The sun revolves around the earth.
Underwear has to be white.
Nice guys finish last.
If you keep cracking your knuckles like that, you'll get arthritis.

Next to each law list one or two ways to break it. Twist the perceptions, shatter the absolutes, prove every "Thou Shalt" and "Thou Shalt Not" wrong. Start breaking laws two at a time, three at a time, whatever presents itself. Be a rebel and break them all at once if you feel the urge. This is your chance to tweak conformity's nose.

Now step back and examine the havoc you've wreaked. Where does it take you? How does it change the situation? In what ways does it liberate the task?

Law Breaker in Action

One of our favorite examples of the success of Law Breaker is a part of the regulation Richard Saunders International Fat and Sassy Hedonist diet—specifically, dessert.

Act II: Eureka! Stimulus Response Explosion

Ben Cohen and Jerry Greenfield broke all kinds of laws when they started their ice cream company.

If you were thinking about getting into the ice cream business and you wanted to introduce a premium product—say, something about twice as expensive as anything else on the market—you would in all likelihood be advised to follow certain rules, among them:

- Stock your factory with gleaming, state-of-the-art equipment.
- Give it a classy, foreign name, like Häagen-Dazs.
- Use only imported ingredients, French vanilla or Swiss chocolate.
- Sell it in upscale places where goat cheese is more popular than Kraft Singles.
- Hire spokespeople with classy Scandinavian accents.

Ben and Jerry ignored these rules. Using an old-fashioned rock salt ice cream maker with a hand crank, they sold their first ice cream at an abandoned gas station in Vermont. They covered their cartons with handwritten labels and cartoon images. Their No. 1 flavor is Chocolate Chip Cookie Dough. Picture the Queen Mother digging into a pint of that. They named a flavor after Grateful Dead lead guitarist Jerry Garcia and promoted it with tie-dyed T-shirts. They gave their employees roller skates to use on breaks and staged free music festivals.

They did everything wrong. But they have the No. 1 selling superpremium ice cream and frozen yogurt in America, and they're very close to overtaking the oh-so-posh New Jersey-based Häagen-Dazs in total sales.

They may be chuckleheads. But they're having the last laugh.

Ben and Jerry's Chocolate Chip Cookie dough is an integral part of any invention process; for that matter, so is Cherry Garcia, Rainforest Crunch, Chocolate Fudge Brownie, Wild Maine Blueberry ...

RICHARD SAUNDERS

Law Breaker also has spiritual applications. I was wrapping up a lecture outside Washington, D.C., when a man approached me, introduced himself as George, and told me he'd learned about Law Breaker from one of my earlier talks. He said he'd made it work in his own life.

"When?" I asked.

"At church!" George said.

I retreated a few steps, keeping an eye out for lightning bolts of retribution. I wondered if George had taken matters too far. There are some authority figures you don't want to cross, after all. But George didn't appear too badly cursed. He told me this story.

His church was rapidly outgrowing its building. Its parking lot was overflowing. But it was located in an area where local zoning regulations required a fixed percent of the land to remain green space.

At a meeting of the church deacons, George suggested they look at the problem through Law Breaker. They listed several laws:

- The parish had a finite amount of property.
- Churches are built on land.
- The church was at its capacity in terms of adding to the church.
- They didn't have enough land.
- Zoning laws require that you not exceed your current green-space-to-building space ratio.
- You build on land.

Once the laws were on paper, solutions to the problem began to present themselves. One, the church could buy more land, which would allow it to expand the building so that the ratio of developed land to green space would remain the same. Two, they could build underground.

It turned out that the church was able to purchase a few adjoining properties, tear down a few houses, and add on to their parking lot without running afoul of the city zoning inspector. Should the need arise, the deacons also have a plan to expand the parking lot by building a second-level parking garage.

I was relieved. In this case, George's Authority Figure probably didn't mind a few laws being broken.

BRAIN PROGRAM #17: EUREKA! PHYSICS

For every Simplesse low-calorie ice cream, there's a Häagen-Dazs. For every Yugo, there's a Lexus. For every Mister Rogers, there's a Clint Eastwood. For every entrance, there's an exit. For every filet mignon, there's a slab of bologna. For every one-trick pony, there's a Secretariat. For every Stealth Bomber, there are a million paper airplanes. You get the idea.

Objective

To isolate trends and problem components, carry them forward to their extremes, and then pull them as far as you can in the other direction. Stretch them. Exaggerate them. Treat them like Silly Putty. Blow them entirely out of proportion. Somewhere between here and there is a rainbow of wicked good ideas.

How to Do It

List overall trends or components that relate to your area of interest. Now apply Newton's law to each item on the list:

A BODY IN MOTION STAYS IN MOTION.

Carry each of your trends or elements forward to an extreme. Push it to preposterous lengths. Imagine what the world would be like if the trend continued for 1,000 years.

Turn around and take it the other way using another of Newton's laws:

FOR EVERY FORCE, THERE IS AN EQUAL AND OPPOSITE FORCE.

Invent an idea that's the exact opposite of each of your trends or elements. Search for the mirror image. Take each of the extremes from earlier in the program and imagine if their opposites had been in effect for 1,000 years.

Eureka! Physics in Action

In the summer of 1982, I was assigned at Procter & Gamble to work out a deal with the National Football League designating Coast soap the official NFL brand. At the time, the sports pages were dominated with headlines about the possibility of a players' strike.

Keeping in mind that a body in motion stays in motion, I asked the NFL representative with whom I was negotiating, a guy named Bill, about the likelihood of a strike. Bill said not to worry, that it wouldn't happen.

I took it to the extreme.

"Are you sure?" I asked him.

"Yes, yes," he said.

"Can I be completely confident there will not be an NFL players' strike?" I asked again.

Bill stayed in motion. "Absolutely positively," he said.

It was time for me to take an equal and opposite tack.

"OK, then, how about if for every game the players do strike, just for the sake of argument, I get a rebate on my licensing fee?" I asked. "I mean, seeing as how you're so sure they won't strike and all."

To which Bill agreed, seeing as how he was so sure the players wouldn't strike and all.

The players went on strike. The strike lasted long enough so that Coast soap ended up paying nothing for its licensing agreement with the NFL that year.

Meanwhile, another Procter & Gamble product, a certain food and beverage brand, had entered into a similar agreement with the NFL. Unfortunately, the brand manager was ignorant of the laws of physics and believed Bill's assurances there would be no strike. As a result, the brand manager paid the full licensing agreement for half a season's worth of games.

BRAIN PROGRAM #18: TABLOID TALES

You're the editor of the smarmiest, yellowest supermarket tab in the universe. You're out to out-P. T. T. Barnum. No fact can be blown too far out of proportion, no truth can be stretched beyond all reason in the hunt for a wicked good idea. The closer you get to the extremes, the more fun you'll find.

Objective

To gild the lily. To make it larger than life. To emphasize, magnify, and overstate various aspects of your task to create new applications for individual elements, new approaches to improving the total package, or new solutions for your task. To create new thoughts by reveling in hyperbole.

How to Do It

List four facts about your product, service, or problem in the middle of a sheet of paper. Find ways to make these facts more provocative. Sensationalize them. Pump them full of energy, chutzpah, and excitement. Distort one aspect of each fact, then another, until the parts become greater than the whole. Look for facts that spark exaggeration. Describe them in terms that, while literally true, make the product look larger than life.

If you need inspiration, leaf through one of the fine tabloid publications available at any supermarket. I recommend *Weekly World News*. Find out where Elvis has been hanging out. Get the latest scoop on cannibal aliens from outer space.

Force-associate the wild, the bizarre, the eye-popping with your problem. Which outlandish thoughts and ideas spark potentially powerful ideas? By blowing certain aspects out of proportion, what do you discover about them?

Tabloid Tales in Action

I'm always looking for ideas to draw publicity of all kinds to Richard Saunders International. Tabloid Tales once helped me do that in a fairly big way.

It was after a social gathering at the Mansion one evening—a Junto, in fact. I was yakking with a couple of the Trained Brains, one of whom mentioned it would be fun to land a story in one of the supermarket tabs. But how? What did we have to offer that might pique tabloid interest? Abominable snowmen? Aliens from outer space? Liz Taylor's latest diet?

We didn't have anything quite like that. But we did have a spooky old mansion, which some believed to be inhabited by ghosts. And we did have a legitimate tie to Elvis Presley through my partner, Dave Howe, who once worked as the King's sound engineer. And I've built a career from my connections, at least spiritually, to Ben Franklin. And Elvis and Ben are both deceased, or so it's been reported in most major media outlets, which means that one might reasonably expect the two to be ghosts in some dimension.

What if we had a séance? What if I hired a psychic to exorcise the other ghosts from the Mansion? What if the shades of Ben and Elvis actually appeared, took possession of my body, and fought for control of my soul? What if we could even provide computer-enhanced photographs of the encounter? Might that be the kind of story that would catch the eye of a tabloid editor?

I flew a psychic in from Detroit. We'd pitched the story to the *Weekly World News*, where the managing editor had said he was intensely interested in hearing from us after the séance. But the *Wall Street Journal* scooped him.

The story that appeared in the *Journal's* March 2, 1993, edition was headlined "Elvis Is a No Show but Ben Franklin's in the Air." An excerpt:

> *The Franklin vibes are strong. She [the psychic] tries again to contact the inventor. This time she decides it's best to turn off the lights. "OK, Ben Franklin. Give somebody a message to let us know you're around," she asks. Mr. Hall has a "shocking feeling" in his legs. Could be too many Blue Hawaiians. But he is undaunted. People need to free themselves, he says.*

Scary, hunh? At least the reporter spelled my name correctly.

BRAIN PROGRAM #19: EDISON

Sometimes the right product or solution requires you to invent or adjust an entire system. If you tinker with the whole system, sometimes you can change the way you do business.

Thomas Alva Edison not only invented the lightbulb, he invented the system to make it work—from the power plant to the utility poles to the point where your finger flicks on the switch. Take away the power plant, and the lightbulb is irrelevant.

Edison understood the importance of the "whole solution." In 1880, he formed the Edison Electric Company. His plan was to locate his first power plant near Wall Street—a move that would require the support of City Hall, inasmuch as it meant that streets would have to be ripped up to make way for power lines.

In this case, the city fathers were part of the "whole solution." They had to be able to see the benefit in order to agree to the aggravation that would result from tearing up the streets.

Edison invited the city fathers—not a particularly visionary bunch—to his Menlo Park lab late one day. With darkness approaching, the elected officials began grumbling about the hour. As they entered Edison's lab, he clapped his hands, a switch was thrown, and the lab was flooded with light. The room was set for an elegant dinner party, with waitresses dressed in formal attire. The city fathers got the point, and Edison got his power lines.

Objective

To explore external factors that can influence your task. To identify the elements of the larger world of which your task is a part. To play with these elements with an eye toward improving the context and finding solutions.

How to Do It

Diagram the Big Picture around your task on a sheet of paper. What forces, factors, requirements, constraints, and elements are at work?

Add new elements to your Big Picture. You might explore what could happen if you added, say, a double shift to your system. What would happen if you changed two or three forces or requirements at one time? What ideas does it generate?

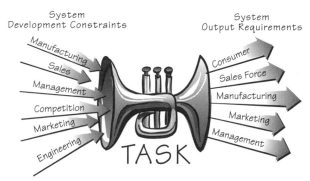

Look again at your system diagram. If all system constraints and requirements were met, the system would be in equilibrium. Now, make a dramatic change to one of the forces acting on your system, sending your system into chaos.

To return equilibrium, make the necessary changes to the other forces. This means some constraints will have to be removed or modified. Once you regain balance, look at the newly created system. How does it look? Does it work? Can you see new opportunities?

Edison in Action

When I launched Richard Saunders International, Eureka! Stimulus Response wasn't the only entrée on my menu. I had to invent AcuPOLL as well. Having a system for inventing thirty ideas for a client in thirty days was of little value if clients had no objective way of knowing whether their customers would buy the ideas. Eureka! Stimulus Response could not survive as an island. It had to function in a larger context.

To be successful, Richard Saunders International had to offer a revolutionary research method as well as a revolutionary creative development system. This research method had to be fast, easy to understand, and able to provide accurate measurements of the consumer response to the ideas we would generate.

AcuPOLL fulfills all three requirements.

For speed, it uses a digital information-gathering computer network. Consumers log their reactions to new product ideas on individual computer keyboards, making it possible to gauge the probable success of thirty new product concepts in three hours—

compared to one concept in three months with traditional research methods.

Additionally, AcuPOLL results are easily grasped. Consumers grade concepts on a scale of 0 to 10. The numbers are then translated to letter grades, A to F. Wicked good ideas are A's; ill-conceived, misbegotten ideas show up as F's, no matter how new and different they may be.

As for accuracy, AcuPOLL's predictions of new product successes and failures have been shown to be correct 89 percent of the time.

The point is, AcuPOLL was the piece missing from a larger system. This same principle was applied when the Eveready Battery Company hired Richard Saunders International to develop a product we called the Eversafe Child Locater Smoke Detector.

We started with the task—to create a new smoke detector—and worked backward, looking at the larger world in which smoke detectors come into play. We began, as we often do, with the obvious questions, which quickly led to less obvious questions:

- *What do smoke detectors do?* Well, they detect smoke. Then they set off a high-pitched alarm to warn people in the house so they can do something about the smoke—or to wake them up so they can head for safety.
- *From a sensory perspective, what don't smoke detectors do?* They don't tap you on the shoulder, they don't carry you out of the house, and they don't light up.
- *Who do smoke detectors warn?* They warn people in the house, not the fire department or neighbors.
- *What if you're a person who is unable to move? What if you're a baby?* A high-pitched alarm isn't going to help you.
- *How could a smoke detector help them?* Maybe it tells other people they're trapped. A fireman, perhaps.
- *What if you take it outside the house? What if you could show a fireman a child's location before he enters the house?* A siren on the outside of the house might work. But a flashing light in the child's window would probably be better.

We thought so, anyway. We engineered a two-part system that included a smoke detector and a separate flashing light that mounted on the window. The client liked it, too.

CHAPTER 207

Franklin Funnel

At some point in your life, usually when your mouth was too full and you looked like a squirrel storing nuts for the winter, you've been advised against biting off more than you can chew. That's the idea behind the Franklin Funnel Brain Programs.

Take a small bite, then chew thoughtfully. Isolate a little piece of the problem and concentrate on it. The idea is to focus on one small part of the task. To mull it over and let your thoughts smooth it like a pebble in a creek. To specialize. To savor, contemplate, and consider it an entity unto itself.

It's a good way to go inventing. Too often, inventors bite off too much. They try to create something that's all things to all people and ends up being nothing to anyone.

The truth is, if you claim complete and unconditional victory in one area, people will believe you can perform in other areas as well. Let's say you're interested in genetically engineering tomatoes in your basement. Instead of trying to create the world's greatest all-around champion tomato, focus on a small bite. Consider the different purposes a tomato can serve. Make your product the best tomato for salads. Or for ketchup. Or juice. Or spaghetti sauce. Or pizzas. Or throwing at politicians whose sentiments you don't share. Or heaving at mimes.

Franklin Funnels are about "er" and "est" claims—comparatives and superlatives. They're not about good. They're about being better at something. Or they're about being the best at one thing.

Be clearly superior. When you're the best at something, you're offering people a solid reason to buy whatever it is you're selling. It's much easier to get people to shout, "Hooray for you!" when you're the best at something. Franklin Funnel is a ready answer to the question "Why should I care?"

BRAIN PROGRAM #20: DO ONE THING GREAT

A Jack of all Trades rarely gets to be King.
RICHARD SAUNDERS

This program is the shortest distance to blunt, highly concentrated, only-a-complete-idiot-could-miss-the-point focusing. It's a shortcut to locating and exploiting your advantages. It will give you new ways to define your assets and help you focus energy on the ones that can make you great.

284

Objective

To isolate one or two facets of the task you can use to burn hotter and shine more brightly than anyone. Do One Thing Great is a fast track to establishing:

- A clear point of difference between you and everyone else
- An area where you can make more money
- An area where consumers aren't fully satisfied
- An opportunity for growth
- An area of technological opportunity
- An area that's more fun
- A direction where no one has gone
- An area where you could stake your claim

How to Do It

The *Guinness Book of World Records* is a mother lode of ideas for ways to Do One Thing Great. Essentially, you want to carve out a niche. To do so, you must corner a superlative. But which one?

Identify areas of exploration that hold the greatest potential—areas you're itching to probe, poke, or push. You can be more trivial in your areas of exploration, since Do One Thing Great is oriented more toward breadth than depth. It's designed to flush out first instincts about lots of different areas, to cover a broad mountain range rather than concentrate on a single foothill.

List every asset you have, the small and the big, the fabulous and the silly. Fill an entire page using both broad and specific categories.

Give each asset an award—Most Exciting, Most Unexpected Yet Appealing, Most Wild and Crazy, Easiest, Most Popular with Your Kids, Most Traditional, Most Like the Competitor, Most Likely to Make Sales Shoot Through the Roof, Most Likely to

Make the Boss Jump out a Window, to cite a few examples. Be generous. Make sure every aspect gets an award.

Now go back through the assets and awards. Select the ones you most want to apply to your task.

Do One Thing Great in Action

When I was a high school junior in Nashua, New Hampshire, I was looking for a way to whip up a dose of inexpensive publicity for my magic show. A short time earlier, a big-time magician named Doug Henning had scored some significant press with a highly touted stunt whereby he levitated a woman atop the World Trade Center, having billed the feat as "The Highest Levitation in the World."

I could levitate people—at least, I knew how to make it look like they were levitating. I knew how to make it look like they were levitating at all sorts of altitudes. Henning had already done the highest in the world; that was his superlative.

I didn't have the financial wherewithal to travel to a higher spot than the Trade Center, which meant I couldn't do the highest levitation in the world. Not in the world as we know it. But I could narrow the venue and, within somewhat more limited confines, achieve highest-ness. I could bring it closer to home.

The tallest building in my world in those days was the Nashua Furniture Barn. It was a magnificent structure: seven stories of sofas, bedroom suites, armchairs, end tables, and dinette sets. It was also one of the tallest buildings in all of Nashua, New Hampshire.

My friend, Mark Armstrong, and my lovely assistant, Sue Shumway, helped me lug a table to its roof. Sue stretched out on the table and I levitated her a height of nearly thirty-six inches. I promoted it as "The Highest Levitation in New Hampshire."

In a rather small niche, it was a shining example of Doing One Thing Great. And it served its purpose. The *Manchester Union Leader* ran a story and a picture.

Ken Eilers is an example of someone else who Does One Thing Great. Around Cincinnati, he's known as The Screen Guy. He drives a screenmobile with the slogan WE SCREEN AT YOUR PLACE stenciled on both sides.

Ken travels around the Cincinnati metroplex and "screens." Screens are his life. If you ask him to help you hang a window box or trim a sill, he shakes his head and says, "Sorry. All I do is screens. That's it."

It is, too. Ken installs window screens, door screens, screens for screened-in porches, and sun screens. He doesn't screen films and he doesn't screen calls. But those are different kinds of screens.

> *I don't want to compare myself to a brain surgeon. But if you only do one thing, you tend to get good.*
> KEN EILERS,
> The Screen Guy

You get the idea. So do his customers. He has established himself as an expert in one thing—screens—and because of his expertise in that area, he's able to charge more. If you want to leave your windows open without having to worry about bugs flying into your house, he's the man to call. Otherwise, he can't help you.

BRAIN PROGRAM #21: BE #1

Like Do One Thing Great, Be #1 is heavy on firsts, mosts, and words ending in "est." How could you become the fastest? The cleanest? The lightest? The safest? The easiest to use? The most fun to use? The sexiest? The most responsible? The most environmentally conscious? The richest? The most decadent? The shiniest? The brightest? The coolest?

Unlike Do One Thing Great, Be #1 doesn't tell you where your strengths are. It shows you what your greatness could be.

Objective

To help you chart your area of brilliance, which is anyplace you can wear the halo. To help you settle on a superlative and plan a route for making it happen. Remember—there are as many ways to Be #1 as there are adjectives in the dictionary.

How to Do It

Consider the various components of your task. What is it now? Make a list of the obvious and the less obvious, the big and the small. Arrange these pieces under the heading "What It Is Now."

Add an "est" or "The Best ..." to each piece and transform it into a winner under a second heading, "Be #1." Address each piece under a third heading, "Ways to Realize."

Say you're inventing a new toilet bowl cleaner. Your Be #1 sheet could look like this:

What It Is Now	Be #1	Ways to Realize
• Fragrant	Best smelling	Add Chanel #5
• A toilet seat cleaner	The best cleaner	Build a brush into the bottle
• A sanitizer	The most sanitizing	Changes color when germs are dead

Bulge and build on each of the items in the best list. Which are proprietary, original, exciting, gold medal winners? Repeat the exercise listing new-to-the world benefits that might be offered. To build on the previous example:

What It Could Be	Be #1	Ways to Realize
• Safe for pets and babies	Safest for everybody	Organic formulation
• Fun to use	The most fun to use	Add multicolor swirl dyes

Be #1 in Action

Inventing is not all fun and games. The Richard Saunders team frequently has to work through the night, consuming a huge tankard of coffee. In fact, we drink so much coffee we decided to create our own bean blend.

We wanted something powerful, something that could enliven the dullest of brains, transform a concept-weary zombie into a fireball of enthusiasm, and raise Jimmy Hoffa from the Meadowlands.

We had a name—Brain Brew. But what was it? We thought, hey, let's make it This World's Greatest Coffee. And let's make it true by blending some of the greatest coffees in the world: java from Java, pure Colombian high-grown Guatemalan, and Tanzanian. The flavor was amazing and the Tanzanian gave our Brain Brew an extra aromatic kick, making it a legitimate Invention Elixir.

We package Brain Brew and give it to clients so they can take a little Eureka! Mansion's energy home. More importantly, when our eyelids droop and our fingers pause over the keyboards, we're able to use it to medicate ourselves. Details on how you too can get some Brain Brew are provided in the back of the book. (What a blatant self-promotion!)

BRAIN PROGRAM #22: PIN PRICKS

Sometimes the best ideas are right there under your competition's nose.

Ouch! What's the single most annoying move you could make as far as your competitors are concerned? What would really cheese them off? Frost their shorts? Stick in their craw?

Pin Pricks is an exercise that brings out the vampire in you. But beware—it can turn timid, tame innocents into bloodthirsty barbarians.

Objective

To spot vulnerabilities elsewhere and turn them into advantages in your own backyard. To engage in one-upmanship. To make the other guy gnash his teeth, pull out his hair, and curse the day he was born.

How to Do It

Identify potential candidates for Pin Pricking. List anyone with whom you compete for dollars, time, or attention. Select a specific target. Map out a plan of action to gig your rival in any one or more of the following ways:

- What is your competition's greatest source of pride?
- Who could endorse your effort and, in so doing, most annoy your competition?
- How could you change your product to annoy the competition?
- What customers could you steal to most annoy them?
- How could you irritate the competition by changing pricing and sizing?
- What element of its product, package, marketing plan, or advertising could you learn from?
- What humorous or outrageous claim could you make to drive the competition crazy?
- How could you shame them into taking steps they'd rather not?

Pin Pricks in Action

Spic & Span Pine had exceeded all its goals during the first year of its test market effort in St. Louis. It was ready to go national. There is a tendency among the sales staff in such cases to rest on their ample laurels and lighten up in the second year. My task was to keep the sales people excited.

At the same time, Mr. Clean, also a Procter & Gamble product, was about to launch a "new and improved" version in the same market. The question for me was, How could I most annoy Mr. Clean and own the hearts and souls of our joint sales people?

A dinner meeting for the sales staff was scheduled where I would make my pitch and the guy with Mr. Clean would make his. Before the dinner, the sales folk had planned a softball game. I flew to St. Louis three hours early with neon-colored baseball caps with the Spic & Span Pine logo displayed prominently above the brims, which I distributed in a sort of impromptu pregame ceremony.

When the Mr. Clean guy showed up at the game, all the sales people were sporting my headgear. He was beaming when he arrived. Then he saw the hats. Oh, how I wish I had before and after photographs to document the change in his expression!

That evening when we were making our presentations, I announced the Spic & Span Diamond Anniversary promotion plan to put a one-third-carat diamond or cubic zirconium in every box and bottle of the product in time for Valentine's Day. This, too, came as a surprise to the Mr. Clean guy.

The upshot is that, during its second year, Spic & Span Pine easily surpassed its sales objectives in the St. Louis market. Indeed, the sales staff was so highly charged that the momentum of Spic & Span Pine helped push Mr. Clean over the top, too.

BRAIN PROGRAM #23: SKYBRIDGING

You can Jump Start Your Brain by putting your head in the clouds. I call it Skybridging. It's a system that allows you to work your way to your objective in forward and reverse. In technical circles, it's called reverse engineering.

Real World Adults often are under the impression that only one road leads through the wilderness—that is, the road their plodding feet travel most often. In fact, there are almost always many roads, but they go unnoticed, untried, or undiscovered.

Objective

To help you discover more realistic as well as more imaginative solutions to your task. To help you see that the Yellow Brick Road isn't the only road to your goal. To help you find your way to the seemingly impossible goal.

How to Do It

On the left side of a sheet of paper, define, in a nut, where you are today. At the far right-hand side of the sheet, describe where you want to be. What is your personal Valhalla?

Fill in the steps you need to take to get from Today to the Ideal Tomorrow. The most practical path is a rigid horizontal line. The more impractical steps will carry you farther up into the sky, arching away from reality, then back down as you approach your goal. Try different trajectories with varying degrees of practicality.

Travel the Skybridge in both directions, forward and backward. It's sometimes easier to start at the end and work backward. If you get stuck using the closer-to-earth trajectory, take a step into thin air. Try a higher trajectory, using steps that are vaguely inconceivable. Continue upward, up into the clouds. Once you've reached the apex, bring your idea back to earth. You may be surprised at how much more achievable your idea seems once you can see how to get there from here.

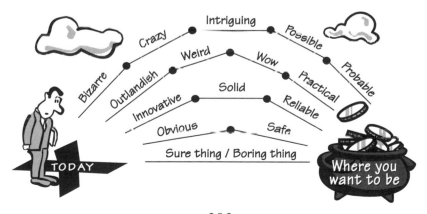

Skybridging in Action

Skybridging did the job on a project to invent a new hot beverage. At the left side of the page, "Today" was defined as "Coffee, Tea, and Cocoa." At the far right end of the spectrum was the pot of gold, "New Hot Beverage."

The first horizontal practical bridge connecting point A to point B looked like this:

Coffee, Tea, and Cocoa—Microwave—Flavored Cocoas—Individual Servings—Colored Marshmallows—New Hot Beverage

A second, slightly convex and slightly less practical bridge followed these stepping-stones:

Coffee, Tea, and Cocoa—Menthol Tea—Self-Contained Disposable Teapots—Built-in Bags—Turn Coffee Makers into Fountain Vendors—New Hot Beverage

A third steeper, more outlandish bridge followed this sequence of thoughts:

Coffee, Tea, and Cocoa—Cocoa in Teabags—Brew a Whole Pot at a Time—Cocoabags that Fit in Coffee Makers—New Hot Beverage

The envelope, please. And the winner? Bridge No. 3!
We called the product Coco Loco.
"Fresh-Brewed Hot Chocolate from Your Coffee Machine," the copy read.
"Now you and your family can enjoy genuine fresh-brewed hot chocolate. Each convenient one-pot filter pack contains genuine ground cocoa beans, Madagascar vanilla beans, and other natural ingredients. In Dark Chocolate, Milk Chocolate, and Chocolate Coffee."
The highest bridge is almost always the best bridge to take, even if it doesn't make the most sense on the surface. Still, it's bound to be the most new and different.

CHAPTER 208

Dr. Disecto

Dr. Disecto is half insane. Dr. Disecto exists solely to hack entities of all kinds into piles of small throbbing, squishy parts. He has a fetish for breaking down whatever crosses his path into their constituent pieces.

> *When I'm stuck for an idea or solution, I try to look at the problem from a different perspective. Tear it apart; turn it upside down.*
> TONY BEVILACQUA,
> Vice President, Marketing
> Eveready Battery Company, Canada

BRAIN PROGRAM #24: DR. DISECTO

Dr. Disecto is an adaptable fellow. The format works with all kinds of tasks.

Objective

To transform your challenge into a solution by applying Dr. Disecto phrases to it.

How to Do It

The process is simple. Add a phrase from one of the Dr. Disecto sample lists at the end of Brain Program #25 to your task, force the two to apply to each other, and out comes an idea. Use as many phrases from as many lists as you like. In mathematical terms, this Brain Program works like this:

$$\text{Task} + \text{Dr. Disecto Pharse} = \text{Eureka! Inventing}$$

To help you assemble your phrases, just go through the Dr. Disecto lists at the end of the next Brain Program and pick out any that relate to your task. Don't be too picky—pick any list that is even remotely related. Here are the main phrase categories to make your search easier:

A. *Geography*
B. *People and Their Parts*
C. *Sensory*
D. *Nature and Science*
E. *That's Entertainment*
F. *Things to Do*
G. *Money and Business*

H. *Intangibles*
I. *Substances*
J. *Product Engineering*
K. *Events*
L. *Home, Friends, and Family*
M. *Actions and Movement*
N. *Wild Cards*

For variety's sake, pick a few numbers from the Dr. Disecto Phrase catalog at random—your choices range from No. 1 to No. 1,090—and add the corresponding phrases to your list. Finally, think of a few custom-made directives that apply solely to your problem.

Take a deep breath and begin force-associating your task with the first Dr. Disecto directive. Just add them together and see what you get. Bend them and twist them until they make sense. Once you're finished, move on to the next directive. Make yourself do each directive. It won't be easy, but you can do it. Keep in mind that the longest stretches usually produce the best results.

Dr. Disecto in Action

Dr. Disecto was the wizard behind the curtain when a guy named Bob was looking for a way to save several million dollars a year in lost sales revenues.

Bob made his living selling chemicals used to print newspapers. He was pretty good at it, too. In fact, he was his company's national sales leader. But he had a colossal problem. One day, he dropped by the Eureka! Mansion to talk about it.

The nature of Bob's product required him to provide serious helpings of technical assistance to his customers. He was having no problem serving his big accounts in major cities. But it was a different story with his smaller customers in the hinterlands. He couldn't tap these lesser markets because his staff simply couldn't get to them as often as they were needed. And it was costing him plenty.

I decided to consult the good Dr. Disecto. My first step was to review the list of categories. This seemed to be a task for category G, *Money and Business* (see Dr. Disecto lists at the end of this chapter).

My next step was to review the list of subject areas included in category G. This led me to Dr. Disecto phrases #611 to #620.

Improving Services
611. Improve your hours
612. Better response time
613. Make it more custom
614. More for the money
615. Sweat the details
616. Hand deliver
617. Mail thank-you notes

618. Enhance quality
619. Baker's dozen
620. Be more personal

We started with the first item on the list, Dr. Disecto phrase #611, Improve your hours. Then Bob and I engaged in a stream-of-consciousness conversation that took this course:

ME: "OK, let's look at ways to improve your hours."
BOB: "How?"
ME: "Give your customers instant service."
BOB: "What?"
ME: "Have a technician available for each printing plant."
BOB: "Can't do it."
ME: "Why?"
BOB: "It costs too much to get there."
ME: "Why?"
BOB: "They gotta drive. It's a long way."
ME: "What if we put a technician in each plant?"
BOB: "How?"
ME: "Beam them there, like they do in *Star Trek*."
BOB: "What do I look like, George Jetson?"
ME: "George Jetson with a Spacely Sprocket space phone."

Dr. Disecto had the answer. Bob's customers could sign a six-month contract for a free "Video Service Station" two-way video telephone service. When his customers had a production problem, they could press a button and a technical support person would instantly appear on the screen to solve it. Because now Bob's technicians could see the problems as soon as his clients did.

BRAIN PROGRAM #25:
DR. DISECTO MUTANT SURGERY

Don't look at the forest; look at the trees. Instead of drawing a bull's-eye on the whole, take aim at small pieces. Put your task under a microscope and consider how the components affect the Big Picture.

Objective

To shake out the bag, juggle its contents, and discover new and better ways to put them back together and make them work for you.

How to Do It

Divide your problem into its constituent parts and write them on a piece of paper, leaving lots of space between them. Next, rip the paper apart so that each piece of your problem has its own chunk of paper.

Take each torn piece and add one of the Disecto directives to it. Like this:

Piece of Task + Dr. Disecto Phrase = Idea

Mutate and modify each piece to invent new ideas, writing down ideas as you go. Apply several phrases to each of your task pieces.

Once you've performed mutant surgery on each part, put the paper back together and see what mutations can work together.

Dr. Disecto Mutant Surgery in Action

Dr. Disecto Mutant Surgery came into play in the development of a board game my friend Kip Knight and I called Pop Opinion.

One fall day in 1989, Kip and I were driving from Indianapolis to Cincinnati when we decided to create a game together and maybe make a few bucks. We began thinking out loud about the elements our task might include—as in *board, fun, more than one player, competition, scoring points, a roll of the dice, sand timer ...*

We started asking questions, responding with whatever answers came to mind. The sequence progressed thusly:

What makes a game fun? Friends getting together.
What do friends like to do when they get together? They eat, they talk.
About what? Sports, news, other people, their opinions. Everybody has an opinion.
Can friends guess friends' opinions? Depends on how well they know them.
What if they can't? Then they take a step back.
What about eating? Could the players eat the board? Then the board is gone.
What if they ate the pieces? Bite-size pieces.
What if the pieces were crackers? Too messy.
What if the pieces were popcorn? Not messy.
How about if you ate to win? The first to finish the pieces wins.

That exchange had us well on the way. Each player starts out with twenty pieces of popcorn. One player tosses the dice and selects an issue from one of 1,000 topic cards. The other players write down their top three opinions on the chosen topic. The first player then tries to divine the other players' opinions. Each correct guess entitles that player to chomp down on a piece of popcorn. Whoever gets through their popcorn first wins.

University Games licensed Pop Opinion and is in the process of introducing it around the country.

DR. DISECTO LISTS

A. Geography

Rooms	Terrains	Africa
1. Parlor	11. Alps	21. Tribe
2. Sauna	12. Sahara Desert	22. Sahara
3. Hallway	13. Mediterranean	23. Safari
4. Cellar	14. Manhattan skyline	24. Jungle
5. Boudoir	15. Rural routes	25. Lion
6. Laboratory	16. Lunar landscape	26. Tiger
7. Foyer	17. Everglades	27. Pride
8. Den	18. Grand Canyon	28. Rasta
9. Attic	19. Rainforest	29. Zulu
10. Breakfast nook	20. Antarctica	30. Medicine man

Asia
31. Tibetan monks
32. Oriental rug
33. Ming
34. Bamboo
35. Chopsticks
36. Saris
37. Curry
38. Marco Polo
39. Forbidden city
40. Himalayas

The West
41. Two-step
42. Conestoga wagon
43. Branding iron
44. Wanted
    dead or alive
45. Coyote howl
46. Cowboy poetry
47. Six-shooters
48. John Wayne
49. Chaps
50. Rodeo

Midwest
51. Great Plains
52. Heartland
53. Corn
54. Patriotic
55. Traditional
56. Mom and
    apple pie
57. Tract housing
58. Tractors
59. Breadbasket
60. Married with
    children

Northwest
61. Logging
62. Fishing
63. Seattle
64. Pine trees
65. Old growth
    forests
66. Granola
67. Constant rain
68. Flannel
69. Outdoor
    survival
70. Yellowstone

South
71. Plantation
72. Scarlett O'Hara
73. Mississippi River
74. Molasses
75. Spanish moss
76. Magnolia
77. Dixieland
78. Barbecue
79. Swanee River
80. Confederacy

Southwest
81. Adobe
82. Sagebrush
83. Tumbleweed
84. Saguaro cactus
85. Hypoallergenic
86. Indian motif
87. Dry heat
88. Colorado
    River
89. Turquoise
90. Mesas

Locales
91. San Francisco, CA
92. Liverpool, England
93. Washington, D.C.
94. Sydney, Australia
95. Atlanta, GA
96. Hometown, USA
97. Cicely, AK
98. Istanbul and Constantinople
99. Graceland, TN
100. New Orleans, LA

B. People and Their Parts

Target Audiences
101. Kids go krazy
102. For the mature
103. 90s consumers
104. Old-fashioned type
105. Penny pinchers
106. Fat cats
107. Trendy teenagers
108. Plain folk
109. Mr. Executive
110. Roseanne

Facial Features
111. Mustache
112. Plucked eyebrows
113. Warts
114. Cauliflower ear
115. Karl Malden's nose
116. Cleft lip
117. Dimple
118. Bright smile
119. Furrowed brow
120. Jowls

Body Styles
121. The Hulk
122. Linda Hamilton
123. Fatty Arbuckle
124. Pee-Wee Herman
125. Cadillac
126. Marilyn Monroe
127. Twiggy
128. Hulk Hogan
129. Jane Fonda
130. Kermit the Frog

New Age
131. Meditations
132. Crystals
133. Harmony
134. Eastern
135. Channeling
136. ESP
137. Organic
138. Inner child
139. Vegan
140. Visualization

Generation X
141. Flannel
142. Dumpster dive
143. Doc Martens
144. Espresso
145. In your face
146. Eastern religion
147. Grunge
148. Slacker
149. McJob
150. Live with parents

Modern Maturity
151. Geritol
152. Metamucil
153. Medicare
154. Condos
155. Winnebago
156. Grecian Formula
157. Cadillac
158. La-Z-Boy
159. Golden Girls
160. I've fallen and I can't get up!

Body Parts
161. Neck
162. Head bone
163. Elbows
164. Biceps
165. Belly button
166. Knees
167. Funny bone
168. Adam's apple
169. Shins
170. Big toe

Shoes
171. Sneakers
172. Patent leather
173. Hobnail boots
174. Wing tips
175. Pumps
176. Cowboy boots
177. Stilettos
178. Doc Martens
179. Keds
180. Loafers

C. Sensory

Textures
181. Grainy
182. Satiny
183. Glassy
184. Cottony
185. Sinewy
186. Gritty
187. Furry
188. Bumpy
189. Scratchy
190. Prickly

New Colors I
191. Neon
192. Flavoricious
193. Cosmetics
194. Gauze
195. Many layers
196. Chalk
197. Max out the spectrum
198. Invisible
199. Color therapy
200. Seasons

New Colors II
201. Color me beautiful
202. Exotic dyes
203. Naturals
204. Chameleon
205. Sports
206. Transparents
207. Opalescent
208. Watercolor
209. Oils
210. Rose-colored glasses

New Colors III
211. Chartreuse
212. Burgundy
213. Grape
214. Burnt sienna
215. Tan
216. Olive
217. Canary
218. Hazel
219. Pearl
220. Teal

Aroma Action
221. Max out a skunk
222. Max out roses
223. Exotic spices
224. Mom's cooking
225. Aromatherapy
226. Tie a scent to a place
227. The smell of Mars
228. Bring back memories
229. Clear the sinuses
230. Rainfall fresh

Scents
231. Sandalwood
232. Zanzibar
233. Prom corsage
234. Clover
235. Sulfur
236. Juniper
237. Armpit
238. Firecracker
239. Orange blossom
240. Snow

Shapes
241. Thin
242. Circle
243. Triangle
244. Blob
245. Blemish
246. Droplet
247. Oval
248. Orb
249. Block
250. Long

Sounds
251. Crackle
252. Squeak
253. Grunt
254. Squirt
255. Pop
256. Bang
257. Burst
258. Smooch
259. Shriek
260. Scratch

Flavor Action
261. Country store
262. Italian ices
263. Super sour
264. Spice a fruit
265. Regionalize it
266. Concentrate it
267. Liquors
268. Make it farm fresh
269. Bubble gum it
270. Relaxation

Fun Flavors
271. Mango
272. Pomegranate
273. Ginger
274. Curry
275. Bing cherry
276. Plantains
277. Sassafras
278. Avocado
279. Gooseberry
280. Pine nut

Tastes
281. Hot
282. Sour
283. Salty
284. Sweet
285. Spicy
286. Fermented
287. Rancid
288. Bitter
289. Rich
290. Tart

D. Science and Nature

Science
291. Shrink the computer
292. Brain surgery
293. Genetic engineering
294. 1984
295. Rocket science
296. Microscope
297. Chaos theory
298. *Star Trek*
299. Animal talk
300. Laser optics

Trees
301. Oak
302. Willow
303. Coconut
304. Apple
305. Olive
306. Pine
307. Joshua
308. American chestnut
309. Sequoia
310. Aspen

Bugs
311. Bunny
312. Mosquito
313. Honeybee
314. Tarantula
315. Scarab
316. Butterfly
317. The Beatles
318. Termites
319. Charlotte's Web
320. Computer bugs

Forces of Nature
321. Tornado
322. Blizzard
323. Heat wave
324. Santa Ana winds
325. Earth quake
326. Lightning
327. Tsunami
328. Monsoons
329. Jet stream
330. Glaciers

Go Natural
331. Make like a tree
332. Give it wings
333. Make it hibernate
334. Seasons
335. Give it natural selection
336. Shape it like a pine tree
337. Make it simple like a daisy
338. Give it a sound like a stream
339. Reproduce like rabbits
340. Max out its crunch

Plants
341. Fern
342. Venus flytrap
343. Bloodroot
344. Bonsai
345. Ginseng
346. Jade plant
347. Witch hazel
348. African violet
349. Nightshade
350. Spider plant

E. That's Entertainment

Heroes
351. Zorro
352. Batman
353. Capt. Kirk
354. Arnold
355. Elvis
356. Moe or Curly
357. Wonder Woman
358. Babe Ruth
359. Christ
360. Wile E. Coyote

Monsters
361. The Blob
362. Dracula
363. IRS
364. Wicked Witch of the West
365. Jack the Ripper
366. Godzilla
367. The Elephant Man
368. Lurch
369. Frankenstein
370. Mothers-in-law

Superstars
371. Pete Rose
372. Madonna
373. Jimi Hendrix
374. Beethoven
375. Harry Truman
376. Magic Johnson
377. Andy Warhol
378. Al Capone
379. Jim Morrison
380. Henry Kissinger

Act II: Eureka! Stimulus Response Explosion

TV Tribute
381. *The Ed Sullivan Show*
382. *Cheers*
383. *The Simpsons*
384. *Saturday Night Live*
385. *Jeopardy!*
386. MTV
387. *Donahue*
388. *Bonanza*
389. *Mr. Wizard*
390. *I Love Lucy*

Movies
391. *Gone With the Wind*
392. *Lethal Weapon*
393. *Night of the Living Dead*
394. *Stand By Me*
395. *Wizard of Oz*
396. *Terminator*
397. *Naked Gun*
398. *Faces of Death*
399. *Citizen Kane*
400. *The Little Mermaid*

In the Media
401. *60 Minutes*
402. *Boy's Life*
403. *Soldier of Fortune*
404. *National Enquirer*
405. *Rolling Stone*
406. *Cosmopolitan*
407. *Reader's Digest*
408. *Oprah Winfrey*
409. *Modern Maturity*
410. *USA Today*

Cartoon Pals
411. Mickey Mouse
412. Bullwinkle
413. Foghorn Leghorn
414. Daffy Duck
415. Flash Gordon
416. Betty Rubble
417. Speedracer
418. Papa Smurf
419. The Dwarves
420. Snoopy

More Cartoon Pals
421. Ren and Stimpy
422. Smurfs
423. Bart Simpson
424. Bugs Bunny
425. Garfield
426. Steamboat Willy
427. Betty Boop
428. Toucan Sam
429. Teenage Mutant Ninja Turtles
430. Scooby Do

Music
431. Classical
432. Folk
433. Techno
434. Grunge
435. Jazz
436. Big band
437. Calypso
438. Country
439. Reggae
440. Rock and roll

Music Maestros
441. Vivaldi
442. Joan Baez
443. Jimi Hendrix
444. Nirvana
445. Doc Severinsen
446. Bob Marley
447. Lawrence Welk
448. Billy Ray Cyrus
449. Rolling Stones
450. The Beatles

F. Things to Do

Kid's Entertainment
451. Play games
452. Fresh air
453. Get wet or muddy
454. Tell stories
455. Bake cookies
456. Make a tape
457. Make crafts
458. Explore old trunks
459. Make believe
460. Lemonade stand

Relax
461. Bubble bath
462. Caribbean island
463. Soap opera
464. Baby-sitter
465. Massage
466. Deep breath
467. Chill out
468. Car drive
469. Hobby
470. Woods

Happy Feet
471. Cha-cha
472. Slam dance
473. Swan Lake
474. Jitterbug
475. Do-si-do
476. Two-step
477. Charleston
478. The swim
479. Minuet
480. Tango

Beating Boredom
481. Rent a wild movie
482. Do something artistic
483. Go to nature
484. Craft a wild food
485. Bake wild stuff
486. Be a tourist
487. Have a water fight
488. Play a practical joke
489. Take a class
490. Join a Nonprofit Group

All About Athletics
491. Contact
492. Individual
493. Cheerleading
494. Spectator
495. All-stars
496. Competition
497. Statistics
498. Injury
499. Championships
500. Uniforms

Sports
501. Hockey
502. Tennis
503. Curling
504. Skiing
505. Soccer
506. Baseball
507. Golf
508. Trail biking
509. Crew
510. Football

Ways to Wake Up
511. Coffee
512. Electric shock
513. Take a nap
514. Go outside
515. Change rooms
516. Play music
517. Take a shower
518. Do the sunrise
519. Play a video game
520. Call a 900 number

Vacations
521. Feel it hot, hot, hot
522. Exercise
523. Education
524. Road trip
525. Elvis last tour
526. Robin Leach videos
527. Survival skills
528. Dude ranch
529. Foreign languages
530. Festivals

Car Trip Activities
531. Songs
532. Counting
533. Cards
534. Competition
535. Crayons
536. Sightseeing books
537. Etch-A-Sketch
538. Cameras
539. Make a book on tape
540. Alphabet game

Home Alone
541. Create food
542. Film festival
543. Crank calls
544. Good books
545. Write
546. Old friends
547. Channel surf
548. Self spa
549. Fix it
550. Clean

Themes
551. Wild West
552. Swingin' 70s
553. Blasphemy
554. Whine & cheez
555. Mardi Gras
556. Hollywood
557. Opposite day
558. Suburbia
559. Movie madness
560. Kentucky Derby

Getting Into College
561. SAT tutoring
562. Alumni
563. Interviewing
564. Volunteer work
565. Resume service
566. Illustrate your essay
567. Send a sample
568. Talk to students
569. GI Bill
570. Newspaper clippings

G. Money and Business

Making More Money
571. Raise prices
572. Lower costs
573. Sell more at once
574. Get new customers
575. Sell faster
576. Expand services
577. Get repeat business
578. Get another job
589. Go on a strict diet
590. Trade with others

Fund-raising
591. Silent auction
592. Celebrity night
593. Carnival
594. Beauty workshops
595. Speaker series
596. Balloon rides
597. Sell snacks in cafeteria
598. Computer exchange
599. Marathon
600. Telethon

Making More Money at Home
601. Baby-sit
602. Catering
603. Accounting
604. Entering contests
605. Coupons
606. Illustrate
607. Crafts
608. Computers
609. Avon
610. Repairs

Improving Services
611. Improve your hours
612. Better response time
613. Make it more custom
614. More for the Money
615. Sweat the details
616. Hand deliver
617. Mail thank-you notes
618. Enhance quality
619. Baker's dozen
620. Be more personal

Inventing Names
621. Name after a person
622. Name after a place
623. Articulate the benefit
624. Use a nonsense word
625. Use numbers and letters
626. Make it rhyme
627. Use an established icon
628. License a name
629. Use a foreign language
630. Use a long, long name

Where to Find Stimuli
631. Go to the library
632. Videos
633. Ask your mother
634. Follow a child
635. Ask a consumer
636. Grocery stores
637. Visit a construction site
638. Visit the mall
639. Survey a college class
640. Watch it being made

More Stimuli Sources

641. Watch more TV
642. Infomercials
643. Hire your competitor
644. Go to a PTA meeting
645. Go to the plant
646. Ask the youngest employee you have
647. Ask the oldest employee you have
648. Go to a retirement home
649. Buy trade magazines in your own trade
650. Buy trade magazines in another trade

H. Intangibles

Emotions	Motivations	Punctuation
651. Joy	661. Greed	671. ?
652. Fear	662. Money	672. !
653. Loathing	663. Sex	673. .
654. Anxiety	664. Fame	674. /
655. Giddiness	665. Peace of mind	675. &
656. Shock	666. Personal growth	676. ()
657. Sadness	667. Attention	677. ;
658. Love	668. Jealousy	678. ,
659. Regret	669. Goodwill	679. " "
660. Awe	670. Popularity	680. :

Symbols	American Icons
681. American flag	691. Statue of Liberty
682. Madison Avenue	692. Bald eagle
683. Ball and chain	693. Cowboys
684. Electric guitar	694. '57 Chevy
685. Crucifix	695. Log cabin
686. Lightbulb	696. Confederate flag
687. Hammer and sickle	697. The Capitol
688. Christmas tree	698. "We the people ..."
689. Convertible	699. Betsy Ross
690. Snake	700. Fireworks

I. Substances

Liquids
701. Juice
702. Oil
703. Syrup
704. Niagara
705. Milk
706. Splash
707. Drip
708. Shampoo
709. Coffee
710. Rain

Fuel
711. Petrol
712. Peat moss
713. Coffee
714. Plutonium
715. Oxygen
716. Cheeseburger
717. Trees
718. Coal
719. Liquid
    hydrogen
720. Cheerleading

Material World
721. Ugly
722. Soft and squishy
723. Bubble plastic
724. Spray on
725. Recycled
726. Hard as nails
727. Crystal
728. Pliable
729. Rigid
730. Temperature
    extremes

Materials I
731. Rubber
732. Steel
733. Sand
734. Silicone
745. Water
746. Gel
747. Graphite
748. Teflon
749. Cork
750. Wood

Materials II
751. Sandalwood
752. Leather
753. Plastic
754. Cardboard
755. Paper
756. Nylon
757. Chain mail
758. Foil
759. Marble
760. Netting

For the Carnivore
761. Beef
762. Free-range chicken
763. Turkey
764. Venison
765. Pork
766. Veal
767. Rabbit
768. Duck
769. Pheasant
770. Steak

Meat Products
771. Slim Jim
772. Smoked
    sausage
773. Jerky
774. Hot dog
775. Ground beef
776. Nuggets
777. Lunch meat
778. Gravy
779. Fish sticks
780. Patties

Cuts of Meat
781. Prime
782. T-Bone
783. Strip
784. Loin
785. Rump
786. Breast
787. Flank
788. Filet
789. Chuck
790. Steak

Booze It Up
791. Peppermint
    schnapps
792. Midori
793. Everclear
794. Moonshine
795. Vermouth
796. Champagne
797. Aged Scotch
798. Raspberry liqueur
799. Absolut
800. Grenadine

J. Product Engineering

Make It Fun
801. Slapstick
802. Practical jokes
803. Funny faces
804. Contradictions
805. Parody
806. Caricature
807. Make fun of
808. Sarcasm
809. Silly noises
810. Freakish facts

Make It Exciting
811. Add aroma
812. Make music
813. Add an element of surprise
814. Add a touch of romance
815. International flavor
816. Add an element of danger
817. Add anticipation
818. Make very emotional
819. Take your body to the limit
820. Enter a contest

Mechanical
821. Dovetail
822. Screw
823. Thread
824. Aerate
825. Lathe
826. Grind
827. Press
828. Mill
829. Corrugate
830. Puncture

Packaging
831. Canister
832. Value packs
833. Reusable
834. Recycle
835. Collector's item
836. Collapsible
837. See-through
838. Hangable
839. Part of the product
840. Ziploc

To the Max
841. Tastiest
842. Highest
843. Cheapest
844. Poshest
845. Farthest
846. Cutest
847. Freshest
848. Wisest
849. Youngest
850. Fun-est

Delivery Systems
851. Transdermal
852. Aerosol
853. Pump
854. Aqueducts
855. Dryer sheet
856. Squeeze tube
857. Federal Express
858. Pour spout
859. Grain silo
860. Air tubes

Mechanical Motion
861. Piston
862. Swing
863. Explode
864. Collapse
865. Spin
866. Fall
867. Pound
868. Jolt
869. Pry
870. Sway

Energy
871. Solar
872. Oil
873. Electric
874. Wind up
875. Rubber band
876. Wind
877. Hydroelectric
878. Geothermal
879. Battery
880. Pull string

Fasteners
881. Glue
882. Rubber cement
883. Hinge
884. Book binder
885. Grommet
886. Rivet
887. Snap
888. Velcro
889. Carpet tacks
890. Paper clip

Closures
891. Zip lock
892. Resealable
893. Balloon disk
894. Milk carton
895. Flip top
896. Drawstring
897. Zipper
898. Button
899. Vacuum hatch
900. Hermetic

K. Events

Occasions
901. Halloween
902. Easter
903. Fourth of July
904. Winter
905. May Day
906. President's
   Day
907. Groundhog
   Day
908. Birthday
909. Homecoming
910. April Fools'

Days of the Week
911. Sunday morning
912. Payday
913. Monday
   morning
914. Saturday
   afternoon
915. TGIF
916. Hump day
917. Saturday night
918. Wash day
919. Saturday
   morning
920. Friday the 13th

Goose Bumps
921. Bungee jumping
922. A walk through
   The Bronx
923. Cemetery at
   midnight
924. Roller coaster
925. Tightrope walking
926. Saying "I do"
927. Listening to
   Pavarotti
928. Watching *Psycho*
929. Someone's out
   there
930. Climbing a
   ladder

First Times
931. First kiss
932. First child
933. First day in kindergarten
934. First day of work
935. First driver's license
936. First steps
937. First night of wedded bliss
938. First pet
939. First tooth
940. First Social Security check

L. Home, Friends, and Family

Lighting
941. Neon
942. Flood
943. LCD
944. Black light
945. Candle
946. Fluorescent
947. Sunlight
948. Flashlight
949. Starlight
950. Spotlight

Fences
951. Invisible
952. Chicken wire
953. Picket
954. Barbed wire
955. Chain-link
956. Hedge
957. Electric
958. Stone
959. Iron
960. Guardrail

Decor Styles
961. Art deco
962. Victorian
963. Cubist
964. Impressionist
965. Egyptian
966. Native American
967. Celtic
968. Shaker
969. Minimalist
970. Bauhaus

Great Gift Elements
971. Gift certificate
972. Message delivery
973. Homemade
974. Ongoing
975. Raw materials
976. More, more, more
977. Charity
978. Fine arts
979. Sports
980. Themes

Great Gifts (Adults)
981. Mail-order catalog
982. Inside jokes
983. Dance lessons
984. Ferrari
985. A year's lawn service
986. Flowergrams
987. Tickets
988. Gallery gift certificate
989. VCR tapes
990. Masseuse

Great Gifts (Kids)
991. Their special day
992. Horseback riding
993. Puppet kits
994. Goldfish
995. Juggling set
996. Tape recorder
997. Day at work
998. Trip to Grandma's
999. Tree house
1000. Legos

M. Actions and Movement

Cooking Styles
1001. Fried
1002. Mesquite-grilled
1003. Flambé
1004. Ginsu-knifed
1005. Oven-baked
1006. Sun-dried
1007. Brewed
1008. Smoked
1009. Steamed
1010. Dutch oven

Transportation
1011. Subway
1012. Hang glider
1013. Unicycle
1014. Rolls-Royce
1015. *Starship Enterprise*
1016. Camel
1017. Roller blades
1018. Mom's chauffeur service
1019. Greyhound
1020. Scooter

Transportation II
1021. BMW
1022. Air Jordans
1023. Concorde Jet
1024. A litter
1025. Monorail
1026. Space shuttle
1027. Checker cab
1028. Tarzan's vine
1029. Barge
1030. Mack truck

Ingestion
1031. Sip
1032. Chug
1033. Nibble
1034. Chomp
1035. Intravenous
1036. Gobble
1037. Inhale
1038. Slurp
1039. Gulp
1040. Shotgun

Displays of Affection
1041. Kiss
1042. Squeeze
1043. Kick to the shin
1044. Hearty handshake
1045. Noogies
1046. Caress
1047. Flowers
1048. Longing glances
1049. Burping
1050. Pat on the back

Movement
1051. Zip
1052. Fly
1053. Sprint
1054. Disappear
1055. Blur
1056. Drift
1057. Sail
1058. Waltz
1059. Jog
1060. Leap

N. Wild Cards

Miscellanea	More Miscellanea	Even More Miscellanea
1061. Puppet shows	1071. Beam me up	1081. Team
1062. Coffee, tea, or me	1072. Fun, fun, fun	1082. Flip-flops
	1073. Party with a purpose	1083. Shampoo
1063. Atomic bomb		1084. Call waiting
1064. Birthday cakes	1074. Davenport	1085. Winter wonderland
1065. Submarine	1075. Queen bee	
1066. Baptist preachers	1076. Monster truck	1086. Elijah the prophet
	1077. Michelangelo	
1067. Redwood forest	1078. 2,000 flushes	1087. Oregon Trail
	1079. Hammerhead	1088. "X" marks the spot
1068. Joker, smoker	1080. Germany	
1069. School bus		1089. Mouse
1070. Mouseketeers		1090. Tractors

BRAIN PROGRAM #26: DR. VANGUNDY'S P.I.C.L. LIST

Another method for listing attributes and using them to shape the skyline is Dr. Arthur VanGundy's Product Improvement Check List.

I've tried every computer program and device to enhance creative thinking I could find. Most are too slow or too boring or unreliable. P.I.C.L. works. It's easy to understand, easy to use, and effective.

Available in poster form, the list contains more than 700 stimuli. If you'd like a P.I.C.L. List to call your own, call me at the Eureka! Mansion (513-271-9911) and I'll forward your request to Dr. VanGundy.

> *The human mind thinks of ideas using chains of associations. Many of these associations arise from random thoughts, with one concept leading to another. A simple illustration would be how we view an object such as a tree. Right away, the tree prompts us to think of any number of associations. We might think of leaves, then tables, then chairs, then eating, and so forth. The P.I.C.L. process builds on this tendency of the mind to free-associate by channeling your associations to resolve a problem. You select a word at random and then consider how the concept might suggest a solution.*
>
> ARTHUR B. VANGUNDY, PH.D.,
> University of Oklahoma

The P.I.C.L. poster is divided into two parts. BASIC P.I.C.L. contains 102 questions oriented toward improving products, organized in such categories as:

Who ...
• uses it?
• doesn't use it?
• would never even try it?

What ...
• are its most important features?
• do customers suggest?
• is altered by consumers?

Where ...
• is it used?
• is it stored?
• is it first tried by consumers?

When ...
• is it liked most?
• is it misused?
• couldn't it be used?

Why ...
• is it better than a competitor's product?
• do people stop using it?
• was it developed?

The second part of the poster is called P.I.C.L. JUICE, a compilation of some 600 idea triggers divided into four categories, each capable of spurring new thoughts and associations by the wheelbarrow. Here are a few samples:

Try to ...
• bend it
• inject it
• divide it
• weave it
• assemble it

Make it ...
• adjustable
• pocket size
• self-destruct
• grow
• portable

- spread it
- wind it up
- dehydrate it
- ventilate it
- dissolve it

- collapsible
- magnetic
- unbreakable
- striped
- triangular

Think of ...
- genetic research
- hot coffee
- credit cards
- televisions
- rain
- turtles
- toothpaste
- banks
- disappearing ink
- silent alarms

Take away or add ...
- handles
- turbulence
- ball bearings
- baskets
- padding
- pipes
- elastic
- keys
- accessories
- decorations

My compatriot, David Wecker, used a P.I.C.L.-like process to do some lifting one day when he and a friend, Terry Sawyer, were dismantling an old log house to reassemble on the Wecker compound in Kentucky.

A piece of equipment they'd planned to use to lower the oak logs one at a time from the house and load onto Terry's 1951 International flatbed had broken down. Each log weighed anywhere from 400 to 500 pounds and, at least at the beginning, would have to be lowered from a height of about sixteen feet. The only tools they had were hammers, crowbars, a couple of ropes, some old boards, their backs, and their brains.

They sat down and contemplated their predicament over a pair of warm beers. They'd pretty much given up for the day and resigned themselves to finishing a case of beer when David started joking about "how Doug would do it."

In what Terry later told me was a scathing, derisive, elflike imitation of yours truly, David started rambling excitedly through one P.I.C.L. phrase after another. "Add ... Pipes!" David squeaked at one point. In the middle of a cheap laugh at my expense, the boys realized they might have something.

"Pipes" led to "channel," which led to "flow," which led to "fast," which led to "slow."

The logs couldn't be dropped because they would break. They couldn't be lowered straight down with ropes because they were too heavy. But was there a way to channel the logs' downward trajectory so that they could be lowered slowly enough to the ground without breaking on impact? Was there a way to adjust gravity's pull?

The boys leaned a half-dozen of the old boards at a forty-five-degree angle against one side of the house from one corner to the other. Then they tied a rope to either end of the topmost log and slowly lowered it down the boards. In this way, they were able to dismantle the whole cabin in about the same time it would have taken had the equipment they'd expected been in working order.

Sooner or later, the boys probably would have arrived at the idea of building a ramp on their own. But the P.I.C.L. List approach helped them get there faster.

CHAPTER 209

Borrowing Brilliance

Great thoughts are sometimes borrowed from other brains. At the Eureka! Mansion, we're an equal opportunity borrower.

Steal as much as you can. Don't reinvent the wheel. And don't think other people don't have any idea what you're going through. You'll find solutions to problems in all sorts of other fields if you just open your eyes. It's hard to do because, in your day-to-day job, you're forced to focus on business as usual. But if you can take a piece of your day and look at what another part of the world is doing, you'll be surprised at what you'll find.
DAVE HOWE,
Richard Saunders Technologies

Borrowing Brilliance is about taking principles and ideas from other fields and applying them to your task. I'm not suggesting plagiarism. I'm talking about searching for ideas in one category and putting them to work in another.

The wise man draws more knowledge from his enemies than the fool from his friends.

BEN FRANKLIN

Some of your best ideas may already have occurred to the other guy. This doesn't mean you can't tailor, tweak, and tuck them until they're truly your own. A clever observer can narrow the gap between himself and Big Time Corporate America. Let the competition spend the money on market research. By watching the other guy, you can learn what he knows. Granted, research tends to be based more on the past than the future. But by understanding the past and by understanding the competition's reasons for doing what it does, you can home in on the future like my two-year-old zeroing in on a plate of brownies.

A favorite source of information for our inventing efforts is the Marketing Intelligence Services new product database. The MIS computers are crammed with information on significant new products in hundreds of categories from hundreds of countries. We often request printouts of innovative products introduced in a particular category or related categories around the world during the previous five years. These printouts are awash with ideas. We also mine idea ore from the results of AcuPOLL Reports monthly tests of major new products.

The key to using this kind of data is to keep it simple. Focus on translating the information into trends, principles, and new ideas. Don't get swept up in the numbers.

BRAIN PROGRAM #27: WINNING WAYS

Winning Ways is a collection of Brain Programs aimed at borrowing brilliance from examples that people bump up against every day.

Winning Ways is a rich assortment of power sources for jumpstarting your brain. They pound with the pulse of the American attitude. They hinge on the premise that America is obsessed with the most, the biggest, and the

best—in short, that America loves a winner. The point is easily supported; our on-line search of newspaper abstracts turned up more than 11,000 articles with the word *best* in the headlines in 1991 and 1992.

Objective

To identify and leverage the principles of success that have been applied successfully in related and unrelated categories.

How to Do It

Assemble a Winning Ways list of superstars, models of perfection, or any item or person that inspires either respect or jealousy. You're looking for the best of the best. Now execute a Stimuli Two Step.

Step 1: Identify the traits and component parts of your Winning Way models that make them successful. Ask questions. Why does each model work? What does it do that's right? Where is its focus? What makes it different? What makes it a certifiable best? Look, too, for characteristics that the models have in common.

Step 2: Catapult from the elements identified in Step 1 to new feels and tocs of imagination.

A number of subsegments of Winning Ways can be applied to the creative process. Here are a half-dozen of my favorites:

1. Best of ...
You can glean inspiration from best-seller lists in the areas of literature, TV ratings, movies, and the various music categories. These lists are one of the most democratic methods I know of for getting a reading of the American consumer's view of life.

Let's say your mission is to invent a new coat hanger and your "best" stimulus list is the Nielsens top 10-rated TV shows. The process might run along these lines:

Top TV Show: Roseanne
Traits: Irreverent, loud, earthy, big, salty, disrespectful, working class, family.
Coat Hanger Idea Translation: Extra-strength coat hangers for large or bulky clothes.

Top TV Show: 60 Minutes
Traits: Exposes, shocks, champions the little guy, ambushes, confronts.
Coat Hanger Idea Translation: A hanger with a special heating tube that dries clothes still wet from the wash, thereby putting an end to scandalous shrinkage and the blight of dryer wrinkles.

2. Classic Themes for the Ages

Fads die quickly, but classic themes live forever. I'd rather build a new product around a theme that has endured for generations than tie it to a hot flash in the pop culture.

Classic themes for the ages are those you can remember from childhood. They're the ones that still apply today, and they'll still apply for your children's children.

Consider the *Star Wars* trilogy. Do the two robots strike you as vaguely reminiscent of other comedy teams where there was a fat guy and a skinny guy?

Look for themes and characteristics that have lasted for generations in your area of exploration and/or with your target customers.

In a search for a new candy product, the Richard Saunders team was asked to develop a five-pack for Air Heads chewy candy—and to do it in such a way that the value of the pack would be greater than the sum of the five pieces.

Each Air Head is a flat piece of taffy, about an inch wide and five inches long. A bit of Kitchen Chemistry experimenting found that Air Heads look like tongues when you leave them hanging from your mouth. Couching this revelation in terms of themes that have been around since the wheel, we hit on the concept of tongue twisters.

A box was designed with a new Air Heads Tongue Twister

326

logo. Original tongue twisters, 150 of them, were featured on each Air Head wrapper—among them:

- Rick's six slick small snails left six slimy snail trails!
- Loco Larry loves a lumpy load of living limp livers!
- Bug-eye Bill blew Bud's blue bugle badly!
- Pity plucky Pinky's poor plump pleading prairie dogs!
- Mitch pitches fits, Fitz picks nits, and Rich just itches!

3. David and Goliath

A common challenge is one that pits an underdog against a giant. These situations are based on relationships, reactions, and counterstrategies between warring factions. Exploring these dynamics can give you insight into ways that you, as David, might slay the Philistine. By looking at other Davids who have done battle and won, you can learn a lot. A list of classic David-and-Goliath confrontations includes:

Wal-Mart vs. Sears
Apple Computer vs. IBM
Burger King vs. McDonald's
Pepsi vs. Coke
Ben & Jerry's vs. Häagen-Dazs
Toyota and Honda vs. the Big Three automakers
The Cincinnati Reds vs. the Oakland As in the 1990 World
    Series
The Revolutionary Army vs. the British Army
Truman vs. Dewey
The tortoise vs. the hare

4. Superstars

We can't help comparing ourselves to those who have made a mark. We measure ourselves against athletes, actors, rock stars, flamboyant billionaires, or that pesky "supermom" across the street. What do they have that we don't?

I took this approach in designing and selling my first board game ONCE: The Storytelling Game for Family and Friends to Western Publishing. Identifying the winning traits of what was at the time the king of board games, Trivial Pursuit, led me to the invention of a successful original game.

5. Street Sense

Much can be learned by watching the competition. Let's say you have an idea for a delightful new low-calorie carbonated prune juice. Your first step should be to visit the prune juice aisle at your local supermarket. After all, you don't want to repeat history.

Study the dynamics at work on the shelf. Look at how the various brands are displayed, packaged, and presented. Recognize that America's leading prune juice companies have spent millions of dollars on market research to nail down the tiniest, seemingly most insignificant details.

For instance, if you're contemplating artificial flavoring for your prune juice, look for flavors the big boys may have recently introduced. Odds are that those flavors—or at least their names—have been researched extensively, resulting in findings of huge potential.

6. The Sure Six

Having written and tested thousands of concepts, I've put together a list of rules that my own experience and AcuPOLL test results single out as the keys to generating consumer interest in new products.

- **Start with a Difference:** It's nearly impossible to get people interested in a new idea unless it offers something that's significantly different from what's already out there. There's little room and even less tolerance for the same old stuff.
- **Basics Work:** Be careful not to toss out the basics in your campaign to change the world. Some fundamentals, like chocolate, will always draw a crowd. In the early 90s, chocolate experienced a renaissance with the introduction of such products as Hershey's White Chocolate Hugs and Swiss Miss White Chocolate Hot Cocoa Mixes.
- **Keep It Simple:** In a complex world, simplicity is a snug place to be. Consumers are bombarded with information overload.

They tend to discount much of what they hear. Focusing on one thing and doing it well gets attention. A prime example is Betty Crocker's Twice-the-Blueberries Muffins. Inside each box are two individual cans of wild Maine blueberries. The two cans reinforce the idea of "twice as much" far more effectively than one large can. After all, who's to say that one large can doesn't contain only one and a half times as much?

- **Fun Is Fundamental:** Left to its own devices, life is fundamentally boring. If you give your customers more fun and excitement, they'll love you for it. There's no category or creative challenge that can't be improved by making it more fun.

- **Common Senses:** Tie your area of opportunity to something your customers can see, feel, touch, taste, or hear. It helps them believe. The more radical your idea, the more people will have to experience it to believe it.

- **Invisible Technology, Health, and Environmentalism:** People are, fairly universally, drawn to technology, good health, and doing right by the environment—as long as it doesn't cost too much, taste bad, or hassle them. People want to feel good without any pain or hassle. The ease of sending a fax is an example of invisible technology at work. The confusing process of programming most VCRs is not. Super concentrated Tide is invisible environmentalism. Bio Pure shampoo in unwieldy quart milk cartons is not.

CHAPTER 210

Party Time

Roll up the rug and crank up the tunes. Party Time Brain Programs are designed for team play. While almost all of the other Brain Programs you've seen so far can be carried out in group settings, the ones in this chapter have been tested and approved by an impartial panel of judges—myself and the Trained Brains—exclusively for use in collective problem-solving efforts.

BRAIN PROGRAM #28: DEAR MR. PRESIDENT

When it comes to understanding what a company can and cannot do, twenty minutes with production line workers is worth twenty days with most management groups.

RICHARD SAUNDERS

One of my pet techniques for inventing ideas and creating solutions is to challenge an entire hierarchy. In other words, let the whole organization be your Flapdoodle sheet.

Objective

To enlist an entire organization in a safari for new ideas.

How to Do It

Challenge all employees, members, or volunteers in your organization to submit their most wicked good ideas. Make it a contest. Offer a prize. It needn't be expensive—perhaps a dinner for two at a nice restaurant. Make sure the contest is judged on merit. If you can't involve the U.S. Supreme Court or Arthur Andersen, arrange an independent panel to handle the judging.

Dear Mr. President in Action

When I was the brand manager for Safeguard soap, we were looking for a new way to display the product in grocery stores without having to stack the bars by hand. While many grocery store products can be displayed in "cut cases," where the tops of cardboard cases are simply cut away, leaving them exposed in the resulting "bottom tray," you couldn't do that with bar soap. Or so we thought.

The corporation had recommended special shrink-wrap trays, a particularly expensive option. I remember discussing the problem at the soap plant in Quincy, Massachusetts, with one of the technicians. We'd commandeered a conference room and, using my standard feel-it-touch-it modus operandi, we had before us four dozen cases of Safeguard.

Thirty minutes and fifteen cases of soap later, the technician blurted out an idea whereby the case would be split down the middle into two trays, like the two halves of a clamshell. One case could then be stacked on top of the other. The technician's idea was ten times more efficient than management's best recommendation, for about a tenth of the cost. Further, test markets showed the new case design increased Safeguard's sales by 40 percent over three months.

It was inspired. And it taught me that the people at the ground level, the ones who do the actual work, know what they're doing. They ought to—they're plugging away at it every day. Unfortunately, the corporate hierarchy usually is more interested in covering their backsides than opening their minds. Fortunately, it's hard to keep a good idea from happening.

When I started at the plant, I suggested lots of new ideas for our production area. The bosses weren't interested. They wanted to do it the way they'd been doing it for twenty years. After being told no a dozen times, I stopped making suggestions. I still try out ideas, but only when the bosses won't notice what I'm up to.

AN INVENTIVE AMERICAN
who prefers to keep
his name to himself

On another occasion, after a presentation to the Monsanto Company, I was pleased to hear that its Innovation Team had launched a three-month Dear Mr. President–style idea generation campaign called "It's In There Alright," in which employees were asked to submit ideas. The best ideas were awarded $1,000 savings bonds.

We ended up with over 300 ideas. Of those, we have several we're seriously looking into. One guy got so excited, he sent in fifteen ideas. It's been great getting ideas in from around the world—India, Australia, Denmark, Korea, France, Japan ...

LINDA MOENTMANN,
Monsanto Innovation Team

When you're in a bind and you need help, it's no time for machismo. Use all the resources at your disposal. Tap other imaginations.

BRAIN PROGRAM #29: PASS THE BUCK

At some point in your search for the wicked good ideas, you're bound to slide into a slump, a slippery slope of a slimy slump, and you'll need a blast of energy to help you over the top.

When you sense a slump coming on in your Eureka! Stimulus Response session, it's time to pull out Pass the Buck. This is genuine Acme TNT designed to blow away the blahs.

I like to accompany Pass the Buck with music. Not the chamber musings of Beethoven or Bach. I mean head-banging, pulse-pounding rattle-and-roll

that makes your feet move and your arms flap. Maybe it's rap, maybe it's metal, or maybe it's straight-ahead rock. For the terminally rhythmic, there is always, ahem, disco. Whatever it takes to start your engine. Don't be shy. The musical accompaniment to Pass the Buck is best played at a decibel level comparable to that of a 747 at takeoff. You'll know when you're getting the most out of it when your neighbors call the cops.

Objective

To transform the wild and whacked-out into practical, wicked good ideas. Sometimes Pass the Buck produces a world-class idea. Other times, its value is simply as an energizer or as a means to show Real World Adults how to find brilliance in the bizarre. Either way, you can't lose.

How to Do It

Divide into four groups. Give each a Pass the Buck sheet. It looks like this:

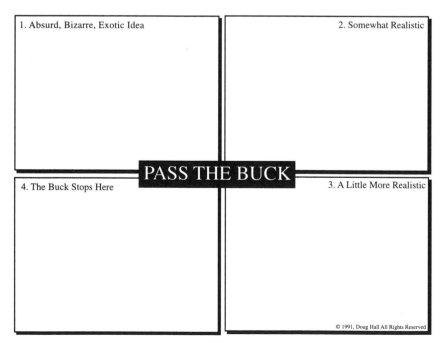

1. Absurd, Bizarre, Exotic Idea

2. Somewhat Realistic

PASS THE BUCK

4. The Buck Stops Here

3. A Little More Realistic

On your mark, get set, GO! Each team fills in the Absurd, Bizarre, Exotic Idea window, then passes the sheet to the next group, under the frantic exhortations of the Eureka!meister to move it, move it, move it!

As the sheets are passed around the room, each team takes a turn refining the initial unrealistic ideas into concepts that are by stages more realistic.

After three passes, the buck stops with the final group, which has to turn the idea into a practical, tactical idea that will send fear into the hearts of competitors and take no prisoners.

Ask each team to read its sheet out loud, from beginning to end. See what falls out—you are sure to be surprised.

Pass the Buck in Action

I sprang a Pass the Buck at the Eureka! Stimulus Response party held to invent this book. The object of the exercise was to come up with an idea to land an appearance on the mother of all TV talk shows, Oprah Winfrey's syndicated TV show. I love Oprah. To me, she's a queen, an enchantress, a video goddess. My life will not be complete until I've been a guest on her program.

Included here is one team's sheet from that session. This team was not particularly respectful, either to Ms. Winfrey or myself. I apologize to Ms. Winfrey for their behavior. But the final idea is one I'm determined to carry out.

Goal: An idea for getting Doug on *Oprah*.

In the Absurd, Bizarre, Exotic Idea window, Group 1 wrote: Doug naked on *Oprah* talking about The Naked Mind.

Group 2 made it Somewhat Realistic: Oprah and Doug naked; they go on crash diets for Fathead program.

Group 3 made it A Little More Realistic: Doug and Oprah on brain food program featuring ultimate diet for your brain/life.

For Group 4, The Buck Stops Here: Doug and Trained Brains on *Oprah* doing Eureka! Brain Programs live with kids who don't think they're creative.

Wicked cool! When I get on *Oprah*, I promise to wave. The idea stirs emotions for me.

I once ran two Eureka! Stimulus Response sessions in one day with two distinctly different groups of ten-year-olds. The children in the first group were miniature RWAs, future corporate Americans and pre-preppies. They were from an upwardly mobile neighborhood with an upwardly mobile school, where they'd been enrolled in an upwardly mobile program for gifted students. They'd been convinced they were creative. Boy, were they smug!

The second group was made up of ordinary kids culled from an ordinary school, and that's how they thought of themselves. No one had told them they were creative, and they most definitely didn't think of themselves as such. They were shy, withdrawn, unnurtured, and untapped.

But when this latter bunch was given the proper Eureka! Stimulus Response Brain Programs, stimuli, and sufficient emotional support from the Trained Brains, who are pretty much kids themselves, we saw ordinary children become supernovas of raw creativity. They bloomed and blossomed and flowered in wonderful, magical ways. Their small faces beamed as they filled the session with glittering ideas that far outstripped those of the "gifted students" in the first group.

The specifics of the ideas that came out of that session have to remain shrouded in secrecy until the client chooses to expose them. But I can tell you that, of the twenty ideas we took to the client from the two sessions, fifteen of them had originated in the second group.

The Trained Brains fell in love with the ordinary kids. I wanted to make them my own. They told me they never got to do creative stuff at their school. The experience was another illustration of the many ways the traditional system of education snuffs the creative spirit. At that moment, I resolved one day to translate the Eureka! Stimulus Response approach to creativity into a program for elementary and secondary schools across America. It is my life's mission. That, and being a guest on Oprah's show.

BRAIN PROGRAM #30: CENTER STAGE

Let's pretend. It's a great way to bend the world into whatever shape you want it to take. Pretending is a step or two beyond mere imagining. When you pretend, you put yourself in the picture. Pretending requires that you believe, at least a little. In that sense, pretending is pathological. That's OK. The important thing is that there are no limits when you pretend, as long as you pretend it's so.

Objective

To stimulate original thoughts through acting out the process of doing what you most desire or most need to do.

How to Do It

Pretend in the way you used to pretend when you were small—back when you were able to transform yourself instantly into a cowboy or a ballerina or a bird or a giant or a cloud or Zorro or Cinderella or Godzilla, with all those ant-size people running away from you, screaming your name in terror.

In those days, you believed you were what you pretended to be. You asked questions, then you answered them. What would Zorro do in this situation? How would Cinderella behave under these conditions? Which fleeing ant-size people would Godzilla squash? Which would Godzilla spare?

You could untangle all sorts of knots by pretending. You invented scenarios and you created solutions. Once you jump-start the part of your brain that controls the ability to pretend the way your childhood self used to pretend, you'll tap into a megaresource of wicked good ideas.

Any number of scenarios can be acted out on center stage: First-timers, old-timers, long-time users of your product, new friends, old friends.

My favorite scenario is that of a buying committee from Mars. Martians have no understanding of your task, your mission, your product or service, seeing as how they're not from around here. It's all they can do to understand your language.

The Martian buying committee's job is to be befuddled. "Huh?" the Martians say.

The rest of the team's job is to explain it and make them want it. What is it? Why should they care? What could it do for them? How would they use it? What good is it?

The Martians' role is most valuable when the Martians become increasingly absurd and cantankerous. Martians should ask basic questions that cut to the center marrow:

- What's being sold?
- What makes it different?
- Why should I care?
- Why would anyone want one?
- How will it make their lives better on Mars?

Stop, look, and listen closely. In the process of explaining and selling a thing, you'll discover new paths, angles, and perceptions.

After five to ten minutes of role-playing, allow an equal amount of time for the small teams to huddle and discuss:

- What surprised them?
- How did the earthlings feel while selling?
- How was the product perceived?
- How could the product or service have been more clearly presented?

Center Stage in Action

The challenge involved a company with more than $10 billion a year in sales. For many years, the company had achieved double-digit growth in sales and profits. But its sales had been dipping on a regional basis over the previous two years as more and more small entrepreneurial competitors did battle with it.

We assembled a group of the company's best and brightest sales and marketing executives. To help them see their situation through other eyes, I invited them onto Center Stage, specifically asking them to role-play the Martian buyer sales process.

To our shock, it was a disaster. When the Martians started prodding, it became obvious that this sales and marketing crowd didn't really believe in their own product. They actually didn't think the product was worth what they were charging for it. Indeed, they admitted that they thought what they were selling was a sham and only a small step removed from stealing.

We were near a crisis at this point. The sudden realization of the lack of faith in the product flattened the group's morale like a hurricane flattens a straw hut. As I write these words, the memory of that moment still sends a chill up my spine.

The group fell into a heated, argumentative debate. I had to do something to shift the momentum, but fast, before knives were pulled. I asked one of the few believers, a local market field rep, to give an emergency testimonial on the value of the company's products.

She spoke with passion about the impact the products had on real-world people and how it made their lives better.

Slowly, the group's confidence returned. The tide of self-assurance brought with it a vision for a series of marketing programs in which the company offered bold new guarantees of performance and satisfaction. The ideas were refined and tested with customers, and the response was universally positive.

But more importantly, the team now has a grasp of the lack of faith among the ranks of employees, and it's doing something about it.

BRAIN PROGRAM #31: PASS THE HAT

Extraordinary ideas have come from mixing and marrying categories. Wine coolers are a matched mix of wine and fruit juice. Video stores are libraries for movies. Singing telegrams combine theatrics with communication. Eureka! Stimulus Response weds fun to creating ideas.

Objective

To stimulate new thoughts by dismantling the benefits of associated categories and reassembling them in new-to-the-world categories.

How to Do It

Divide into small teams and give each team a hat. Have each team fill out five or six slips of paper listing individual traits of a range of aspects that relate to a problem you're trying to solve. These aspects might be sensory in nature—as in sights, sounds, smells, tastes. Or they might be based in emotions—as in fears, expectations, hopes, and any number of likes or dislikes. Or you might look at your problem in terms of its physical aspects—such as height, width, depth, weight. In any case, you are looking for the components of your problem, those aspects that give it individuality.

Each team folds its slips and places them in its hat.

Ask each team to pass its hat to the next team. The teams each pull two slips from the hat and arbitrarily bring together—or force-associate—one or more trait on each slip with one or more trait on the other slip to invent new ideas. Teams continue pulling slips from the hat, one at a time, until no slips remain.

Pass the Hat in Action

There we were, working on ideas for a new bath oil, four small groups engaged in writing down characteristics, emotions, behaviors, perceptions, benefits, and anything else they might associate with bath time, romance, being pampered, and relaxing.

Some of the traits we jotted down included:

- Characteristics—"Silky," "Luxurious," "Suds Mountain," "Rose Petals."
- Emotions—"Ecstasy," "Romance," "Warm Solitude," "In the Clouds."
- Perceptions—"Return to Womb," "Cozy," "Surrender," "Royal Treatment."

One team connected the idea bits "Royal Treatment" and "Rose Petals." The juxtaposition prompted one team member to blurt out, quote, *Princess Anne roses!* That spark led pretty much directly to a concept called Princess Anne Pedigreed Rose Water, which would feature actual petals of pedigreed Princess Anne roses in the bottle. Wicked good idea! As of this writing, the concept is under development.

BRAIN PROGRAM #32: OUT-OF-THE-BLUE LIGHTNING BOLT CLOUD BUSTER

This exercise pushes the playfulness button in your brain. It gets people off their derrieres, then puts them back down again. This exercise works great with small groups. One of my fondest dreams is to one day do this exercise in a stadium filled with people and hundreds of thousands of airplanes.

You'll need paper airplanes. The Out-of-the-Blue Lightning Bolt Cloud Buster is piloted by the amazing Obatala, the Yoruban deity of creativity, a mythical hermaphrodite who is held in high regard among members of the Yoruba people in Nigeria. He/she looks like this:

Technically, Obatala is not the world's finest pilot. She/he has trouble landing, which can be an emotional strain for the passengers of her/his Out-of-the-Blue Lightning Bolt Cloud Buster, although it isn't a problem as far as she/he's concerned since, in some incarnations, she/he has wings in the middle of his/her back. To her/his credit, however, she/he's highly skilled at flights of fancy. Let Obatala be your copilot.

Objective

To give people a fun, immature, and high-spirited way to build on others' thoughts on a one-on-one, confidential basis.

How to Do It

Make up enough paper airplanes ahead of time to fill the runways at LaGuardia, O'Hare, and LAX. You can develop a model of your own design or, if you're an RWA who has forgotten how to make a paper airplane, you can assemble a Lightning Bolt Cloud Buster from the following schematics:

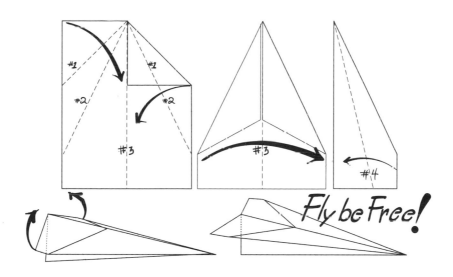

Fly be Free!

Crank up a lively piece of old-fashioned rock and roll to a ridiculous level and toss out the planes. Have your participants write their thoughts and/or ideas on the wings of the planes. Fill the air with aerodynamic origami. Ask each sessionaire to pick up any planes that come his or her way and jot a note, an idea, or a bulge on the wing.

You're looking for gut reactions, not considered responses. You want people to feel as if they're flying by the seat of their pants. Each time an idea or bulge is added to an airplane, it should be immediately relaunched. Allow enough time for each plane to take four or five flights.

Enough music, already! Gather up your planes for review and analysis another day or, if you must come to completion, ask everyone to take a plane and retreat to his or her team to enhance and refine the cargo of ideas from the various aircraft.

Another use for the planes is to ask people to use them to record any ideas they might hear during a session that they think may have gotten short shrift and merit special consideration, then have them fly the planes into a box or other safe harbor. At the Eureka! Mansion, we tell clients to fly their planes into the fireplace if it's not lit.

Remember that when the brain hears a good idea, it clings to it for a while, which keeps it from taking hold of new thoughts. Writing these ideas on paper airplanes helps reduce the risk of mental constipation.

Out-of-the-Blue in Action

The scene was the Eureka! Stimulus Response party to invent methods to promote this book. The planes flew.

As they landed and took off again, the ideas grew. One plane in particular took off. I later unfolded it and read:

"Nothing beats seeing the book on the shelf."
"Seeing someone reading it on a plane would be better."
"Give out pictures of Ben Franklin and Doug to anyone Doug sees reading it."

"Forget Doug. Give out $100 bills with Franklin's picture on them."

Wicked good idea. As I said in the first chapter, I think I will, to the first dozen people I see reading this book outside Cincinnati.

BRAIN PROGRAM #33: BATTLE OF THE SEXES

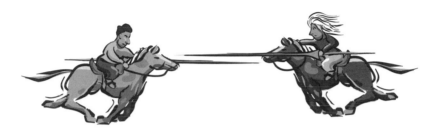

Battle of the Sexes is a Brain Program that never fails to astound me with the angst it evokes between males and females. It always causes a big commotion. I don't know why. It must be just another of those things we're not meant to understand. But when you segregate the girls from the boys, you end up with a blend of imagination and libido that fires the creative furnace.

Objective

To stimulate new thoughts through the differences between the sexes and through competition between the two. To mine the distinctly male and female points of view for ideas.

How to Do It

Put the boys on one side of the room, the girls on the other. Invite each side to develop two ideas to satisfy these requirements:

- The perfect solution to the task from their perspective

- The perfect solution to the task from the perspective of the opposite and opposing sex

Sprinkle liberally with stimuli. Give the girls a collection of men's magazines, such as *Esquire, Men's Health, Field & Stream, Soldier of Fortune*. Likewise, give the boys a handful of women's magazines—*Redbook, Cosmopolitan, Mademoiselle,* and *Better Homes & Gardens* will do for starters.

Stand back! Get set for some major explosions. When you split up the sexes, each quickly reverts to its lowest common denominator. My experience when I've introduced this drill into the Eureka! blender is that the girls become giggling flibbertigibbets and the boys become obnoxious juvenile delinquents, menaces to society and to themselves. But both sides usually come up with killer ideas.

Battle of the Sexes in Action

Our task was to build a winning concept for a new mouthwash. The boys were asked to dream up the ideal mouthwash for women; the girls, the perfect mouthwash for their Neanderthal counterparts.

In casting about for a way to sum up the male impetus for using mouthwash in the first place, the girls hit on the idea of "Dragon Breath." Their underlying premise: The only way to effectively detoxify the breath of the typical American male is to use a three-stage approach involving gasoline, a flamethrower, and an industrial-strength disinfectant.

The trail quickly led the girls to Dragon Slayer, a mouthwash for men with triple levels of cleaning, deodorizing, and freshening to make "the man in your life that much more kissable." Initial consumer research showed the idea a winner on both ends—female consumers immediately latched onto the idea of dragon breath, while male consumers were willing to do just about anything to make themselves more kissworthy.

BRAIN PROGRAM #34: ROLL CALL

This exercise is shoot-from-the-hip in its purest form. It's a good energizer, stimulates the creative flow, and eliminates the middle-man of the conscious mind. Roll Call should be done at a full gallop.

Objective

To energize minds through force-associating unrelated elements.

How to Do It

Divide into small teams. Arbitrarily select three team players to holler out a word, any word. In three minutes, force-associate the three random words to form a common (or uncommon) denominator. Instead of leaping to a conclusion, leap to an idea.

Roll Call in Action

Roll Call came into play when the Eureka! Stimulus Response team applied itself to developing a public relations strategy for the Leukemia Society of America. At one point during the Eureka! Stimulus Response session, one participant blurted out, "Kids," followed by another participant who blurted out, "Astronauts," followed by a third participant whose blurt was "Blast off."

That three-link sequence led us to the idea of sending a child with leukemia and a researcher on a space shuttle launch, the purpose being to study the effects of weightlessness on the disease itself, on current treatments of the disease, and on experimental treatments.

The Leukemia Society is exploring the concept—not so much in its concrete terms, but in terms of looking at new approaches for treatments of the disease. It's just a thought, but it has helped the society look beyond its traditional boundaries.

BRAIN PROGRAM #35: SPIN THE BOTTLE

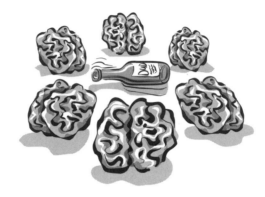

This exercise is an amusing method for letting individual participants come up with stimuli for inventing. You may have played a variation on this theme when you were thirteen or fourteen. It's a great way to get unconditional team support for bulging, smoothing, and polishing personal pet ideas.

Objective

To get the group working on individual favorite ideas that participants feel have a good chance of succeeding.

How to Do It

Get a supply of empty bottles. The best kind of bottle to use, from a spin perspective, is an Original Coors long neck—or, if you're in search of less substantial ideas, a Coors Light. Have your small teams sit on the floor in circles, each with a bottle in the center.

Spin the bottle. The person to whom the bottle points blurts out an idea, either a spontaneous creation or a thought borrowed from an earlier Brain Program. The team explores the idea for a limited time. A three-minute egg timer would come in handy here. Repeat the process until everyone in the team has had multiple blurts.

Spin the Bottle in Action

We spun bottles when a major food company stopped by the Eureka! Mansion in search of ideas for new products. This company was built around a large fictional character along the lines of Snuggle Bear, Speedy Alka-Seltzer, Reddy Kilowatt, and the Sta-Puf Marshmallow Man. One member of the client's team, a woman named Jane, had long harbored a pet idea for a livelier, sprightlier, younger version of the aforementioned icon—sort of a kid brother.

Her colleagues thought Jane was suffering from a hormonal imbalance. But she had a point—the original icon had grown long in the tooth, while a kid brother–type version could provide a spunkier, fresher face for the 90s.

So Jane persevered. Spin the Bottle gave her the opportunity to present her idea in a neutral, Eureka!-ized format. In the process of pushing and prodding her initial embryonic thought, we arrived at an idea for a new line of food products with sharper, spicier, more vivid flavors—the kinds of tastes an upstart could go for in a big way.

We tested the concept and it scored huge! I would dearly love to be able to brag about it here, but the client insists on keeping it under cover till they're good and ready to expose themselves.

CHAPTER 211

Extra Brainpower

The final chapter of Act II is devoted to two miscellaneous methods of bulking up the muscle inside your head. They're not as direct as the others listed in Act II; they just sort of happen. Putting them to work for you is a matter of recognizing them when they occur. One involves allowing your brain to rub up against other brains in a specialized social setting. The other is a matter of turning off your conscious mind and letting the hazy, innermost forces of your brain take over.

> *The best way to jump-start your brain is to get out of the situation you're in and do something totally different and fun. Clear your mind of everything and the solution will come to you.*
>
> PAM AND MARK TWIST,
> my sister and brother-in-law

Before we get into these last two methods, let's reinforce an overriding principal—that of exercising your brain. There are two ways to do this.

First, you can expose your brain to new experiences. Each of us is born with a certain number of brain cells, but you can increase the connections between brain cells by stimulating your brain, making it possible for you to process more information and, in general, become more mentally agile.

This can be accomplished in any number of ways. Visit a museum. Take up hang gliding or beekeeping. Sit in on a law class. Become an amateur archeologist. Strike up conversations with strangers. Climb a mountain. Learn to cane a chair or dance the tango or scuba dive. Join the circus. Buy a unicycle. Cultivate an herb garden or an ant farm. Build a treehouse. Hop a freight train.

Secondly, you can exercise your body. Recent studies indicate you can build a better brain by breaking a sweat and pumping up your muscles. An article in the November 30, 1993, edition of *USA Today* had this to say on the subject:

> *Aerobic activity builds capillaries, increases blood flow to the brain and prevents cell death. So, what's good for your heart is also good for your head.*

BRAIN PROGRAM #36: STIMULATING THE SUBCONSCIOUS

The power of the subconscious to create, clarify, and refine ideas is immense.

It doesn't take much to clog up the mental food processor with emulsified thoughts. When that happens, it helps to walk away from the problem and let your subconscious mind find the solution. We've all had the experience of having a name or a thought on the tips of our tongues. The more you consciously try to dislodge it, the deeper it becomes embedded—only to have it come to you once you stop chasing it. What happens is that your subconscious mind continues to process the data request even though your conscious mind has let go.

> *I back away from conscious thought and turn the problem over to my unconscious mind. It will scan a broader array of patterns and find some new close fits from other information stored in my brain.*
> ART FRY,
> corporate scientist,
> cocreator of Post-it Notes,
> 3M Corporation

The answer to your problem is often in your subconscious. The problem is that we make so much noise in our conscious minds that the subconscious doesn't get heard.

It's possible to program the subconscious. The key is to engage in an activity unrelated to the task at hand.

When I was stumped on a particularly tough engineering problem in college, I'd leave the room and spend twenty minutes juggling—not simple juggling, mind you, but difficult tricks with four or five balls or clubs, the kinds of stunts where, if you didn't focus your complete concentration, you'd be clunked on the head. Afterward, especially if I didn't get clunked, the gears in my brain would turn more smoothly and the ideas would flow.

> *I sit on the back porch, smoke a cigar, and watch the stars come out.*
> AUSTIN T. MCNAMARA,
> Group Vice President,
> Chiquita Brands International

I make it a point to go out for recess during the day, especially during group Eureka! Stimulus Response sessions, when my
mind has to be tightly focused for long stretches. Go outside and
play if it's a nice day. Climb a tree, bounce on a pogo stick, toss
the old pigskin around, take a seventh-inning stretch.

Another way to make your subconscious work for you is to
take a nap.

> *I can usually see the answer in my dream, because I do*
> *a lot of lucid dreaming. So it's like, even if I've already*
> *slept and I'm not even tired, I take a nap. I think cre-*
> *ative endeavors need a very receptive mind to show*
> *themselves. And when I have a deadline, I just turn*
> *everything up and take shorter naps. It's sort of like*
> *sleeping quickly.*
>
> SARK,
> friend and author

SARK is in good company. The ranks of history's dedicated
nap-a-holics include Thomas Edison, Eleanor Roosevelt,
Winston Churchill, and Presidents Truman, Kennedy, Ford, and
Reagan. Not that SARK has taken naps with any of those people.

> *HOW DO YOU JUMP START YOUR BRAIN? I take*
> *a nap.*
>
> JERRY MATHERS,
> "The Beav"

When I've got inventor's block, I sometimes find that if I close
my eyes, relax, and let my subconscious give me the answer, it
will. Not long ago, I was stuck on a name for a new food product. The client liked the overall concept, but not the name I'd
picked for it. I had twenty minutes to get back to the client with
alternatives.

I took a deep breath, wiped my conscious mind clean, and
waited. After a few minutes, the right name bubbled up from my
subconscious. The client loved it, and consumers loved the concept. It'll be on store shelves by the time you read this.

BRAIN PROGRAM #37: JUNTO

The Junto tradition fits nicely into a Eureka! setting. The two philosophies are both dedicated to the premise of unfettered exploration. In the case of the Junto, it's to gather in a safe forum for discussion, where no topic is taboo.

TRACY DUCKWORTH,
Trained Brain,
President, Junto Society

One great idea begets many others.

An example of a great idea is Ben Franklin's Junto Society. He conceived of the Junto as "a club for mutual improvement," whereby he could gather his brightest, most articulate, artistic, and creative pals "to spend a social evening together discoursing and communicating such ideas as occur'd to us upon a wide variety of subjects." The first Junto Society members were "leather-apron men"—artists, printers, explorers, barristers, and writers, all with a hunger for learning and a desire to improve themselves.

The Junto was one of the earliest adult education programs, a combination lecture series and party time. Franklin required "a pause between speeches so one might fill and drink a Glass of Wine." The wine flowed. So did the ideas. The Junto Society was a boon to Philadelphians. It was responsible for the creation of America's first public library, the first fire department, and the first plan for paving, lighting, and cleaning the city's streets. The group also established Philadelphia's city hospital, the American Philosophical Society, and the University of Pennsylvania.

To be eligible for Junto membership, one had to observe four criteria, as Franklin defined them:

- "To love truth for truth's sake, and to endeavor impartially to find and receive it personally and communicate it to others, without fondness for rudeness or desire for victory."
- "To not harm any person in his body, name or goods, for mere speculative opinions, or his external way of thoughts."

- "To love mankind in general no matter what the profession, beliefs or opinions."
- "To have respect for all other members and invited guests."

The concept is two centuries old, but the principles still apply. All you need is a place and people who are willing to expose their minds to the leading edges of philosophy, art, religion, politics, and any other area of thought you might wish to pursue.

The Eureka! Mansion convenes a junior version of the Junto Society the third Saturday of every other month, with a membership comprising about forty friends and employees of Richard Saunders International and AcuPOLL Research, along with spouses and significant others. Speakers are culled from whatever fields the members care to explore—from paranormal psychology to square dancing, from yoga to sleep disorders, from computer law to politics.

Our approach is to invite two speakers to talk for fifteen to twenty minutes each, then have an interactive discussion the rest of the evening. We find that we learn most from the two-way discussion. Given the size and diversity of our group, it's not uncommon to have relatively heated discussions between believers and nonbelievers, Republicans and Democrats, and many other yins and yangs. But we're careful to follow Franklin's example in these discussions and express neither fondness nor rudeness, nor desire of victory.

One of the more memorable Juntos was the time we brought in a psychic to put us in touch with the spirits of Ben and Elvis, and to make a clean sweep of sundry spirits that some Richard Saunders International staffers were convinced were inhabiting certain corners of the Mansion.

The psychic—she was one of those first-name-only types, like Cher, Charo, and Madonna—impressed the Juntonauts with her ability to divine the names of their dearly departed family members. She conveyed to their various survivors that they were fine and generally enjoying themselves in the afterlife, which was rather nice of her.

Unfortunately, she was unable to draw the spirit of Elvis—a circumstance she felt was probably due to numerous other psychic efforts in other locations to contact the King, thus distracting his spirit.

Ben never actually appeared either, although I'm pretty sure I felt his presence. At least, I felt a definite tingling in my legs.

Late in the evening, our psychic invited thirty Juntonauts and a reporter from the *Wall Street Journal* to accompany her to a tiny office on the third floor, where she aimed to release the spirit of a young woman who, in fact, had become pregnant out of wedlock around the time of the Civil War and hanged herself in that room.

Except for the light of the moon shining through the windows, the room was dark. One woman in our group began weeping. She told the psychic of a soft, frightened female spirit who had been in the room for many years and was afraid to leave. At that, the psychic's voice deepened two octaves as she took on the persona of her "spirit guide," a Native American she called White Feather, and directed the frightened spirit to, I don't know, someplace else.

The Juntonauts were afflicted with goose pimples the rest of the night. I decided that at the next Junto, we'd explore the mysteries of square dancing.

The headline in the *Wall Street Journal* gave the psychic the benefit of the doubt. "Elvis Is a No-Show," it read, "but Ben Franklin's in the Air."

Searching for Elvis might not have been the sort of subject matter Franklin had in mind when he created the Junto. But it was a lively evening, for believers and nonbelievers alike.

Franklin didn't have a patent on the Junto. Think about forming one of your own. All you have to lose are your preconceived notions. Gather your friends, gather your family, and explore new elements of the world you were not previously familiar with.

Go to see an opera, see a ballet, see a heavy metal band, visit the art museum, the starving artists' gallery, take a class in yoga, take a class in computers. Take a trip, try a new restaurant, rent a foreign film. Whatever you do, do something.

The key to jump starting your brain is a spirit of adventurousness. To be truly alive, you need to fill your mind continuously with new stimuli and new experiences. From this comes a passion for life, learning, and love.

ACT III

Go4it!

Former Procter & Gamble marketing whiz...Doug Hall goes to any length to encourage a fresh perspective...clients say it works.

Wall Street Journal

Over the past year, its Eureka! division...has developed more new products (or off-shoots of existing ones) than any other organization in America.

New York magazine

Act III

Go4it!

Well done is better than well said.
BEN FRANKLIN

Your brain has been jump-started, and you can see your dream. You have an idea—a shimmering, ephemeral killer of a wicked good idea destined to realign the planets and rewrite history.

Talk is cheap because supply exceeds demand.
RICHARD SAUNDERS

But you're the only one who can see it. If you want to show it to the world, if you want to make your dream happen, you have to make it real.

In life, you have a choice—you can enjoy the scenery of the merry-go-round or the thrills and terror of the roller coaster.
RICHARD SAUNDERS

You'll be taking a route that departs radically from the much less scenic, far more regimented one favored by Classic Pro Forma Management 101 Corporate RWA America. And once you get there, you will have become a full-fledged member of the countercorporate culture.

It's not easy.

Trust me.

You're blazing a trail, after all. You need courage and conviction. You need a vision. The idea you have today may be different from the idea that actually happens—that's OK. But you have to see a way to get there from here.

First things first. You have the idea. Now you have to make a decision. Do you go for it or don't you? Do you put your safe, snug career on the line and take a leap of faith? Do you step out to the edge of the nest and jump?

It's a thorny one, all right. But you'll never be younger.

It's a challenge to know when to hold them and when to fold

them. In the end, it almost always comes down to an unsettling combination of rational thought and gut instinct. Here are a couple of ways to help arrive at a decision:

The Franklin Ledger

When Ben wrestled with a decision, he would weigh the options in print. Note how he would use time to smooth out emotional impulses.

> *My way is to divide half a sheet of paper by a line into two columns; writing over the one Pro, and over the other Con. Then during three or four days' consideration, I put down under the different heads short hints of the different motives, that at different times occur to me, for or against the measure.*

When I have thus got them all together in one view, I endeavor to estimate their respective weights; and where I find two, one on each side, that seem equal, I strike them both out. If I find a reason pro equal to some two reasons con, I strike out the three. If I judge some two reasons con equal to some three reasons pro, I strike out the five; and thus proceeding I find at length where the balance lies; and if after a day or two of further consideration, nothing new that is of importance occurs on either side, I come to a determination accordingly.

And, though the weight of reasons cannot be taken with the precision of algebraic quantities, yet, when each is thus considered, separately and comparatively, and the whole lies before me, I think I can judge better, and am less liable to make a rash step; and in fact I have found great advantage from this kind of equation, in what may be called moral or prudential algebra.

The Writings of Benjamin Franklin
ALBERT HENRY SMITH, editor

Freud Flip

In his book, *What a Great Idea!*, Chic Thompson describes a wicked cool system for making emotional, instinctive decisions:

> *Sigmund Freud came up with a unique way to test out his gut feeling on a problem. He would flip a coin. First he would assign heads and tails to a yes/no decision. Then he'd flip. If the coin said yes and his gut said, "Let's go two out of three. I'm not comfortable with that decision!" then his intuitive reaction had just revealed itself.*

Real World Survival Guide

The trick to surviving and thriving in real-world corporate America is to be yourself. Insist on it.

You might say Procter & Gamble qualifies as a large corporation. The way to be the most effective in P&G's chrome-glass-and-soap environs is to be distinctively yourself. Be a personality. Think of yourself as a product. You'll rise faster on your own abilities than you ever will by trying to fit the official corporate personality mold.

The more you establish yourself as an expert in a distinct area, the more valuable and successful you'll be. Averageness doesn't cut it. You have to be exceptional in some area.

> *He that hath a trade, hath an estate.*
> BEN FRANKLIN

Use your energy, your enthusiasm, and your smile as if they were weapons. Sadly enough, most people in the cold, gray corporate world lead what Henry David Thoreau called lives of quiet desperation. If you sweep in with high-voltage enthusiasm and a 100-watt grin, these people will gravitate to you. They will make you their champion. They will try to be like you.

Don't be afraid to take risks. Corporations have an amazing array of checks, balances, and safety nets to prevent you from hitting the wall at ninety miles an hour. As long as you've looked at both sides and measured the risk against the benefits, be bold and brash. Develop a reputation for it.

In big corporations, you'll run into big obstacles. But there are ways to get around them.

In the early days of a development project for an all-purpose spray cleaner at Procter & Gamble, I was having trouble winning support from management.

So I set up a scam to have all the members of senior management take a bottle home and test it on the domestic front. When the families of senior management types tried the prototype product in their homes, the logjam began to splinter. Their reactions kept hope alive and laid the foundation for what years later became the highly successful Cinch spray.

In another case, a group of us were shackled with an unbearable boss, the kind of guy where, if you hold a flashlight up to one ear, the beam shines through the other.

We decided to trumpet his virtues. So we did—to every executive recruiter we could find. We showered him with laudatory adjectives and generally let it be known to the recruiters that here was a guy who wouldn't be content to stay where he was much longer on account of he was just too darned sharp. We put the spit polish on him. We lathered him up thoroughly.

By the end of the week, our boss let it slip to me, "Boy, I've been getting a lot of calls lately from headhunters." Really? I said.

The upshot is, he was gone within a month. He got a big raise and, dingdong, the wicked witch was dead.

Be like Frank Sinatra. Do it your way. That means, among other things, not worrying about looking like everyone else. In my case, I gave up suits. People used to ask how I got "Them" to give me permission to not wear suits. The answer is, I didn't ask. Whenever you ask "Them," whatever it is you want to do becomes Their responsibility. If you press forward on your own authority, they'll look the other way.

Once I had stopped wearing suits, I gradually became known as That Eccentric Inventor Guy. I was seen as a slightly mad step-cousin who was best left alone. Simply by being myself, I came to define the corporate lunatic fringe.

At one point, the Procter & Gamble gods decided to ease up on the corporate dress code and handed down a memo outlining the premise of "casual Fridays." The idea was to give employees the option of laying back, kicking out the jams, and, once a week between Memorial Day and Labor Day, wearing something to work other than the de rigueur navy or gray wool suit. Naturally, casual Friday was not unqualified. Jeans and sneakers were still verboten on casual Friday.

It was all very confusing to me. But I adhered strictly to the policy and restricted my wearing of jeans and Nikes to Mondays, Tuesdays, Wednesdays, and Thursdays. In keeping with the letter of the law, I wore shorts and sandals on casual Fridays.

Avoid fitting in. Whenever possible, make the structure adapt to you.

OK, it's time to kick it in gear. Time to step on the gas and rip into the big bad world. Here are ten commandments to help you on your way.

The Ten Commandments of How to Turn Your Dreams into Reality

COMMANDMENT #1. BUILD A PROTOTYPE

Roll up your sleeves and craft your idea into a tangible model that can be seen, felt, and touched. It doesn't have to be pretty. This isn't a beauty contest. Just rough together something that people can see, feel, touch.

Where prototypes are concerned, "works like" is more important than "looks like." If your idea is for a new fund-raising event for your organization, draw up the poster and draft a letter to explain it. If your idea is for a service, put it in a brochure and let people reach to it.

Sketch it out and take a good look. If your idea involves board games, cannibalize parts from Monopoly, Yahtzee, Risk, and Trivial Pursuit that you need to make the game work. Think about it.

The cartoonist who dreamed up Garfield and Friends agrees:

> If we have a truly different idea, the best way to sell it is to help the client visualize it. We'll take our idea, dress it up, draw it, paint it, set it to music, and prototype it. Many times we go to dramatic lengths to demonstrate our ideas. If our clients can see it as we see it, chances are they'll embrace it.
>
> JIM DAVIS
> Paws Incorporated

368

Building a prototype is a learning process. You'll learn about trade-offs and challenges. Don't let them scare you. Keep your dream in focus. As you define your idea, you'll discover bumps in the road you hadn't noticed earlier.

> *By making the thing real, you then have a "thing" to do something with.*
>
> SARK,
> *A Creative Companion*

Involve yourself in the prototype's construction. Doing so will help you understand the three-dimensional dynamics of your vision. It'll also be your salvation when it's time to sell your idea to the real world.

> *Hammers and screwdrivers have built more ideas than all the meetings and paperwork in the world.*
>
> RICHARD SAUNDERS

Make a little, sell a little, learn a heap. Line up a small supply of prototypes, put them in stores, and watch the reaction.

Many's the time I've talked a good line. But when I write it down in black and white or built a prototype, many's the idea that has suddenly lost its luster.

> *Before leaping from a plane, it's best to have seen and felt the parachute.*
>
> RICHARD SAUNDERS

COMMANDMENT #2. YOU MUST BELIEVE

You're the Gipper, with apologies to Knute Rockne and Ronald Reagan, and you're the Gipper's team. And you can't allow yourself to stop anywhere short of The Best.

You must be willing to stake your name, your reputation, and your family jewels on your vision. You'll have to fight for it.

Because if you don't put your total energy behind it, if you aren't willing to reach way down deep, no one will pay attention.

> *If you don't believe, I don't believe.*
> RICHARD SAUNDERS

What's your dream worth? What are you willing to risk? The cost of achieving is always greater than you expect it to be. At the same time, the exhilaration is greater than you can imagine.

I marvel at the faith my forefather, Lyman Hall, showed when he signed his name to the Declaration of Independence, agreeing to declare war with the most formidable power on the planet. He and his fellow revolutionaries didn't believe in excuses. General George Washington had no army, no arms, no uniforms. But he had men who agreed to mutually pledge to each other their lives, their fortunes, and their sacred honor.

Imagine the outcome at that meeting in the summer of 1776 if the heads of Chrysler, General Motors, and Ford had been asked to add their names to the parchment.

Nothing cheeses me off more than hearing corporate Americans whine about the raw deal they're getting from the Japanese. If the former devoted as much energy to providing vision and leadership as they do to whimpering, they wouldn't have anything to mewl about.

Short of winning the lottery, there's no such thing as instant wealth. In order for greatness to occur, you have to do something great. You have to be the catalyst.

> *Do nothing, and nothing happens. Do something, and something happens.*
>
> RICHARD SAUNDERS

Do you wake up in the morning ready to attack your task? Do you stay up late sweating details? If your task totally consumes you, you're sufficiently committed. If you have no trouble separating the task from the rest of your life, you probably aren't. I don't mean to suggest you should rip up your life. But you'll never start the engines of a new-to-the-world idea with a 50-percent effort and half a heart.

Believe me, the energy and commitment are worth it. No amount of money, fame, or hedonistic pleasure matches the feeling of walking into a store and seeing a product you've created on the shelf. I can think of only four moments that surpass the rush I experience whenever I see a product of my own making awaiting shipment at the loading dock—namely, the day of my marriage and the births of my three children. Of course, my children are the most complex things I've ever helped create. They're also the most expensive and exhilarating inventions conceivable. In both senses of the word.

Still, when my board game ONCE... first arrived on store shelves, I stood in the aisle of Swallen's department store in Cincinnati staring at the boxes for four hours. I spent two more hours pointing them out to anyone who happened down the aisle. I might have been a happy dad gazing through the big window on the maternity ward.

COMMANDMENT #3. TAKE RESPONSIBILITY

> *Fish stink from the head down.*
> BEN FRANKLIN

You are the Chosen One. It's up to you, Geronimo, to blaze the trail as you head westward ho! into the wilderness. As your own CEO, you're not merely the Chief Executive Officer. You're the Chief Energy Originator.

C.E.O. =

Chief Energy Originator

371

I'm merciless on CEOs. People want to do the right thing. They want to take pride in their work. If a business isn't performing properly, the fault lies with the person atop the pyramid.

> *Corporations are like monsters; heads enough, but no brains.*
>
> BEN FRANKLIN

The buck stops with you. You alone are responsible for the success of your venture. By definition, you're responsible for making sure your people succeed. When they succeed, so will you.

Leadership is dangerous, scary, lonely, fun, and exhilarating. It's not for everyone.

The best leaders are easy to spot. Wicked good leaders:

- Inspire people to perform above themselves.
- Create confidence among customers.
- Are maniacs when it comes to quality.
- Have the guts to get it done. Sometimes, they have a gut, too.
- Have equal proportions of heart and brains.
- Love people.
- Lead by example.
- Take responsibility for everything.
- Accept neither praise nor money that are not deserved.
- Are honest, with themselves and with others.

Leading is not the same as managing. Managers are concerned with style and process. Leaders concentrate on substance and imagination. Managers shy away from aggression out of an inborn terror of chaos. Leaders know that nothing gets accomplished without aggression. At the same time, leaders are willing to risk bruising a few egos because they direct their aggression at ideas, not people. Leaders realize aggression is a necessary ingredient of the chemistry of motivation.

> *Trust thyself, and another shall not betray thee.*
>
> BEN FRANKLIN

I was twelve years old when I staged my first paid magic show. It was for a six-year-old's birthday party at York Beach in Maine, and I was paid $5.

I'd practiced for weeks before the show, imagining that my audience would react with wild applause and perhaps even carry me off on their shoulders. As it turned out, my reception was, at best, tepid.

After the show, an old man who came to the beach every day and who had watched me teach myself to juggle asked me how the show had gone. When he was younger, he'd traveled the famous vaudeville circuits in New England. So we had something in common.

"I was great," I said. "My audience wasn't so hot, though."

He smiled.

"Let me tell you something, sonny," he said. "There's no such thing as a bad audience—only poor performers. If they didn't like you, it's because you didn't give them the right show."

He was right. If you want it to happen, you have to make it happen. If you make excuses, you'll never make anything happen. Excuses flow freely from the fountain of noncommitment.

COMMANDMENT #4. HAVE A SIMPLE VISION

The first step to greatness is believing you've already arrived.

RICHARD SAUNDERS

The vision is what will sell your new-to-the-world idea. The vision has to be a story with a beginning, a middle, and an end. It must depict your idea so that investors, customers, family, and friends can see your destination. Or a reasonable facsimile there-of. Wicked good visions breathe life into dreams.

A good vision is as exciting as the idea it defines. It should dazzle, amaze, tantalize, and tease. It should swoop, plummet, and soar like a roller coaster. It should make your heart pound and your audience catch its breath.

No matter what your task, you must have a vision of the end result. You must know where you're headed and what you're trying to accomplish. You have to see it, feel it, and know it in your heart.

Your vision can change along the way. You may need to fold, spindle, adapt, and modify as you go. No problem. Visions aren't chiseled in mahogany. They're alive and fluid. The important thing is to have one. If you do, you'll be able to cash in on the serendipities. If you don't, vast networks of dead-end streets lay waiting to swallow you up.

> *Without a vision, you'll never know if you're moving toward your goal or away from it.*
>
> RICHARD SAUNDERS

Another way to gauge your vision is to close your eyes and form a picture in your mind. Athletes routinely use this technique, imagining the ball falling through the hoop, sailing through the goalposts, catching the inside corner of the plate. I've used it to build my business and my clients' businesses.

When I was looking for a new planetary headquarters for Richard Saunders International, I came across a rambling old ramshackle brick mansion. Logical, rational advisors urged me to keep looking. But in my mind's eye, I saw a world-class invention facility, a place in the country that could be an island of originality. It took a few months to clarify the vision to the point that I could articulate it to the company team. But by that time, the people on my team were having visions of their own. The visions flirted, mingled, and blended. The result, the Eureka! Mansion, is as fine a planetary corporate headquarters as any I've seen.

When you have one vision, you can develop dozens. Once you have a vision of a potential solution, your mind will open and other answers will come tumbling out. The first vision often turns out to be a mirage. But by then, it has served its purpose, stoking your confidence and providing direction.

COMMANDMENT #5. CHECK YOUR MOTIVES

If your overriding motive is money or fame, you may as well call it a day. The journey is too hard, and there are too many other ways to make money or win fame.

> *'Tis easy to frame a good, bold resolution. But hard is the task that concerns execution.*
>
> BEN FRANKLIN

Changing the world or your portion of it is hard work. It's fatiguing. And fatigue is a big hairy grizzly bear. To overcome it, you have to be internally motivated to make a difference. Otherwise, the first of the hundreds of obstacles you confront will most assuredly drop you like a sack of ballpeen hammers.

The kind of motivation I'm talking about comes from a profound conviction that you're doing the right thing, that you're going to make the world better. Never mind what the world thinks it needs—you have to believe the world needs your idea.

The purity of your motivation is vital to your success. Procter & Gamble emphasizes the importance of doing the "right thing in the right way." The core principle of doing the right thing is presented as standard operating procedure to new recruits. It's a big reason Procter & Gamble is as successful as it is.

So your idea has to be The Best in its class. The crowd—the bankers, the manufacturers, the sales staff, the store owners, and the average Josephs—has to believe you have an idea of significance. If the crowd doesn't believe, it won't rally around you.

When your goal is pure, you won't have to concern yourself with looking for money and fame. They'll find you.

Before you blast off, you should know how to lead, manage,

and sell to "Suits." A Suit can be a corporate executive or a banker or a client. A Suit is a RWA with sufficient money and power to make your idea happen.

If you have a job in a corporation, don't leave simply because you can't stand working within the hallowed halls. If you can't make things happen inside a corporation, the odds of being successful on the outside are against you. When you leave, you'll be substituting one kind of Suit for another. Instead of management Suits, you'll face client, banking, and governmental Suits.

Study your motivations. Why are you really leaving? If it's because the money isn't good enough or because you're angry, don't do it. If it's to accomplish a significant goal, to realize an inner passion, then what's kept you this long?

Never be pushed into anything. In America, you have the freedom of choice. You can be a slave to corporations, bankers, and investors only if you consent to it. Never run away from a Suit. Have the courage to run toward opportunity.

> *Necessity never made a good bargain.*
> BEN FRANKLIN

COMMANDMENT #6. SELL, SELL, SELL

> *He that would catch Fish must venture his Bait.*
> BEN FRANKLIN

Your million-dollar idea isn't worth ten cents until you sell it.

People have to want it. They have to see that it's in their best interest to buy it. They need to believe your product or service is better able to meet their needs than what they already have.

Your role is to make them understand. The process is a friendly mix of cajoling, inspiring, instructing, and wooing. The most important rule to remember when selling is to be likable.

> *If you would be loved, love and be lovable.*
> BEN FRANKLIN

People like to buy from likable people. They like to buy from companies that are friendly and fun. They will occasionally buy from jerks, idiots, scumballs, and slimebuckets if they have no choice. But they'd rather not.

People will like you if you're reliable, honest, conscientious, relaxed, and friendly. Chances are, they'll like you if you're simply yourself.

Fun is fundamental to selling. Life is fundamentally boring. Most people don't have a lot of on-the-job fun. If you can add a little fun to their lives, they'll love you passionately and deeply.

Friendliness is the key. And I don't mean a you-scratch-my-back-and-I'll-scratch-yours greasy kind of friendliness. Nor am I referring to the patronizing type of suck-up-brownnosing friendliness so popular at used car lots and in corporate boardrooms. I mean a true, genuine, loyal friendliness, more along the lines of a do-unto-others-as-you-would-have-done-to-you sort of friendliness.

Unless you're selling trousers to aborigines, you and your wicked good idea are destined to encounter at least one Suit on the sales trail.

For the most part, the Suit has not arrived at its lofty position by embracing new-to-the-world ideas such as your own. The Suit may have championed one or two relatively radical ideas in its career that turned out to be successful—but for the most part, whatever status the Suit has achieved has been by way of the safe bet.

By virtue of your entrepreneurial spirit, you're probably an alien being to the Suit. You and your idea are out there at the lunatic fringe. You're living, eating, and breathing your brave new universe. The Suit, meanwhile, has little time and less tolerance. The Suit is not easily impressed.

The question, then, is how do you sell a Suit?

Suits come in two basic types. It's important to know which type you're dealing with in order to tailor your pitch to fit. The key is in determining what's beneath the Suit's suit.

> *Initially, you want to believe that under every suit, there's a T-shirt. You can tell immediately. It's like, your pupils get dilated. You can tell when someone understands. All of a sudden, a light goes on and they say "yeah."*
>
> GUY KAWASAKI
> Macintosh software evangelist

If your Suit's suit is hiding a T-shirt, summon up your formidable supplies of energy, enthusiasm, and passion to paint the vision. This type of Suit will quickly get the picture.

If, on the other hand, you suspect that your Suit is wearing a suit beneath its suit, the challenge is much steeper. A Suit with a suit under its suit is a Suit through and through, even when it's naked. The spirit of such a Suit is governed by fear, uncertainty, doubt, and despair. They tend to be tightly wound butt coverers whose natural posture is defensive. Their No. 1 priority is protecting what they have, which has little indeed to do with risk taking.

T-shirt Suits smile easily. They roll up their sleeves. They react. There is light in their eyes. They offer you coffee and get it for you themselves. Suits with suits beneath their suits are poker-faced individuals. They wear their suit coats as if they were bulletproof shields. They don't react. Their eyes are glazed, like doughnuts. They offer you coffee, then they buzz their secretaries to get it for you.

Change is the enemy of Suits with suits beneath their suits. It's the one dynamic they fear above all else. And since change is a fact of life, they live in fear. They're constantly looking over their shoulders, less concerned about doing what's right than with how they're perceived by their bosses above them and their subordinates below them.

It's not a pretty picture. Pity the poor double-suited Suit.

Frequently, they're mere conduits in the corporate plumbing, through which ideas percolate up from the bottom and bubble onward to upper management. These doublesuited Suits lack the power and, generally speaking, the initiative to make decisions. For all practical purposes, a Suit with a suit beneath its suit often contains a brain-dead human being.

Selling to this second type of Suit requires almost monumental strength. In fairness, they're able to grasp the incremental ideas— the unscented product, the new flavor, the idea that transforms pie into pie à la mode. But their minds are closed to any idea that takes a quantum leap forward. They have to be spoon-fed the proper sensations in order to see, feel, and touch your new world order.

Always show a suit your idea in three dimensions. Give them the experience. If it's a direct mail campaign, show them the mailing piece. If it's a new product, give them a sample. If you're selling cars, let them take a test drive. Once a Suit has experienced the wicked goodness of your idea, you're halfway to making the sale.

COMMANDMENT #7. BE PERSISTENT

There are no gains without pains.
BEN FRANKLIN

If we are industrious, we shall never starve, for at the working man's house hunger looks in, but dares not enter.

BEN FRANKLIN

Sell like the wind. Do it. Over and over and over again until you break through. If your vision is good and if you're calling on the right people, you'll make it. Here's the secret: Don't allow quitting to be an option.

It took three years to sell my first board game. It took two presentations to sell the second. Today, toy companies call me asking for ideas. The key is to keep looking for new clients. In most cases, sales(wo)manship is a matter of spreading the word and ringing doorbells. It's a tough, lonely road, fraught with frustration. It requires equal measures of faith and courage to keep going. The only way you maintain sanity in the face of adversity is to develop an unshakable faith in what you're selling. Otherwise, a mind is a terrible thing to waste.

It is true that there is much to be done, and perhaps, you are weak-handed; but stick to it steadily, and you will see great effects; for constant dripping wears away stones; and by diligence and patience, the mouse ate in two the cable; and little strokes fell great oaks.

BEN FRANKLIN

Nothing is more important to your business growth than a continuous marketing effort. Marketing is not something you turn on and off.

The effect of marketing efforts is cumulative. This letter illustrates this point:

> *"Dear Mr. Hall," it read. "I was intrigued by an article I read in the* Wall Street Journal *regarding your business. Your whole creative approach struck me not only as novel but as fun. I clipped the article to put in a 'think-about-someday' file. Since that point, I've seen two further articles on you and your business and have decided I need to learn more."*

COMMANDMENT #8. INSPIRE EXCELLENCE IN YOUR TEAM

You must know yourself to be a wicked good leader. That means knowing your limitations. You have to know when to hold your ground and when to yield.

> *Three things extremely hard: steel, diamonds, and knowing one's self.*
>
> BEN FRANKLIN

Wicked good leaders set examples that inspire people to perform above their abilities, to make them better than they ever thought they could be. Prove to your team that they're champions. Once they believe it, they will be it.

Instill a feeling of togetherness and support. Give your team players the strength to fend off armchair naysayers who continually tell them their efforts are futile.

> *To be a good leader, you have to be nice. You have to be nice and take turns. Good leaders don't push and shove.*
>
> KRISTYN HALL, age 5

You're not a dictator. You're more of a listener. Lead not just by example, but by collecting thoughts from those around you, then incorporating them into the vision so that your people can achieve. Give them credit for having functioning brains. After all, you hired them. You didn't hire them because of their ability to say yes; you hired them because they're capable of greatness.

Understand that Lincoln freed the slaves. You're no one's master. America is a free country, which means that everyone who works with or for you is free to take a hike at any time. Great leaders work with people, not at them.

Success, it is said, is 10 percent inspiration and 90 percent perspiration. Ideas don't perspire, no matter how wicked good they are. People perspire. It follows, then, that your odds of success are tied directly to assembling the right people.

The important thing is not to hire the smartest, the most likable, the most persuasive, or the fastest. It's more a matter of spirit, passion, and an ability to persevere in the dead of night.

The right people aren't clones of yourself. The right people have a range of skills and strengths different from your own. Your team should reflect a wide portfolio of talents. But everyone on it should have the same basic value structure.

Think of it as a basketball team, where the key is consistency between the players. Some prefer a fast-break, run-and-gun style. Others like a slower tempo, where the ball is passed until someone has an open shot. Either is effective. Both aren't. When you begin to mix playing styles, you end up with chaos.

At Richard Saunders International, I look for people who want to move quickly. I look for a low tolerance for bureaucracy and a desire to change the world, as opposed to simply making money. And I look for confidence. In short, I look for people who share my own fundamental values. A profile of Celtics legend Red Auerbach in the May 1989 edition of *Yankee* magazine put it this way:

> *Before Red drafts a player, he calls his coach, coaches who have opposed the player, his family, friends, teachers, anyone who can tell him not only how good that player's jump shot might be, but what kind of character he has.... Red has never been a coach who judged performance by scoring or rebounding statistics. "You can't measure a ball player's heart, or his willingness to sacrifice by statistics," he once said. "I always had only one statistic. When this guy's in the game, does the score go up in our favor or down?"*

I look, too, for people with a yen for adventure. I tell my newly hired to expect thrills and chills, spiced with plenty of highs and lows. I tell them that we'll make up the rules as we go and that what exists today will look a lot different tomorrow. I tell them they'll be expected not only to do their job, but to look for ways to make it faster, smarter, quicker, and, yes, more fun.

COMMANDMENT #9. SWEAT THE DETAILS

> *Glass, china and reputations are easily crack'd, and never well mended.*
>
> BEN FRANKLIN

It's one thing to talk the customer into giving you a shot. It's another to keep him coming back.

Surprisingly big issues aren't key to your success. The major screwups won't bring you down. You'll take care of those. It's the tiny details that will jump up and bite you in the throat. Your ability to deliver wicked good customer service hinges on your attention to details.

> *A little neglect may breed great mischief. For want of a nail, the shoe was lost; for want of a shoe, the horse was lost; and for want of a horse, the rider was lost, being overtaken and slain by the enemy. All for want of a little care about a horse shoe nail.*
>
> BEN FRANKLIN

In today's world, customer service is absolutely, positively non-negotiable. The customer is the boss. By customers, I'm referring to the blessed saints who give you the money to do what you do. In a corporate setting, the customer is often company management. If you're out there in the entrepreneurial stratosphere, the customer is your client.

You may fool a customer once with now-you-see-it-now-you-don't sales techniques. But once they find out your idea isn't as good as you told them it was, you'll never trick them into coming back. And the cost of a lost customer is immense.

> *Tricks and treachery are the practice of fools that have not wit enough to be honest.*
>
> BEN FRANKLIN

There's no trick to getting a satisfied customer to return. Customers *want* to believe that their faith in you is well-founded. It's human nature. Your job is to prove them right.

When a customer feels slighted, it doesn't matter who's right and who's wrong. Because you lose. And the expense of finding a new customer is far greater than the cost of maintaining one you already have.

Stay focused on delivering the wicked good product that was your vision. If cost problems drive up your price, seek ideas to modify your vision. But maintain a focus on greatness instead of compromising to mediocrity.

Act III: Go4it!

'Tis easier to prevent bad habits than to break them.
BEN FRANKLIN

Demand excellence in all areas. Don't let a flimsy bottle cap, a crappy wrapper, or a faulty whompus ruin a brilliant product.

The worst wheel of the cart makes the most noise.
BEN FRANKLIN

Sweat the details. Properly sweated details will generate buckets of brackish saline solution, which will breed success. The people in the pinstriped suits usually notice sweaty details. Even if they don't, sweat the details anyway. Because it's the right thing to do. Otherwise, you won't be the best. A commitment to details often is the difference between success and failure.

If a consumer makes a mistake with your product, it may be the consumer's problem. But it's your problem, too. Moreover, it's not the consumer's fault. The fault is yours.

RICHARD SAUNDERS

As a wicked good leader, you set the moral and spiritual tone for your effort.

You're the lightning rod. You bear the blame when something goes wrong. Conversely, you share the credit when you succeed. If you follow that pattern, your successes will far outnumber your failures.

The larger issues of ethics, customer service standards, and corporate culture flow down from the top. If you accept a 10-percent consumer complaint level, your team will see it as an objective, not a maximum.

There was a righteous man, and he walked a righteous mile,
He built a righteous fortune with a righteous brainchild;
Then he started cutting corners,
His priorities grew confused.

So he lost his brainchild fortune,
Which was righteous through and through.

RICHARD SAUNDERS

COMMANDMENT #10. BE SPEEDY

Whatever the marketplace pace is, double it. The fact that most of those engaged in your area of interest are huge lumbering giants is a fact that can work to your advantage.

Consider the components of momentum. In physics, momentum is a function of mass and velocity.

$$Momentum = MASS \times Velocity$$

It doesn't matter how big, how huge, how overweight your competition may be. If you're quicker on your feet, you'll get the lion's share of the market. If you and your band of Gypsies move with enough speed, you can go out and test it and fail and try it again and fail again and keep failing until you get it right before the corporation can make its first move.

There has never been a better time to change the world than right now. You occupy a unique point in history. It's called the computer age. This machine is the great equalizer. It can put you on a par with GM, AT&T, and IBM. It can make you larger than life. With it, you can be in two or more places at once. With your computer, you can. Whether it's from an executive suite or a corner of your basement, you can. I did.

Listen to Your Heart

We've come a long way, you and I. Thanks for bearing with me. I hope this book helps you move a few steps closer to realizing your dreams.

I'd like to know what you think of it. If you'd care to, please send a picture postcard—that's right, a PICTURE POSTCARD. I love picture postcards, and I hereby promise to make every effort to respond, depending on how many postcards I end up receiving. If I can't write, one of the Trained Brains will—unless we get 50 gazillion picture postcards, in which case I'll think of something else. You can write to me directly in care of:

Send To:

Doug Hall
Eureka Mansion!
3851 Edwards Road
Cincinnati, Ohio 45244

At the same time, please don't send inventions or ideas for new products. I hate to sound like a jerk, but if you do, they'll become my property. Legally, it's a tangled mess to get ideas and inventions in the mail. Besides, you'll be much better off if you push your ideas forward on your own, using the principles contained in this tome.

As you sail forth into the Real World, please remember to listen to your heart. Regardless of what the experts say or the accountants calculate, the most critical elements to your success are your faith, energy, and enthusiasm.

> *Wealth is who you are, not what you have.*
> RICHARD SAUNDERS

If you choose to push forward, you'll experience higher highs and lower lows than you ever imagined. You'll work harder and longer than you ever thought you could.

> *God helps them that help themselves.*
> BEN FRANKLIN

If you believe that your task is right, don't hesitate—no matter what you hear from the Real World Adults. Look closely at the numbers, look closely at your strategy, look for a path to success, and, most of all, look into your heart. If you can't see any path at all, put your plan on hold until you can.

> *If you can see the start of a path to success, even though that path may not be the right one, then go for it. Because where there's one path, there's probably more. When you don't see any path, that's when you better give it up.*
> DAVE HOWE
> Richard Saunders Technologies

As you survey the landscape, don't forget the rest of your world. Don't forget your family and friends. Work is supposed to make life better. The act of carrying a wicked good idea from dream to reality is courageous and commendable. But it's not worth your family, your friends, or your life.

> *Wealth is not his that has it, but his that enjoys it.*
> BEN FRANKLIN

Keep a steady hand on the reins. You'll work twenty hours a day for days on end, but you'll need to take time to play and enjoy. Balance the two. Otherwise, Flash, you'll crash and burn.

> *Drive thy business, let not that drive thee.*
> BEN FRANKLIN

Like Dorothy and her pals in the Wizard of Oz, you already have what you need:

The Heart, The Courage, The Brains.

I have it on good authority that 100 percent of all adults alive today were at one time five years old. That child is still somewhere inside you. Let the child come out. Once you do, you can make your dream happen.

You can do it. I'm convinced of it!

Well, that's about it. The day is done. You've been good. Time to hit the sack. But first, let me tell you a little bedtime story. It's called "Yink's 'It'!" I want Yink to be the last thing on your mind before you drift off to sleep.

So get comfortable. Fluff up your pillow. Enjoy.

I'll be seeing you out there in the Real World. Or as my children Kristyn, Tori, and Brad say every night before they go to bed, "Don't let the bedbugs bite. See you in the morning light—Yeah!"

He thought of umbrella hats,
of an electric ball bat
that never misses
whenever it swings,

of shoes with large wings
and kites without strings--
to name but a few of
Yink's idea things.

But the older he grew,
the less this Yink knew.
Or so he thought when he started in school.
He learned to draw straight,
and to never be late,
but mostly he learned dreams are for fools.

Then one day, Yink's boss,
a Mister Herman McMoss,
told employees the
outlook was dire.
Sales were a-crawling,
Profits were failing.
Said McMoss,
"Our fat's in
the fire..."

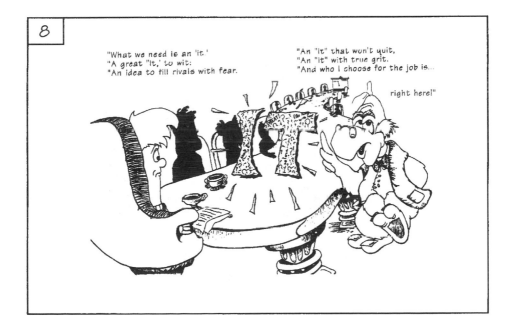

8

"What we need is an 'it.'
"A great "It,' to wit:
"An idea to fill rivals with fear.

"An "it" that won't quit,
"An "it" with true grit.
"And who I choose for the job is...

right here!"

9

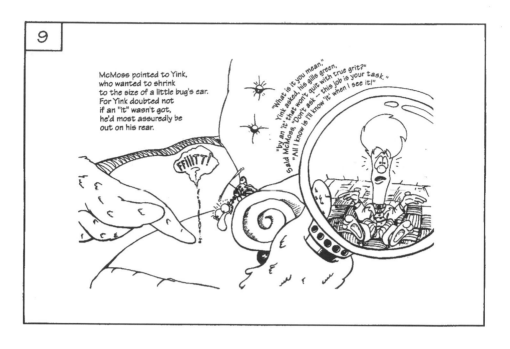

McMoss pointed to Yink,
who wanted to shrink
to the size of a little bug's ear.
For Yink doubted not
if an "it" wasn't got,
he'd most assuredly be
out on his rear.

10

So Yink sat and thought. He was in a tight spot.
He grimaced and grumaced and groaned.
All his "its" were the same, each one of them lame.
His brain dribbled and drabbled and droned.

Yink thought a lot.
So hard did he think,
he practically turned
orange, purple and pink.

And yet ...

11

He could draw a straight line
and be right on time,
but he'd forgot how ideas are made.
Still, he jotted a note
to pass off as "it," so he hoped
to escape the boss's office unscathed.

12

Unfortunately,
Mr. McMoss
did not see
Yink's "it" in a
positive light.
"This 'it' is the
pits,"
McMoss said
in a snit.
"Not even
close --
it's nowhere in
sight!"

13

Then Herman McMoss became
particularly cross:
"I'm not yanking you, Yink.
"I want 'its' that don't clink.
"Your 'it' is rinkydink.
"Furthermore,
your 'it' stinks!"

Yink asked yet
again for a how,
what, why, when,
for some hint
where an "it"
could be found.
Said McMoss, "You
got me. But I'll know
when I see -- please
don't ask me right
now to expound."

Yink grew so morose,
he turned white as a ghost.
He barely kept a stiff upper lip.
That night, his little girl,
a Yinkling named Pearl
said, "Ease up, Dad --
c'mon, get a grip!"

"Let's play, Dad -- it's fun;
"you chase, and I'll run.
"Nevermind all those its, ands and bits.
"Let's run through the yard
"and play really hard."
So they did, and Yink forgot all about "it's."

And after a while, Yink started to smile.
The best "it" this side of Topeka
popped into his head; and Yink instantly said,
"I christen this 'it' a Eureka!"

Yink quickly perked up
and promptly worked up
a Eurekal report right away.
It wasn't hard what he did;
he just thought like a kid.
His boss didn't know quite
what to say.

"Yink, you've done yourself proud,
"I'll say it out loud," said McMoss
on the corporate P.A.

"Your 'it' is pure gold
"Your 'it' breaks the mold.
"It's the best 'it' ever -- hooray!"

19

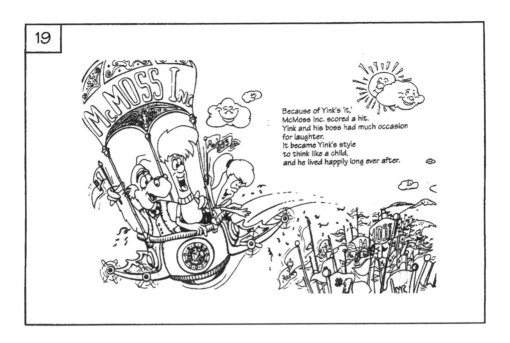

Because of Yink's 'it,'
McMoss Inc. scored a hit.
Yink and his boss had much occasion
for laughter.
It became Yink's style
to think like a child,
and he lived happily long ever after.

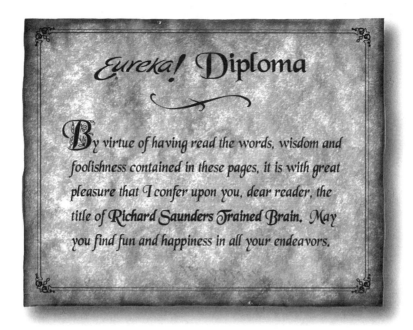

Eureka! Diploma

By virtue of having read the words, wisdom and foolishness contained in these pages, it is with great pleasure that I confer upon you, dear reader, the title of Richard Saunders Trained Brain. May you find fun and happiness in all your endeavors.

Congratulations!
You are now a Trained Brain.

With due respect to the greatest radicals of all time—among them, Benjamin Franklin, Thomas Jefferson, John Adams, George Washington, John Hancock, and my forefather, Lyman Hall—I have created a new Declaration of Independence.

The Eureka! Mansion
Declaration of Independence

When in the course of human events, it becomes necessary for us to dissolve established patterns of thought which have connected us with the conforming world and beyond, a decent respect to the ruminations of mankind requires us to declare the causes that impel us to the separation.

We hold these truths to be self-evident, that all men and women are inventive, that they are endowed by their Creator with certain unalienable rights, that among these are Fun Is Fundamental, Wicked Good Ideas Contradict History, Perception Is the Only Real Reality, Newborn Ideas Are to Be Respected, and You Gotta Swing a Lot to Hit Home Runs, as well as and notwithstanding Life, Liberty and the Pursuit of Creative Freedom. That to secure these rights, Conformity to Conventional Wisdom is instituted among men, That whenever any form of Conventional Wisdom becomes Destructive of these ends, it is our right to alter or to abolish it and to Recapture Innocence, laying its foundation on such principles as shall seem most likely to give wing to Flights of Fancy.

And when a Long Train of Abuses and Usurpations evinces a design to shackle us under the Absolute Despotism of Conformity, it is our Right, it is our Duty, to throw off Conventional Wisdom, and to provide a New State of Mind for our future independent, imaginative thoughts. The history of Conformity is a history of Repeated Injuries and Usurpations, all having an Absolute Tyranny over our Imaginations. To prove this, let facts be submitted to a candid world.

Conformity has enacted Political Correctness, discouraging fresh perspectives.

Conformity views passion, energy, and enthusiasm as lack of self-control.

Conformity puts out a Suggestion Box, but never looks inside.

Conformity discourages risk taking, preferring instead the beaten path of least resistance.

Conformity believes in consensus to averageness instead of debate to brilliance.

Conformity demands identical dress, identical talk, identical thoughts.

Conformity encourages us to toil in jobs we hate so we can retire and live the good life.

Conformity increments our salary upward till we're enslaved to maintaining the status quo.

Conformity confuses orderly, well-managed process for wicked good content.

Conformity regards change and chaos as a result of poor planning rather than a chance to grow.

Conformity whines and whimpers instead of taking responsibility.

Conformity rewards blind acceptance.

Conformity defends acting on precedent as risk-free.

Conformity views honesty, truth, and common sense as negotiable items.

Conformity views factory workers as pieces of equipment.

Conformity believes platters loaded with stale cold cuts constitute real food.

Conformity believes overpriced French cuisine is superior to pizza.

Conformity believes money is a stronger motivator than pride and craftsmanship.

We, therefore, the Representatives of Original Thought and Unfettered Imagination, appealing to the Supreme Judge of the world for the rectitude of our intentions, do solemnly publish and declare, that we are and of right ought to be, Eureka!-ized; that we are absolved from all allegiance to Conformity, and that all ties between us and Conventional Wisdom are and ought to be totally dissolved, not to mention that we no longer wish to wear ties; and that as free and independent thinkers, we have full power to imagine, reason, contemplate, create, and otherwise use our brains as we see fit for the good of mankind.

For the support of this Declaration, with a firm reliance on the protection of Divine Providence, we mutually pledge to each other our lives, our fortunes, and our sacred honor.

Benj.ᵃ Franklin, *Lyman Hall*

Doug Hall

_____

Reader

Thank-Yous and Miscellanea

A WORD FROM DOUG
(never known to be short-winded)

Thanks, World's Greatest Writer, David Wecker.

Thanks, World's Greatest Fairy Godmother and Yink's Guiding Spirit, Sandie Glass.

Thanks, World's Greatest MacMerlin, Randy Mazzola, book illustrations.

Thanks, World's Greatest Illustrator, Ben Sauer, Yink Illustrations.

Thanks, World's Greatest Typist, Loretta Gordon, dictation transcription.

Thanks, World's Greatest Stat Man, Mike Kosinski, BOS statistics profiler.

Thanks, World's Greatest Stat Lady, Lisa Fridley.

Thanks, World's Greatest Angel, SARK, for angelic inspiration and guidance.

Thanks, World's Greatest Creativity Seminar Leader, Chic Thompson.

Thanks, World's Greatest Parents, Buzz and Jean Hall.

Thanks, World's Greatest Brother, Bruce Hall (Boo Boo the Clown).

Thanks, World's Greatest Sister, Pam Twist (The Amazing Saleena).

Thanks, World's Greatest Grandmother, Hazel Hall.

Thanks, World's Greatest In-Laws, Walter and Lillian Chapman.

Thanks, World's Greatest Brothers-in-Law: George Chapman, Chris Chapman.

Thanks, World's Greatest Sisters-in-Law: Sandie Chapman, Wendie Chapman.

Thanks, World's Greatest General Manager, Marc Marsan.

Thanks, World's Greatest Office Team: Miki Reilly, Kari McCampbell, Christina Collct, Margaret Henson, Negia York, Paula Wood.

Thanks, World's Greatest Original Trained Brains: Hannah Buchanan, Tracy Duckworth, Diane Iseman, Bill Vernick, Tessa Westermeyer, Doug Sovonick, Marc Marsan, and David Wecker.

Thanks, World's Greatest Marketing People: Marc Marsan, Miki Reilly.

Thanks, World's Greatest Art Studio, WBK Design.

Thanks, World's Greatest Cover Creators: Lauren Avery (designer), Brian Freeman (production).

Thanks, World's Greatest Package Designers: Bill Avery, Patsy Baughn, Jody Bergman, Kindra Bolsinger, Barbara Carlotta, Theresa Chiodi, Doug Faulkner, Claudia Gladstone, Steve Glaser, Stacy Hyun, Tony Hyun, Steve Klein, Kevin McNamara, John Recker, Jaime Santillan, Tessa Westermeyer, Janet Zack.

Thanks, World's Greatest Trained Brains: David Wecker, Hannah Buchanan, Diane Iseman, Tessa Westermeyer, Kindra Bolsinger, Bruce Hall, Mike Katz, Eric Schulz, Dave Howe, Bill Johnson, Laura Rolfes, Jane Portman, Janet Weisman, Bill Vernick, Roseanne Hassey, Tracy Duckworth, Marilyn O'Brien, Deborah Storz, Liz Nickles, Flick Hatcher, Debbie Hall, Marc Marsan, Sandie Glass, Cathy Wecker, Doug Sovonick, Marie Keaney, Walt Harrell, Randy Mazzola, Michelle Martin, Pam Hall, Marie Keaney, Barb Buck, Dave Buck, Tina Mims, Steve Glaser, Steve Klein, Peter Loyd, Jack Streetmarter, Becki Meyer, Chic Thompson, Andy VanGundy, SARK, Watts Wacker, Jim Taylor, Dennis Speigel, Liam Killeen, Peter de Jager, Paul Rousseau, Lynn Kahle, Jim Hetzel.

Thanks, World's Greatest Catering Company, Village Pantry, Nancy Ward.

Thanks, World's Greatest Macintosh Bureau, Color Copy Center and Photographer, Gil Gray.

Thanks, World's Greatest Summer Intern and Dr. Disecto's Guiding Spirit, Michelle Martin.

Thanks, World's Greatest Clients.

Thanks, World's Greatest Travel Agent, Karen Kelley.

Thanks, World's Greatest Computer, Macintosh PowerBook 180.

Thanks, World's Greatest Word Processor, Write Now.

Thanks, World's Greatest Computer Tech: Brian Rowe.

Thanks, World's Greatest Landscaper, Doug Evans.

Thanks, World's Greatest Mentors: Ross Love, Mark Upson, John McDonald, Phil MacSweeny, Barb Thomas, Bob Gill, Gibby Carey, Kip Knight, Becki Meyer, Chuck Hong, SARK, Tim Feely, John Pepper, Bill Hill, Rod Wyndt, Dave Kilbury, Dave Christie, Doug Williams, Jim Bangel, and my Dad and Mom.

Thanks, World's Greatest Partners: Jack Gordon, Dave Howe.

Thanks, World's Greatest Agents: Mel Berger, Randy Chaplin, Henry Reisch.

Thanks, World's Greatest Attorneys: Tim Riker, Lynda Roesch, Patricia Hogan.

Thanks, World's Greatest Banker, John Dillaman.

Thanks, World's Greatest Accountants: David Cassady, Lillian Ferrante.

Thanks, World's Greatest Coffee Roasters: 7-Hills Coffee, Joe Morris, Andy Timmerman.

Thanks, World's Greatest Editor, Joann Davis.

Thanks, World's Greatest Book Publishers, The Warner Books Team: Grace Sullivan, Maureen Egen, Mel Parker, Nanscy Neiman, Jimmy Franco, Diane Ekeblad, Vincent La Scala, Abraham Matalon, Mari Okuda, Harvey-Jane Kowal, Ann Schwartz, Karen Torres, Kata Bates, Bruce Paonessa, Dina Mastrandrea, Anne Hamilton, Ellen Herrick, Cathy Melnicki, Christine Barba, Susan Moffat, Kathy Baker, Olivia Blumer, Caryn Karmatz, Joann Davis, Larry Kirshbaum, Lisa McGarry, Rachel McClain, Patricia Keim.

Thanks, World's Greatest Book Sales People: Ron Van Winkle, Norm Kraus, Dick Efthim, Peggie Seamen, Christopher Austin, Steve Marz, Linda Wally, Rich Overfield, Conan Gorenstein, MaryAnn Johnson, Judy DeBerry, Judy Nosel Rosenblatt, Marty Conroy, Randy Rosens, Richard Tullis, Carol Loverico, Catherine Wisniewski, and Patricia Guzman.

Thanks, World's Greatest Puppeteer, Jim Henson. His outrageous and utterly original Muppet antics inspired me during my teenage years to take the life trail less traveled. While I was at P&G, I had the honor of meeting with him at the Muppet Mansion in New York City. At that meeting, Jim Henson exhibited a genuine warmth, a natural curiosity, and a childlike innocence that stood in stark contrast to the "Adult Business World." At that meeting he showed me that you could be incredibly successful in business while keeping your heart and soul. In honor of the truly great Jim Henson, the cover of this book uses Kermit Green (PMS #375).

Thanks, World's Greatest_____, Anyone and everyone who I have missed on this list.

Thanks, World's Greatest Life Partner, Debbie Hall. I love you!

Thanks, World's Greatest Kids: Kristyn, Tori, and Brad Hall. I hope you all grow up with the same healthy disrespect for conformity and authority that your mother and I have.

I Love You All!

NOW A WORD FROM DAVID

Thanks, Cathy, for bearing with me. Thanks, Sam and Betsy, for being our babies. Thanks, Bud and Dottie, for bringing me up; Ken Fields for continuing the process; and God for everything else. Thanks, too, to my muse, whose name is Al. Amen, brothers and sisters!

This book is the first in a collection. All books will have the same spirit, tone, and easy access style this has. All will be translated into English by The World's Greatest Writer Who Lives in a Log Cabin in Alexandria, Kentucky, David Wecker.

Jump Start Your Ideas

Jump Start Your Ideas

An entrepreneurial, counterculture guide to turning your thoughts and ideas into reality. This is not a scholarly book, rather it's a practical hands-on guide for survival and success in the real world. Chapters include:

- Westward Ho!
- Harvesting the Seeds
- The Write Stuff
- The Name Game
- Product and Package Development
- Money, Money, Money
- Market Research
- Painting the Vision
- Selling
- How to Sell a Suit
- P. T. Barnum, We Love You
- Courting the Media
- Customer Service
- Chief Executive Officer
- Building the Team
- Motivating
- Corporate Structure and Reward Systems
- Partnerships
- Corporate Interpretation
- Reality Check

Jump Start Your Kids

A guide to helping your children grow up to be happier, smarter, and healthier. Written in partnership with my life partner, Debbie Hall, a registered nurse and all-star mother of three. The book offers real-world experiments in teaching children how to think better, smarter, faster. Chapters include:

- "I Love My Kids Best After Midnight"
- The Differences B.C. (Before Child) and A.C. (After Child)
- Stimulus-Activated Thinking for Kids
- Where Are You, Dr. Seuss, When We Need You?
- Because I Said So
- It's Not a Leave It to Beaver World Anymore. It's Better.
- The Good, Bad, and Ugly of VCRs and PCs
- School System Defense Systems
- How to Make a Firstborn Last Born and Last Born Firstborn
- A Two-Career Survival Guide
- Flapdoodle Note Taking for Schools
- Rainy Day Mondays
- Soccer, Scouts, Ballet, Swimming, Baseball, Football
- I Say Dr., Dr., What Are You Planning to Do with My Child?
- The Big Times ... Ages 2, 8, and 13

THE LEGEND OF EUREKA! MANSION BRAIN BREW

"Official Coffee of Trained Brains"

Travel east on U.S. Route 32 out of Cincinnati and you'll come to a 150-something-year-old estate called the Eureka! Mansion, home to the eclectic and eccentric creativity gurus known as the Richard Saunders International Trained Brains®.

One day, the Trained Brains noticed that a lusty cup of java cleared their heads and helped them embark on fanciful and vivid journeys of the imagination. The Trained Brains are not alone in their findings; throughout history, the likes of Franklin, Voltaire, Twain, Bach, Beethoven, and Brahms have sung the praises of coffee.

Working with a micro-roaster, they blended, brewed, and tasted for three years before arriving at their choice for java perfection. Out of respect for the brew's ability to fuel the creative spirit, they named it Brain Brew. The brew itself is dark, but its power is clear.

> **Brain Brew Coffee** has an overwhelming amount of rich coffee aroma and robust coffee flavor without the bitterness, burn or bite of gourmet coffee "imposters."

Available through selected enlightened retailers or by calling (800) IDEAUSA (433-2872). Major credit cards accepted.

All Profits for Charity: Like Paul Newman and his salad dressing, I'm donating all coffee profits to charity. Your purchase of Brain Brew helps support our Planet Eureka!™ *Ideas for a Better World* public service creativity arm.

Richard / Saunders

International
• • • • • • • • • • •
Professional Inventors

RICHARD SAUNDERS INTERNATIONAL SERVICES INCLUDE:

Eureka!® Inventing *!*

Eureka! Stimulus Response Inventing

Give us your tired, your weary, your most frustrating business challenges and we'll find solutions for them. Within days or weeks, the Eureka! Stimulus Response Inventing system can invent and articulate a strategic and executional program for generating positive business momentum. Clients use Eureka! Stimulus Response for:

• *Creating a* Strategic Game Plan *for revitalizing an existing business*
• *Creating a* Tactical Game Plan *for revitalizing an existing business strategy*
• *Inventing* New Services *&* New Products.

Planet Eureka!

Ben Franklin once said "Let kind offices go round. Mankind are all of a family." To that end, I have founded Planet Eureka!, a nonprofit organization to provide creative services free to public service organiza-

tions—services that normally costs corporate clients upward of six figures. Planet Eureka! clients include The National Leukemia Society, the second Live Aid II concert planning group (WAR, short for World Aid Relief) and even Congressman Rob Portman. In 1995, 20% of Richard Saunders International's creative efforts will be devoted to charitable concerns.

From our sister company, AcuPOLL Research

The AcuPOLL Precision Research System provides the fastest, most cost effective and predictive method available to quantify the customer appeal of business-building concepts.

(Note: Late in 1993, I set AcuPOLL free. The company was sold to its president, Jack Gordon, who continues to operate it according to the demanding standards set forth at its inception.)

To get more information about our services, contact us:

• Via phone (513) 271-9911
• Via fax (513) 271-9966
• Via mail: Eureka! Mansion, 3851 Edwards Road, Cincinnati, Ohio 45244
 • Via Internet: EUREKAM@AOL.COM

GREAT WRITERS, GREAT BOOKS, AND STUFF

SARK
- *Living Juicy.* Berkeley, CA: Celestial Arts, 1994.
- *SARK's Journal and Play! Book.* Berkeley, CA: Celestial Arts, 1993.
- *Inspiration Sandwich.* Berkeley, CA: Celestial Arts, 1992.
- *A Creative Companion.* Berkeley, CA: Celestial Arts, 1991.

For SARK books and posters, contact:
- Celestial Arts, P.O. Box 7327, Berkeley, CA 94707 or call 1-800-841-2665.

For more SARK posters, cards, stationery, and other amazing stuff, contact The Red Rose Collection, P.O. Box 280140, San Francisco, CA 94128 or call 1-800-374-5505

To contact SARK, write:
> SARK
> c/o Celestial Arts Publishing
> P.O. Box 7327
> Berkeley, CA 94707

- SARK's inspiration line (415) 546-EPIC
- Information on wondrous and fantastic SARK speaking engagements (415) 397-SARK

Guy Kawasaki

- *The Macintosh Way.* Glenview, Illinois: Scott, Foresman and Company, 1990.
- *Selling the Dream.* New York: HarperCollins, 1991.

Chic Thompson

- *What a Great Idea!* New York: HarperCollins, 1992.
- *"Yes, But..." The Top 40 Killer Phrases and How You Can Fight Them.* New York: HarperCollins, 1993.

Dr. Arthur VanGundy

- *Idea Power.* New York: American Management Association, 1992.
- *Techniques of Structured Problem Solving,* 2nd ed. New York: Van Nostrand Reinhold, 1988.
- *Creative Problem Solving: A Guide for Trainers and Management.* Westport, CT: Quorum, 1987.
- *Managing Group Creativity: A Modular Approach to Problem Solving.* New York: AMACOM, 1984.
- *108 Ways to Get a Bright Idea.* Englewood Cliffs, NJ: Prentice-Hall, 1983.
- *Brain Boosters for Business Advantage.* San Diego: Pfeiffer & Co., 1994.

Great Software for Stimuli Creation:

- Idea Fisher, Fisher Idea Systems, Inc., 2222 Martin St. 110, Irvine, California 92715 (714) 474-8111